Cycling
in
Victorian Ireland

Cycling
in
Victorian Ireland

Brian Griffin

NONSUCH

First published 2006

Nonsuch Publishing
73 Lower Leeson Street
Dublin 2
Ireland
www.nonsuchireland.com
www.nonsuch-publishing.com

© Brian Griffin 2006

British Library Cataloguing in Publication Data.
A catalogue record for this book is available from the British Library.

ISBN 1 84588 562 7
ISBN-13 978 1 84588 562 5

Typesetting and origination by Tempus Publishing Limited
Printed in Great Britain

Contents

Preface

It gives me great pleasure to acknowledge the help and encouragement that I have received from many individuals and institutions in the course of researching and writing this book. Without their assistance and encouragement this book simply could not have been written. I owe a particular debt of gratitude to the British Academy's Arts and Humanities Research Board for a generous grant at the start of my research. The staff of the following institutions were particularly helpful: the British Library at Euston Road and the newspaper library at Colindale; the National Library of Ireland; Bath Spa University's interlibrary loan department, especially Maggie Collins; the Russell Library, National Library of Ireland, particularly Mrs Penny Russell; the National Archives of Ireland; the Public Record Office of Northern Ireland; Dublin Civic Museum; Trinity College Dublin library and archives; University College Dublin archives; Birmingham Central Library; Niamh O'Sullivan of the Kilmainham Jail archives; Dr Austin M. O'Sullivan, curator of the Irish Agricultural Museum, Johnstown Castle, Wexford; Raymond Refaussé, librarian and archivist of the Church of Ireland's Representative Church Body Library; David Higman, curator of the National Cycle Collection, Llandrindod Wells; and the staff of the British Cycling Museum, Camelford. My colleagues in the School of Historical and Cultural Studies at Bath Spa University kept my enthusiasm alive, both by their interest and their well-meaning banter at my fascination with 'Penny-farthings' and similar arcane subjects – Graham Davis, John Newsinger and Terence Rodgers deserve a special mention here. I am very grateful to Alan Marshall and Fiona Montgomery for facilitating timetable relief for a semester, which allowed me to write in relative peace. I would also like to thank the students who took my sports history module, for helping me to clarify various cloudy issues in the course of seminar discussion. Other individuals who helped by bringing valuable sources to my attention are James McConnell, Donal Lowry, Tom Hunt, Neal Garnham, Joe Casey, Margaret

P. Lennon-Wynne and particularly Tom Hayes, who generously shared with me some of the fruits of his on-going Ph.D. dissertation research on Irish sport in the decades before the formation of the GAA. A heartfelt 'thank you' to you all – any errors in the text are to be laid at my door entirely. I would also like to thank Nonsuch Publishing for according me the opportunity to publish this book, and to Bridgette Rowland, in particular, for editing the manuscript. My greatest debt of all is to my greatest helper, my wife, Sally – without her love and support, not a single word of what follows would have been written.

1

Introduction

In December 1886 a Dublin barrister, one of the pioneers of Irish cycling, described an incident during his travels in rural Ireland astride an 'Ordinary' or 'Penny-farthing' bicycle. He explained that in the autumn of 1878 or 1879 he had been staying in a hunting lodge 'in a wild and rugged portion of County Tyrone', where '[m]any of the natives had never seen or even heard of a bicycle'. One dark evening he was coasting silently and at great speed down a hill when he passed an old woman on the road:

> It was dusk, and I went by without a sound. Down she dropped on her knees like a shot, and, with hands clasped above her head, prayed fervently; and as the people ran out to see what was the matter, they heard her exclaiming, 'Och sure! I seen him, I seen him! [T]he prophecy has come true, and it's the end of the world has come! Shure I seen the devil himself go by without wings or legs, and he sailin' through the air! Och, murdher! murdher! it's the end of the world has come enthoirely!…'[1]

Three brothers from Dublin, who went on a cycling holiday in Galway in August 1883, found themselves surrounded, when they stopped for a break in Kilconnel, by an awestruck crowd who 'gazed open-mouthed' at the 'iron horses' which they were riding. The cyclists proceeded on their way through Galway city and headed for Spiddal. As it was getting dark when they approached the latter village they turned on their lamps:

> It happened to be a Roman Catholic holiday, and, as is customary in that district, the people had assembled in crowds at every convenient place along the roadside to chat or indulge in rustic games. As we noiselessly approached every voice grew silent and they gazed, awestruck, at the mysterious light now seen clear against the murky sky – as we gained the top of one of those sharp, stiff hills which

follow each other in rapid succession on that mountain road – and the next moment flashing swiftly into the hollow beneath, only to reappear, brighter and more distinct, on the opposite summit; but as soon as we had passed, and they saw that we were real flesh and blood, and not a visitation of the Evil One, or a Will-o'-the-Wisp taking a constitutional along the high road, they ran alongside with shouts of delight and exclamations in Irish, so long as they could keep up.

One of the villagers stuck his fingers, out of curiosity, through the spokes of the hind wheel of one of the bicycles, with resultant agony for himself and causing the cyclist to crash.[2] Another cycling pioneer in 1891 told a story of how, some years previously, his father, 'an old Irish country gentleman', had encountered a couple of men 'riding those big spider wheels' near his house. The old man, filled with curiosity about these new machines, threw large stones at the cyclists to see what effect this would have on their progress.[3]

These incidents, while seemingly trivial in themselves, are nevertheless important because they illustrate the tremendous impact of the first appearance of bicycles or tricycles, especially in rural areas of nineteenth-century Ireland. These new machines were exciting and, for some, terrifying novelties. Ireland's pioneering cyclists agreed about the exciting nature of their pastime and frequently considered themselves to be a select or elite group – 'brethren of the wheel', in the words of one Belfast cyclist[4] – who loved to associate together in clubs and go on cycling trips into the countryside or to coastal resorts. Before the 1890s most Irish cyclists were young, middle class, and male. The exclusive nature of their cycling world was reinforced by the high prices of tricycles and bicycles, which meant that most members of the working or lower classes were effectively excluded from participation, while technical considerations and the conventions of female dress meant that almost all of those Irishwomen who engaged in the pastime were restricted to the relatively heavy and cumbersome tricycle.[5] Before the 1890s a 'freemasonry of the wheel'[6] dominated Irish cycling – not only was the pastime socially exclusive, but enthusiasts were convinced that 'cycling creates a stronger bond among its followers than any other sport'.[7]

Technological innovations, especially the invention of the safety bicycle and the development of the pneumatic tyre, revolutionised Irish cycling in the 1890s. The pneumatic-tyred safety bicycle not only rendered the Ordinary bicycle and the tricycle obsolete, but it made the sport more widely accessible to women, and also to middle-aged or elderly men and younger men, for whom the Ordinary bicycle was too daunting a prospect. By the middle of the 1890s much of middle-class and, to a lesser extent, upper-class Ireland was consumed by a cycling craze; cycling agents mushroomed throughout the land and cycling clubs, moving with the times, welcomed female members. In 1896 the *Weekly Irish Times*'s humorous columnist, 'Murty', reflected on what he saw as the insane enthusiasm for cycling which had gripped Dublin:

CHEERING REMARK TO A YOUNG RIDER.

PADDY (*to beginner, who is "all over the shop"*): "Arrah! me honey, an' won't she go aisy thin ? Sure it's meself that'll be afther givin' her a touch up wid the saft ind av me shillelagh."

A peasant offers to 'help' a novice bicyclist in 1881.

> The generation that's comin' into manhood and womanhood will be wore out
> before their bones hardens, and anyone that reaches sixty will be as crooked as
> a cork-screw from bicyclin' or auto-car-in'! I wish even the clergy would take
> a thought and preach repose as a cardinal virtue. But I find some of them also
> – reverend fathers! – on wheels performin' like schoolboys over the suburban
> bye-paths![8]

Not all cyclists looked favourably on the dramatic changes which the Irish cycling world underwent in the mid-1890s. The editor of the *Irish Cyclist*, Richard James Mecredy, in the middle of the cycling craze of that decade, yearned for the early days when cycling had been a much more exclusive activity:

There is scarcely any pleasure left to a poor old cyclist. Wobbling ladies in red faces and any colour blouses come along at the wrong side of the road and ring the bell at you. Getting out of their way, you get right into the thick of embryo speedmen intently studying the pedals and humped up in a way that would shame a dromedary. Farther on detachments of 'hands-off' people are met. We wonder do these young men intend to join a circus, or do they really imagine their performance is unique. Soldiers, by the way, seem to have a strong predilection this way. Going without 'arms' is probably pleasant to them. Then comes the creeping novice of middle age, who knows he carries his life in his hands. His face tells you so. It is a dial of misery. So they fill our park and suburban roads, till one would almost wish the old solid tyre days were back again, when a man monopolised a country.[9]

In 1898 the *Irish Tourist* published an imaginative piece, 'Dublin Fifty Years Hence', in which the author speculated on how the enthusiasm for cycling would affect the capital city if it persisted into the future. In the Dublin of 1953, cycling 'scorchers' and anyone who deliberately sang 'Daisy Bell' would be 'mercilessly shot down by the nearest passer-by', while the Liffey between the Custom House and Capel Street would be pumped dry and the riverbed transformed into a splendid cement cycling track.[10] While cycling obviously never developed to these absurd levels, by the late 1890s it was, nevertheless, no longer viewed as an unusual 'fad' or a 'fancy' but had become a commonplace activity in Irish society.[11] According to the *Irish Cyclist* in May 1902:

> The glory of cycling has departed, leaving in its place only the skeleton of what was once a soul-stirring pastime and sport. True, the remnant is a wonderfully utilitarian means of quick and easy locomotion; but it is as commonplace, by comparison with what it was, as a voyage per steamboat compared to the fun of single-handed yachting.

Cycling in Ireland had developed to such an extent that 'there is nothing uncommon about cycle riding in the twentieth century'.[12]

In the pages that follow, the key features of the development of cycling in Ireland in the late Victorian Age are explored, from the pastime's relatively small-scale beginnings in the 1860s to its explosion in popularity in the 1890s. Cycling's impact on the lives of cyclists and non-cyclists alike is discussed, and the unique ethos of the cycling world in this period is examined in detail. What follows throws light not only on the under-researched subject of sport in nineteenth-century Irish society, but also contributes further to our understanding of Victorian Ireland.

2

The Pioneering Years

Before examining the early years of cycling in Ireland, it is necessary to present a brief overview of cycling developments in other parts of the world. Before the bicycle as we understand it emerged, there were a number of precursors of varying importance and longevity which contributed towards the bicycle's development. The first of these was Baron Karl von Drais's invention of the *Laufmaschine* (running machine) in Baden in 1817, which he patented in 1818. Consisting of a wooden frame and two wooden wheels, the Draisienne (as the machine was generally known on the Continent) was propelled by riders using their feet to push themselves along the ground. A machine based on von Drais's principle was introduced to England by London carriage maker Denis Johnson in 1818. Johnson called his machine, which he patented in December 1818, the 'pedestrian curricle' but it was better known by its nicknames of the 'dandy horse', 'hobby horse' or 'Irish jaunting car'. For much of 1819, fashionable English society appeared to be besotted with Johnson's contraption, and for a brief period a similar craze also affected the eastern seaboard of the United States. However, the physical difficulties of propelling the machine, as well as the ridicule to which those who used the Draisienne were subjected, contributed towards its rapid demise in popularity.[1] Nevertheless, von Drais's invention – short-lived as it was – eventually provided the chief inspiration for the first pedal-propelled bicycle in the 1860s.[2] It is impossible to state with accuracy how popular the hobby horse was in Ireland, although undoubtedly some were used in the country. According to the *Irish Cyclist* in March 1890, the hobby horse appeared in Ireland shortly after it appeared in England, but it 'did not become popular on this side of the Channel, however, and soon went out of fashion'. One documented instance of the hobby horse's use in Ireland concerns the father of James Talbot Power of Leopardstown – who was in possession in 1890 of a hobby horse which his father used to ride in 1836.[3]

A 'hobby horse' or 'Irish jaunting car'.

Kirkpatrick Macmillan, a blacksmith-mechanic from Dumfries, is often credited as being the inventor of the bicycle. Around 1839 he devised a two-wheeled
machine which was apparently propelled by operating foot-treadles at the rear
wheel, and which he frequently cycled in the vicinity of Thornhill.[4] A similar
machine was developed by Alexandre Lefèbvre, a blacksmith from St Denis, near
Paris, around 1842 or 1843.[5] However, as neither Macmillan nor Lefèbvre produced more than one of their bicycles, and their designs were neither copied nor
developed by others, their machines constitute no more than interesting foot-
notes in cycling history – in the words of James McGurn, they represent 'progress
without progeny'.[6]

A more significant and long-lasting development was the invention of the
four-wheeled velocipede or quadricycle by William Sawyer, a carpenter in Dover.
Sawyer produced his treadle-propelled quadricylces – which, apart from the
wrought iron axles, were constructed from wood – from 1845 until 1868.[7] There
is patchy evidence to suggest that the quadricycle was the most common form of

cycle used on Irish roads before the invention of the bicycle. According to David
Harrel, who was born in 1841, when he was a child quadricycles were 'quite
common' in the Ardglass region, so it is likely that they were also used elsewhere
in Ireland, particularly as they were brought to the public's notice by the display
of two machines at the Dublin Exhibition of 1853. Dr W. H. Stacpoole-Westropp
of Lisdoonvarna, for instance, stated in 1887 that he rode one in his youth in the
1840s. Harrel records that on one occasion when he was going for a spin on his
quadricycle he encountered two of the principal barristers of the north-east circuit, James Whiteside (later Chief Justice of Ireland) and Thomas O'Hagan (later
Lord High Chancellor of Ireland), walking on the road near his father's house.
The two men stopped Harrel and took turns riding his machine.[8] By the late
1860s – even after the invention of the bicycle – there were 'numberless varieties
and patterns' of quadricycles on the market, with those produced by a Dublin
manufacturer named Andrews, considered by one source as '[a]mongst the best,
if not the very best'. Andrews's machine, the 'Dublin velocipede', consisted of a
frame made of 'the best inch-square iron', with the other parts made of wood: ash
treadles and felloes, elm wheels and hickory spokes, with a seat made of wicker
or cane work. The selling points of the quadricyle were 'perfect security, space for
a companion, and an imposing appearance'; however, its drawbacks consisted of
'want of control, steering-brakes, loss of power, and expense'.[9]

In addition to mass-produced quadricycles on Irish and British roads in this
period, there was a motley collection of cycles produced by amateur or even
professional mechanics of which little is now known, mainly because these were
produced only for the enthusiasts' own pleasure and use.[10] An 'ancient lady'
from Co. Tipperary produced tantalising but sketchy evidence in 1892 that a
Mullinahone maker of cars and wheelbarrows made his own cycling machine in
the early 1830s, which sounds rather like a quadricycle or possibly a tricycle. She
claimed that:

> …he got *a lot* of little wheels and put thim undher a good sthrong timber frame,
> and begor in a short time he used to be dhrivin' up and down the roads, and he
> sittin' within in it, and workin' it wud his two feet, and all the children runnin'
> after him: and he going as fast!!! 'Twasn't long, thin, till some of the young gin-
> tlemin round the counthry got wans too, only improved on *his*, for they were
> rich and could get what they liked…[11]

There is stronger evidence that William Bindon Blood of Cranagher, Co. Clare, a
professor of engineering at Queen's College Galway and, in 1876, the inventor of
the 'Dublin' tricycle, designed and built a tricycle for his own use in 1852. It was
built of wood, with iron rims on the wheels; according to Blood it was a heavy,
slow and noisy machine, but he was still able to negotiate all of the hills in the
neighbourhood of Galway on it, including those with gradients of one in seven.

Blood rode this tricycle for some six or seven years.[12] There may also have been other amateur enthusiasts making cycles in Ireland before the 1860s, but, if there were, no recorded evidence of their activity appears to have survived.

The breakthrough of the bicycle – a machine with two wheels which the rider propels via pedals – occurred in 1861 when a Parisian, Pierre Michaux (variously described as a cabinetmaker, locksmith and carriage repairer), whilst repairing a Draisienne, realised that a machine along Draisienne lines but fitted with pedals on the front wheel and cranks, would be a marked improvement, allowing riders to propel themselves continuously without having to put their feet on the ground. He and his son, Ernest, built the first prototype of their 'velocipede' in 1861, and in 1862 some 142 machines were produced. In 1865 Michaux's company (which continued in production until 1869) produced some 400 machines, which cost the equivalent of £8 each. The early models were rudimentary affairs, with wrought-iron backbones and iron tyres on wheels of equal size; later models had a front wheel that was somewhat larger than the rear wheel, thus carrying the rider further with each revolution of the pedals, and had tyres of solid rubber. Michaux exhibited some of his machines at the Paris Exhibition of 1867, where they caught the eye of Rowley Turner, of the Coventry Sewing Machine Company. Turner brought one of Michaux's velocipedes back with him to Coventry and persuaded the sewing machine company (which was reconstructed as the Coventry Machinists' Company in 1869) to manufacture 400 machines of a similar type and to sell them in Paris, where Michaux's company could not meet the demand for the new machines. The outbreak of the Franco-Prussian War in 1870 killed off the French production of velocipedes, leaving the Coventry Machinists' Company as the main supplier of velocipedes in the United Kingdom, although several other companies had also entered the market in the late 1860s. The 'boneshaker', as the velocipede was commonly called, proved to have a more enduring popularity in Britain than the earlier hobby horse, even though its retail price varied from £10 to £14.[13] Several velocipede clubs were established and, beginning in June 1869, a large number of popular velocipede races were held for a number of years in various parts of England.[14]

The velocipede was soon superseded by the development of the high-wheeled bicycle. The first of these was introduced to England by James Moore, who had been racing successfully in Paris in the summer of 1870 with a lightweight bicycle (due to its hollow backbone) which had an oversized front wheel of around forty-eight inches in diameter. Following the outbreak of the Franco-Prussian War he returned to England with his new machine, and entered it in a race at the Midland Counties Championship in Wolverhampton in August 1870. Moore easily won his first two heats, but failed to win his race due to an unfortunate fall – nevertheless, his performance was enough to convince eyewitnesses that this new type of bicycle represented the quickest means of two-wheeled locomotion available. William Hillman and James Starley of the Coventry Machinists'

Company took out a patent for a high-wheeled bicycle, the 'Ariel', in 1870; their firm, Starley and Company, of Coventry, began producing the new machines in September 1871. They were followed by a number of other pioneers, most notably Thomas Humber of Nottingham and Daniel Rudge of Wolverhampton. By the middle of the 1870s there were approximately twenty English firms producing high-wheeled bicycles, with front wheels which increased in size from the original forty-eight inches in diameter at the start of the decade to sixty inches or even more by the decade's end.[15] These new machines were being called 'Ordinaries' by the late 1870s, as they were the most usual or common form of cycle in use – the pejorative nickname of 'Penny-farthing' was not coined until around 1891, probably by London 'guttersnipes' who jeered at cyclists who persisted in riding the high-wheeled bicycle at a time when safety bicycles were becoming more common.[16] For the majority of cyclists in Britain and Ireland during the 1870s and most of the 1880s, the Ordinary was the machine of choice.

Some riders in both countries preferred to ride tricycles. While the velocipede or boneshaker was in its heyday, some tricycles, such as the treadle-driven, 80 pounder 'Edinburgh', were developed. The early tricycle was little more than a velocipede which had its rear wheel replaced by two wheels; it was considered 'an extremely dangerous machine, being liable to turn over at corners'.[17] In 1869 two Dubliners named Isaac Farrell and William Turner took out a patent for a tricycle 'which rises and falls in imitation of a rider of a horse', and sent some of their machines to London. In June 1870 some of their tricycles were on view at P. Ledwidge's coach factory on Amiens Street and at Turner's Hammersmith Iron Works.[18] There is no evidence that their tricycle was widely used in Ireland or England, however, and in general the manufacture of three-wheelers lagged behind that of the two-wheeled vehicles, whether of the velocipede or high-wheeled variety. After the Ordinary displaced the velocipede as the principal form of cycle, entrepreneurs realised that there was a market for a less daunting form of machine, one that could be sold to women and middle-aged and old men – to all of whom the Ordinary was an inaccessible vehicle – and also young men who were either less athletic or less adventurous than those who rode Ordinaries.[19] Various tricycles, which were much more sophisticated affairs than the earlier 'Edinburgh', were developed to cater to this market. The first entrepreneur to develop a three-wheeled machine in the 1870s was William Bindon Blood who, as we have seen, already had some experience as a tricycle maker in the early 1850s. In his patent of 3 November 1876, Blood pointed out that his treadle-driven 'Dublin' tricycle, which had a rear driving wheel and two front steering wheels (like the earlier 'Edinburgh' three-wheeler), was suitable for women riders as a frame apron could be added to the front which would conceal their ankles from public view. It was also suitable for disabled riders, including those who had lost the use of their feet, as hand-operated levers could be hinged to the machine's crossbar.[20]

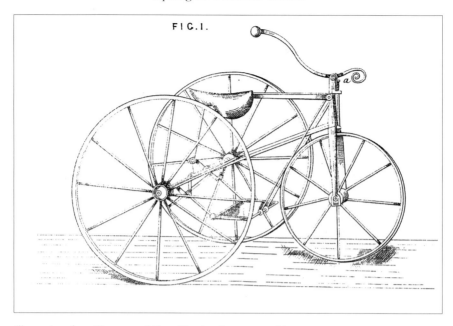

Illustration from Turner and Farrell's tricycle patent, 1869.

Blood claimed in 1889 that his machine was in use 'for a considerable time' before he patented it,[21] but it has not been possible to verify this using other sources. Booth Brothers of 63 Upper Stephen Street constructed the first, experimental machine and then, for a number of years, the 'Dublin' was made by Carey Brothers of St Andrew Street in Dublin, after which it was produced under the name of the 'Challenge' tricycle by the Singer Cycle Company of Coventry. However, 'by degrees it dropped out of favour', and in December 1883 Blood let his patent become void by not paying the requisite stamp duty.[22] The main reason that Blood's tricycle did not receive greater public support was due to competition from machines developed by James Starley, the patent for the first of which – the chain-driven 'Coventry Lever' tricycle – was taken out just fifteen days after Blood's. Starley went on to develop a number of very popular models, the crowning achievement being his 'Salvo' machine, renamed the 'Royal Salvo' in 1881 after Queen Victoria encountered one on the Isle of Wight and ordered two of them. Although she is unlikely to have ridden them, the fact that she acquired two of Starley's machines gave a considerable boost in Britain to the popularity of the tricycle in general, and Starley's makes in particular.[23] Although Blood's invention had largely fallen out of favour by the early 1880s, a small number continued to be produced by Booth Brothers, the leading Dublin cycle agents. Following the death of Carey, the original manufacturer of the 'Dublin', the Booths bought the equipment which he had used to make the tricycle and in 1885 were reported to be making small numbers of the machine,

Advertisement for Booth Brothers of Dublin in 1885.

which was 'still of great use for invalids'. A number of Blood's tricycles could still be seen on Dublin's streets in the late 1880s.[24]

There are several conflicting claims as to who was the first Irish cyclist in the modern cycling era that was inaugurated by the Michauxs' innovation in 1861. As all of these claims were made a considerable time after the introduction of the bicycle they should be treated with some scepticism, and it is impossible now to determine which of the early cycling pioneers was the first in Ireland. In 1886 James Talbot Power of Leopardstown asserted that he introduced the 'first modern velocipede' – 'a miserable forty-two-incher' – to Ireland in 1862.[25] The Michauxs only made 142 velocipedes in this year.[26] The landlord of the Railway Hotel in Shillelagh, 'a most enthusiastic cyclist', showed an English tourist in 1877 an old velocipede which he stated was built in 1863 and bought by him in 1864.[27] Notwithstanding the claims of these two alleged first Irish cyclists, in the Irish cycling world of the late nineteenth century it was generally believed that the first Irishman to ride a bicycle was Dr Austin Meldon, the founder of the first Irish cycling club, in 1869. Meldon learned to ride a velocipede in Paris in 1864, and because he weighed some twenty-four stone in that year his machine had to have special springs constructed to bear his weight. He is reported to have ridden his velocipede constantly and to have visited St Cloud, Versailles and Fontainebleau on it.[28] John Townsend Trench of Kenmare, the Marquis of Lansdowne's agent, claimed that he was also in Paris in 1864 when he saw the 'marvellous' sight of a man quietly riding a velocipede along the street. He ran after the cyclist to enquire about the

Left: Dr Austin Meldon, one of the first Irishmen to ride a velocipede, pictured with a bicycle in 1896.

Opposite: Sketch allegedly made in 1864 of John Townsend Trench's velocipede.

'strange machine', and elicited from him the information that he had just bought it from a blacksmith named Michaux. Trench then proceeded to Michaux's forge and purchased a velocipede for himself, which he learned to ride in Paris before bringing it to England at first and then to Ireland, where he rode it 'constantly' at Kenmare. According to Trench, this was the first velocipede in either England or Ireland. In 1895 he printed a sketch which he stated his sister had made of the machine in 1864. Despite the fact that the sketch bore the date of 1864, it is possible that Trench's memory was playing tricks with him and that he had, in fact, acquired his machine from Michaux at an earlier date. Trench told the *Irish Cyclist* in March 1890 that when he went to Michaux's forge, Michaux said of the velocipedes that 'he had not yet made more than a dozen of them', which 'he had only just invented and brought out'. According to Trench, at the time Michaux was making his bicycles by hand, 'without the aid of machinery of any kind'. In 1895 Trench gave the newspaper a different version of events, claiming that Michaux told him that 'he had only just invented these machines, and had only made six of them, and had sold five of them, and had one left', which is the velocipede that Trench bought and brought to Kenmare. The details suggest that it was possibly early in 1862 that Trench acquired his machine.[29] One cannot now say with certainty which, if any, of the aforementioned individuals was the first Irish bicyclist, but one *can* say with more assurance that they were amongst the very first Irish users of this revolutionary machine in the 1860s.

Some of the first generation of Irish cyclists recorded their memories of the early years of the new pastime, allowing the historian to piece together a picture of Irish cycling in the 1860s and 1870s from these and other contemporary

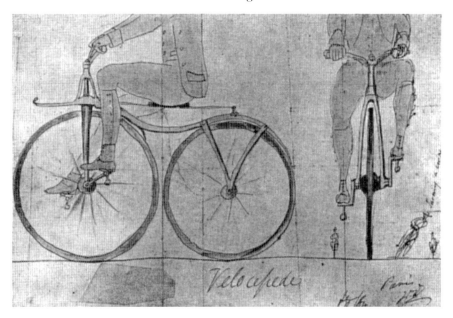

sources. Much of this early cycling activity centred on Dublin, where, as early as 1866, there was at least one business which carried out repairs on velocipedes – William Henderson's of Drury Street.[30] E.J. O'Reilly, a prominent sports journalist in England and Ireland in the 1880s and 1890s, provides a wonderful account of the first time he saw a velocipede being ridden on the streets of Dublin by a Mr Kenny – directly outside the grounds of the Royal Dublin Society – in 1867, and the vivid impression it made on his boyhood imagination:

> I was amazed at the sight, and I could think of nothing else for long enough afterwards. I lived near Ball's Bridge at the time, and soon the gentleman on the bicycle (and the footpath always) became a familiar object, for he constantly passed in the evenings. What puzzled me most was the balancing of the thing. This man's balance on the machine was as great a source of wonder to me then as a balance at the bank would be now. With its heavy wheels and its iron tyres it made a great noise, but it got over the ground at what seemed at the time a wonderful pace. I was filled with the cycle fever, and sighed with the profound sigh of boyhood for the wealth of Midas that I might spend it all on such a machine. Tops, marbles, and india-rubber balls interested me no more. Paper balloons and kites lost their charms, that were at one time so seductive. I no longer delighted in driving the baker's horse, or in accompanying the milkman on his afternoon rounds. At home I rebelled, in the hope that by establishing a domestic reign of terror I might find the wherewithal to purchase a velocipede. I did everything that was wrong. I put my elbows on the table at dinner, I held my knife in my left hand. When strangers were present I purposely clamoured

for anything of which the supplies had run out. I spilled my glass of milk on the table cloth; and proclaimed loudly in the presence of visitors, that my new knickerbockers were not the latest thing from Paris, but had in reality been made from a pair of discarded bed-curtains. All in vain! The only result of this policy was that my hours out of bed were curtailed of their fair proportions, and my little body was made more tender by external applications of birch.

Having failed to bully his parents into buying him a velocipede, O'Reilly skilfully planted the desire for a bicycle in the mind of a friend who lived in Sandymount Avenue, whose father was more indulgent of his offspring than O'Reilly senior was towards his. The stratagem succeeded and O'Reilly and other boys learned to ride on the newly acquired machine, 'and joy reigned in the land'.[31] O'Reilly subsequently acquired a boneshaker of his own, which he rode until 1875. This was called 'the hearse' or 'the gun-carriage' by his friends, because of its weight and the noise that it made. He replaced it with a wooden bicycle which had solid-rubber tyres – when these became loose from the wheels O'Reilly would affect repairs by the simple expedient of hammering a nail into the loose tyres.[32]

In 1867, the same year in which O'Reilly saw his first velocipede, Michael Walsh, a coachmaker from Portlaw, built what was probably the first bicycle to be made in Dublin that had pedals and rubber tyres. Before this, no velocipedes in Dublin had rubber tyres. Walsh was inspired to build his bicycle after seeing a woodcut illustration of a velocipede in an English magazine.[33] Another pioneering cyclist who built his own machine was P. Kavanagh, a coachbuilder from Arklow, who not only constructed his own bicycle but entered it in one of the first cycling races to be held in Dublin, in June 1870.[34] Most cyclists did not build their own machines, of course, but procured them from a number of retail outlets or commissioned coachbuilders, such as Walsh, to construct bicycles for them. The latter course of action was taken by Thomas Mayne in 1867, when he had a Brunswick Street coachmaker build him a boneshaker 'which he trundled about for some considerable time in a very energetic manner, often covering twenty miles in an evening'.[35] The first Dublin bicycle retailers included Robinson's toy shop on Grafton Street, which began selling velocipedes in 1867. Robinson initially acquired his machines from Paris, but after a few months these were supplied by John Roberts and Company of Bridgwater. Robinson is also recorded as offering bicycles for hire in 1870.[36] William Bindon Blood, who moved to Dublin in 1860, left his tricycle behind in Galway 'where it rotted away, and departed this life eventually full of rust and years'. In 1868 he heard of the bicycle which Michaux had invented and shortly afterwards he saw a Mr Meade riding one in Stephen's Green, which he had bought from Robinson's establishment on Grafton Street. Blood bought one from Robinson also, 'but soon wore it out', whereupon he procured wheels from the coachbuilding business of Thomas Maxwell Hutton and Lucius Octavus Hutton in Summerhill,

An early Irish illustration of a velocipede.

and got Booth Brothers of Stephen Street to build him a new machine.[37] Before 1870 the 'chief emporium' for bicycles in Dublin was Fredric Bapty's sewing-machine shop on Grafton Street. Bapty had a riding school for learners in a gallery of the Exhibition Building in Earlsfort Terrace, where novice cyclists paid a shilling each for an hour's lesson from the instructor, Bapty's son, who also demonstrated some trick riding to the budding cyclists.[38] Another important concern which was connected with the Dublin cycle trade in the early years was that of a well-known carriage axle manufacturer named Neal, who started a bicycle factory on Clarendon Street around 1869, as well as a riding school for learners. Louis Meldon, Austin Meldon's brother, was taught how to ride a bicycle there by Neal in December 1869. Early in 1870 – in which year there was 'a regular craze for bicycles', according to Michael Walsh – Neal moved his bicycle factory to the Exhibition Buildings in Earlsfort Terrace. Its turnover was seven or eight bicycles per week. Neal emigrated at the end of 1870 and Walsh, who had been Neal's foreman, opened his own bicycle factory at 18 Nassau Place, which he ran for three years. In addition to supplying local customers he also provided machines for a customer in Clara who bought them for postal use, a Dr Churchill who brought two of Walsh's machines to India, as well as sending machines to customers in England and, on one occasion, to a customer in Paris.

One of his sidelines was converting iron-tyred bicycles to rubber-tyred bicycles for the Booth brothers. Walsh's wooden bicycles cost about £8 10s to produce and were guaranteed for a year. His business was overtaken by the advent of the 'Ariel' high-wheeler; although Walsh became an agent for the 'Ariel', he decided to emigrate to America in 1873.[39]

The evidence regarding cycling in the rest of Ireland at this period is scarce in comparison to that relating to Dublin, but enough survives to allow one to build up a sketchy picture at least. In the South, the most prominent cyclist was Richard Edward Brenan, a post office employee in Dungarvan, who formed Ireland's second or third cycling club – and one of the world's first – in that town in June 1870. At this time it was common for people who sent newspapers through the post to write messages in the folded-up newspapers, and it was one of Brenan's duties to check newspapers that were posted to Ireland from abroad to ensure that this illegal practice was not being carried out. While engaged in this duty he came across an advertisement in a French newspaper that contained an illustration of a bicycle, and he was transfixed. His father gave him £5 towards the purchase price and his first bicycle was acquired from Paris. His next machine, 'an improved boneshaker', was purchased from Robinson's of Dublin, rather than from Pierce's, the agricultural implement factory in Wexford, which began producing boneshakers in the late 1860s.[40] His next velocipede was purchased from Neal's of Dublin, who, according to Brenan, 'did what was then considered a large "velocipede" trade, and, we young Irelanders of that period, took much pride in our home manufactured mounts'.[41] Brenan, like so many of the first cyclists, was an avid devotee of the new pastime. In 1868 he went on the first documented cycling holiday in Ireland, starting from Dungarvan and passing through Youghal, Midleton, Queenstown, Cork, Ballincollig, Blarney and other towns. On the return journey he rode from Cork to Dungarvan in one day, during very wet weather, 'a performance which was thought something wonderful in those days'. When he was in Cork he was followed 'everywhere' by crowds, on one occasion having to take refuge in the *Cork Examiner* office – a sure indication that the bicycle was extremely rare, if not unknown, in Cork at that time.[42] In 1896 R.B. Baker, owner of a cycle depot at 48 Patrick Street, was described as 'one of the oldest, if indeed he cannot claim to be the first, cyclist in the southern capital'. His first bicycle was 'of the timber variety, iron-tyred and ungeared', which he bought from an army officer who, in turn, had brought it with him on his return from India. Baker rode this machine 'until it actually and literally fell asunder'. It was credited as being one of the main means by which the velocipede was popularised in Cork.[43] Another of the southern pioneering cyclists was W.G.D. Goff of Waterford, who, some three decades later, was described by one source as the second person in Ireland to have ridden a bicycle. This retrospective claim can be easily discounted, however, as Goff's first mount was a wooden boneshaker which was brought over to Ireland for the lord lieutenant, Earl Spencer, in 1870.[44]

At the other end of the country, cycling in Ulster in the early years mainly involved a number of Belfast enthusiasts. According to Harry Hewitt Griffin, a Canadian of Irish descent who wrote several works on cycling in the late nineteenth century, an occasional boneshaker might have 'found its way' to the North by 1869, but the sport was still 'practically unknown here in that year'.[45] One of the first velocipedes in Ulster was the bicycle with a thirty-six-inch driving wheel which Joseph David Everett, professor of Natural History at Queen's University Belfast, saw exhibited in the window of John Riddell's ironmongery and hardware shop in Donegall Place in the summer of 1868. It cost £15.[46] Everett waited until cheaper English makes came on the market before purchasing a bicycle – made by the West of England Carriage Company, of Bridgwater – in the summer of 1869, for £10, 'after looking at all the kinds that were available', including those offered by Bapty and Robinson in Dublin. He took a lesson in Bapty's riding school at Earlsfort Terrace, but most of his first practice efforts were made in the lanes near his home. When he found that he could manage to coast downhill without wobbling he put his feet on the pedals and 'by degrees learned the stroke'. In that summer Everett rode to numerous towns within easy riding distance of Belfast, including Bangor (where the hostler at a hotel informed him that he was the first cyclist to have visited the town), Lisburn, Hillsborough, Carrickfergus, Whitehead, Newtownards, Ballyclare, Antrim and Randalstown, proceeding at a pace of about five miles an hour on level roads. According to Everett, riding velocipedes was tiring on riders' knees and there were other problems which novice riders had to overcome:

> It was an amusing sight to see learners practising. There were no such things as headers, but there was plenty of sideways falling, and the driving wheel was not limited in its steering range as at present, but could turn its back where its front should be, and pinch the rider's leg against the [bicycle's] backbone. This was a very common occurrence in tumbles. I twice had my own leg jammed in that way, and had some difficulty in extricating myself from the trap.[47]

Harry Hewitt Griffin moved to Belfast in March 1871 after securing a position at the head office of the Belfast Bank, and joined the Belfast Gymnasium. According to Griffin, 'This was the real centre of cycling energy in the North. The wheel fever was just taking root, and here it was aided and encouraged'. The gymnasium's equipment included a couple of boneshakers, and on these the gymnasium's expert riders 'took much trouble to teach the "duffers" and perfect the "middlers"', probably in the grounds of the Belfast Academical Institution, to which the gymnasium members had access. Griffin was considered a 'middler' as he had already done some tricycling and bicycling in his final school holidays at Bridlington Quay in Yorkshire – his rudimentary riding skills were perfected by R. Garrett, Ireland's record holder for a one-mile race in 1870. Griffin acquired his own bicycle in April or May 1871, which he had ordered the previous year from Underhill's of Newport. In 1894 he observed of cycling in the early 1870s in Ulster that:

> The sport made but slow progress, however; riders were scarce and machines not very attractive, although many is the jolly ride I had on the mass of iron, steel, and wood which constituted my bicycle. Reckless coasting was a special delight, and at the top of the hill I used to spurt, then throw up my legs on the long projecting leg-rests, and let the machine 'go' in a manner that dare not be attempted on the dainty cycles of today.[48]

The early velocipedes, which weighed over 100lbs in 1868,[49] originally had wooden wheels and iron 'tyres' or rims, but 1870 saw the emergence of bone-shakers with iron wheels. These were easier for youths with iron-working skills to construct, and, according to Professor Everett, 'lads' in ironworks in Ulster began making their own bicycles. The disapproving academic noted that 'Rough fellows of this sort soon formed the majority of riders and put bicycling rather out of fashion', and he gave up the pastime 'for a few years, as it was not considered respectable'.[50]

Improvements in bicycle technology, and particularly the 'Ariel' high-wheeler, soon meant that the boneshakers which these youths were constructing were obsolete and that cycling once again became the preserve of mainly well-off, middle-class young men. Although at least one engineer in Mossley Mills, Belfast, succeeded in making his own Ordinary bicycle, including the ball bearings,[51] the new machines were generally too sophisticated for most youths in iron foundries to make. The 'Ariels' were also too expensive for foundry youths to buy – the early models of 1871 cost from £8 to £12,[52] and the later and more sophisticated models were even more costly. By 1873 the 'Ariel' was being produced by Haynes and Jefferis of Coventry. The firm introduced a clever advertising gimmick by establishing the Ariel Bicycle Club, with its headquarters in Leamington Spa and with branches throughout the United Kingdom – it was a rule of the club that members rode 'Ariel' machines, which were supplied at discounts to club members. Harry Hewitt Griffin joined the Ariel club in late 1873 and began organising a Belfast branch, which was successfully accomplished early in 1874 – this was the first cycling club in Ulster. Griffin not only cleverly used the new club's name when trying to persuade sports committees in Ulster to put bicycle races on their sports programmes, but he also secured a liberal discount for the Belfast branch of the Ariel Bicycle Club – which was, in effect, a syndicate for acquiring cheaper bicycles for its members – when he placed an order for fifteen or sixteen machines from Haynes and Jefferis. Some five per cent of the discount went to the club's funds, part of which went towards hiring a room to store members' bicycles in a building behind Donegall Place, which was used as a rendezvous where the members gathered before club runs.[53] Because it was the first cycling club in Ulster (changing its name to the Belfast Bicycle Club in 1875) its first run to Larne 'created great excitement' in that town.[54]

The huge impact made by the bicycle's first arrival in a rural district is captured by Robert Cromie's description of his machine's delivery to a village in Ulster, possibly in Co. Antrim, in an account which he sent to *The Wheel World* in 1883:

> 'She's coming! She's coming!' The speaker was an excited urchin, who, in the hurry of his race to be first with the news, had out-run his breath. He belonged to a class which is now only to be met with in out-of-the-way country villages… She was a bicycle, the advent of which was regarded by the entire youth of the place with unaffected interest, and now that she had arrived there was no small stir concerning her. The important intelligence alluded to had been no sooner conveyed than the carrier appeared wheeling the machine before him, and surrounded by a guard of honour whose tender years would scarcely prepare one for the utter gravity of their demeanour. Each individual seemed to feel a certain responsibility, as if the safe delivery of the bicycle depended, less or more, on his especial escort, and when the, to them, marvellous vehicle was handed over to me they stood around with the air of men who knew their duty and had done it. The peculiar interest which the machine possessed for them lay in the fact that although an occasional tourist may have passed through the village on his wheel, never yet had any such fearfully and wonderfully made construction taken up a permanent abode amongst them. It was to them a thing of mystery, and in truth it was little else to myself, for I had never previously bestrode even a boneshaker.[55]

Cromie's account is not atypical, as numerous other pioneering cyclists recorded broadly similar impressions of the stir which was created when bicycles or tricycles appeared for the first time in Ireland's towns, villages and rural districts around this period.

For instance, Edward O'Toole records in his memoirs that when George Knox, from near Rathvilly, used to cycle into the aforementioned village on his Ordinary bicycle, the first bicycle seen there, around 1872, 'he was always followed by a crowd of youngsters who were delighted with the novel sight'.[56] In 1875 two cyclists who were en route from Bangor to Killyleagh to visit the Killyleagh regatta, accepted a challenge to race from a car driver they encountered on the road, who believed that his mare could outdistance 'them things':

> Killyleagh was crammed with strangers, but catching a long sight of our 'dust-up', in more senses than one, aquatics were forgotten, and they formed up into cheering lines as we dashed into the village, the wheels a bit ahead. It was the first time a modern bicycle had ever been seen in the place, so the excitement can be imagined. The country folk fairly swarmed round the riders, to touch and handle the machines, and to ask questions.[57]

When Thomas Hiram Holding of the Banbury Bicycle Club passed through Millstreet on his cycling holiday in 1876, he was followed by 'hundreds of people surging down the street after the machine, yelling and laughing'. Some of the inhabitants ran with him for almost a mile outside of the village.[58] When Patrick Fagan, a cycling tourist on a 1,100-mile trip through the west of Ireland, proceeded through Ballygar en route to Oughterard in September 1876, he found that the village's fair stopped so that the inhabitants might gaze at him as he passed through. On reaching Mulranny some days later, he was 'delayed a good deal from the insatiable curiosity of the natives', as he was only the second cyclist to have travelled through the Mayo village; when he reached Kilcar, Co. Donegal, he 'collected such a crowd as filled up the whole street', and on leaving the village he was 'accompanied for some distance by the villagers in the rear'. At Carrick he delighted the constabulary by speeding through the village.[59] On much of his trip Fagan was either the first or the second cyclist to have passed through the villages on his route (he was occasionally told that he had been preceded by the president of the Limerick Bicycle Club),[60] which accounts for the sensation that his arrival caused at various points. Two cycling tourists from Newark, who made their way southwards from Greenore in August 1877, were a novelty to the local inhabitants when cycling from Ardee to Kells, as they found that, 'The labourers at work in the fields, when they caught sight of us, even from the far side of a field, would throw down their implements and come running up to the road to see us pass'. They made their way from Kells to Clonmellon one evening, creating a particularly vivid impression in the latter place. Clonmellon was:

> …a large village, through which it seemed to us that bicyclists seldom or never passed, from the manner in which the natives saluted us. We considerably frightened the natives during this moonlight ride; two men jumped clean over a hedge in their anxiety to get away from us, and some old women who saw us pass that night told their friends that they had seen 'two witches riding on nothing'.

On their arrival in Delvin the two cyclists went for a drink of ginger beer in a draper's shop; they had to bring their machines into the shop to protect them from the curious throng who gathered outside to take a closer look at their bicycles.[61]

A Limerick cyclist who went on a bicycling holiday through counties Limerick, Cork and Kerry in the following month wrote:

> …since I left Lombardstown my bicycle and myself were the admiration of all the peasantry; in fact, it was a regular triumphal march – the Russians entering Kars the other day was nothing to it! Everyone left their work and ran with all their might to the ditches to get a better view of the 'man on wheels'. Some of the old women muttered blessings as I flew past, the girls looked coy, smiled and wished me all kinds of luck, while the men who had the good fortune to be on

the roadside waved their hats and cheered most lustily; with such good-will on all sides I did not feel the miles passing by.[62]

There is other evidence from the 1880s which illustrates the gradual, if uneven, spread of cycling in the country and the sheer novelty of tricycles and bicycles in various districts in that decade. For instance, a Limerick tricyclist who passed through the village of Loughill – 'a depressing collection of a few dozen cabins' – at some point in 1880, recorded that 'Every inhabitant of it who was not bedridden rushed out to see me, but I went at too great a rate to be pursued, save by four boys whom I lured on for about a mile, and who then dropped off from sheer exhaustion'.[63] James Bennet of the Northern Bicycle Club, who went on a cycling tour throughout Ulster in October 1880, stopped by the roadside near Gweedore for a rest when he was cycling through Donegal. He wrote that 'in a comparatively short time, quite a crowd of natives gathered around me to examine the "curiosity of a horse" that I was riding', and they asked him many 'foolish questions' concerning the bicycle's construction and how he rode it.[64] A Dublin cyclist, who went on a three-day bicycling tour through counties Kildare, Kilkenny and Waterford in 1881, was astonished when he was abused by a group of elderly women whom he met on a mountain road between Fiddown and Waterford – he recorded that the women used 'no very choice adjectives in their denunciation of bicyclists in general and myself in particular'. An explanation for the women's behaviour was gleefully provided by a man whom he encountered further along the road. A few evenings previously a local cycling club had been returning to Waterford and came upon the same group of women on the same stretch of road, as they were carrying butter, milk, eggs and other produce to a local market. As it was evening the cyclists had their lamps turned on:

> The women, seeing strange and various coloured lights flitting noiselessly about the road, became terribly alarmed, believing it was [a] 'will-of-the wisp', or the devil. The bicyclists, unconscious of the cause of the old ladies' alarm, and, seeing them rushing away screaming, increased their speed to inquire of them what was the matter. Seeing the lights gaining on them augmented the superstitious terror of the women who threw away eggs, butter, milk and everything they had, and sprang into the ditches, many falling into the water and being thoroughly drenched. When the ladies discovered the cause of their alarm their rage knew no bounds, and the cyclists were obliged to save themselves by a hasty flight.

This afforded the Dubliner an insight into the women's antipathy towards cyclists. When he was returning from Waterford to Kilkenny on a different mountainous route through the villages of Dunkit, Kilmacow and Mullinavat, his passing created a considerable stir amongst the local inhabitants, which is testimony to the rarity of bicycles in this district at this time:

William Hume of the Cruisers Cycling Club and J.B. Lindsay of the Northern Cycling Club depicted on a tandem tricycle, a machine which had a dramatic impact in Limerick when it first appeared there in September 1885.

> In passing through the villages the natives of these wild regions flocked to the doors of their cabins to see the strange machine speeding along, and several children who were loudly repeating their tasks in a village school flew to the open door, oblivious of books and everything else, to gaze, with wonder stamped on every lineament of their ruddy faces, at the flashing spokes of the bicycle as it sped swiftly through the village, down the steep mountain road.[65]

Another cycling tourist who went on a summer holiday trip in counties Armagh, Monaghan, Fermanagh and Donegal in 1883, stopped for a break at the Monaghan village of Middletown, where his bicycle 'produced a sensation as it innocently lay at rest against a refreshment-house door'.[66] William Henry Duignan of Walsall, who travelled by tricycle from Dublin through several Leinster and Munster counties in August 1883, noted as he passed through the Laragh-Rathdrum region that 'My machine was the continued admiration of the farmers on the way, and they were never tired of examining it, always pronouncing it to be an "iligant yoke", the best they had "ever seed", etc.; indeed, from the attention it received throughout, I should doubt if any "Humber" had previously travelled south'.[67] Tricycles were also a rarity in Co. Tipperary, judging from an incident in 1892. A tricyclist on a Sunday night-time spin near Slievenamon surprised a party of the local peasantry who were secretly digging an old rath which was reputed to contain buried treasure – not having seen a tricycle before, the peasants 'could not understand the weird apparition' and presumed that the devil had arrived in person to carry them away for their sacrilegious conduct, and they 'stampeded in extreme disarray'.[68]

The terrified response of the Tipperary peasants was an unusual reaction, as most areas of Ireland must, by then, have witnessed the passing of a tricycle or an Ordinary bicycle at least once. What was more common from the mid-1880s onwards was for people who were already familiar with the sight of tricycles or Ordinary bicycles to become excited by the appearance of new makes of cycles. For example, the Newry agent for the Rudge Cycle Company 'created quite a sensation' when he rode through the town on a new Rudge 'Bicyclette' (a safety bicycle with a large front wheel) in May 1886.[69] When the first tandem tricycles arrived in Ireland in the mid-1880s they also often astonished those who saw them for the first time. Two Englishmen, Henry Sturmey and a colleague, went on a cycling holiday in the west of Ireland on a tandem tricycle in the summer of 1885. Sturmey's record of this holiday reveals the impact of their new machine as they cycled through Co. Clare:

> About midway between Miltown and Kilrush...is a village of which I do not know the name. It is built on the side of a hill, and as, with feet up and gong sounding, we flew through the long street at about fifteen miles an hour, the inhabitants left their work *en masse*, and when at the bottom of the hill, we turned right over a bridge, we saw the street above thronged with a gaping crowd, evidently thunderstruck at the novel sight.[70]

The first tandem tricycle to appear in Limerick also had a dramatic impact when it was ridden through the city by a member of the Cyclists' Touring Club in September 1885.[71] When A.J. Wilson and a colleague from London visited the Wexford Gaelic Athletic Association sports meeting in August 1888, they were prevailed upon by the organising committee to cycle around the race course on their tandem tricycle, the first to be seen in Wexford.[72] Some years later, the first tandem bicycle to appear in Sligo, on 31 August 1894, also attracted a lot of attention from locals.[73] Perhaps the best-known innovation in cycling technology in this period was the development of the pneumatic tyre and its subsequent application to safety bicycles. A pneumatic-tyred safety's first arrival in a district was a particularly noteworthy event – indeed, according to Edward O'Toole of Rathvilly, the pneumatic-tyred bicycle which he purchased in the spring of 1892, the first one to appear in Co. Carlow, 'created almost a greater sensation than George Knox's Penny Farthing of twenty years previously'.[74] It is instructive that the arrival of the pneumatic tyre in Bruree was one of the few memories which Eamon de Valera detailed in a lecture on his boyhood years which the aged politician gave in the Co. Limerick village some sixty-five years later.[75]

Evidence of the startled reaction of animals to the first appearance of tricycles and bicycles reinforces the sense of the tremendous impact that these machines often had in rural Ireland. A bicyclist on an Ordinary who travelled from Dublin to Arklow on 7 August 1877, recorded that his machine gave a tremendous fright to a horse on the road near Avoca, and that in that district 'horses are very timid about bicycles', from which he inferred, almost certainly with accuracy, that bicycles were scarce in the neighbourhood.[76] William Henry Duignan, whose tricycle tour through several Leinster and Munster counties in August 1883 has already been referred to, noted when he reached New Ross that 'The farther

A carthorse bolts at the approach of an Ordinary bicycle.

I go south the more my machine excites attention, and the more it frightens animals; donkeys stop suddenly at the sight of it, horses are alarmed, and mules, which are very numerous, become unmanageable.'[77] Animals in Wexford were also scared of the first safety bicycles, as a cyclist who travelled from Templeshelin to Enniscorthy in December 1890 found out:'I made the discovery that nearly all the beasts of burden in the Co. Wexford are afraid of [safety] cycles, and I had to dismount at least a dozen times en route to allow horses and even donkeys to pass the dreaded machine', he recorded.[78] Even as late as 1899 cycling tourists were warned that bicycles were still scarce in some parts of Donegal and that carthorses and plough-horses were likely to shy at bicycles which they encountered on the roads.[79] Horses shying at their first encounter with a bicycle was a sufficiently common occurence to inspire Percy French to write a short story, 'The First Bicycle in Ballymachugh', the main action of which involves a mare taking fright at the sight of an Ordinary bicycle. In the words of Mr O'Hanly, the fictional farmer who witnessed the incident, 'She gin' one snort and haway wid her down the road, like the devil went thro' Athlone, in standin' leps'.[80]

3

Who Cycled?

As we have seen, while there is plenty of evidence that the first appearance of
cyclists was often a startling novelty for many Irish people, they gradually became
accustomed to the sight of tricyclists and bicyclists on the roads. The emergence
and spread of cycling clubs throughout the country was undoubtedly an important factor in this transformation. In a speech to fellow cyclists in Cork in June
1887, Dr Stacpoole-Westropp of Lisdoonvarna observed that 'Cyclists are gregari-
ous beings, who forcibly illustrate the truth of the old adage, "Birds of a feather
flock together". Let a few cyclists crop up in any locality, and their first instinct
is to form themselves into a local club.'[1] Although Stacpoole-Westropp, in his
enthusiasm for cycling-club activity, probably exaggerated the extent to which
cyclists organised themselves in clubs, there is no doubt that the club was a distinctive and important feature of the Irish cycling world. An examination of the
development of cycling clubs thus provides the historian with a useful means of
charting where and when cycling had planted relatively strong roots in Ireland in
the late nineteenth century.

Ireland's first cycling club, the Amateur Velocipede Club, was organised in
Dublin by Dr Austin Meldon in 1869. Its first two meeting places were Meldon's
house at 10 Weston Row and the house of a pawnbroker, Edward A. Hayden, at 43
Clarendon Street, before a permanent club premises were found at the Exhibition
Palace Annexe at Earlsfort Terrace on 26 November 1869. The club met on
Wednesday evenings, when as many as seventy members often assembled for prac-
tice and also to learn various cycling tricks. Meldon's club – one of the first in the
world – petered out in 1873, due to the premises having to be given up and the
club's inability to find suitable alternative accommodation, as well as the death
of some of the principal members.[2] Another Dublin club, the Earlsfort Terrace
Machinery Court Club (which was either the second or third to be established in
Ireland) was formed in 1870,[3] possibly connected with Neal's riding school in the

Exhibition Palace building, but it does not appear to have lasted as long as Meldon's club. By 1875 two other clubs existed in Dublin – these were the Dublin Amateur Bicycle Club, the older of the two, which had its headquarters in Dublin city, and the County Dublin Bicycle Club, with its headquarters in Kingstown. According to one source, the former club 'had little life in it' by 1875, whereas the latter club (whose members included Austin Meldon's brother Louis, a solicitor) engaged in such pursuits as paper chases to Bray, Little Bray and Enniskerry, racing, playing the dangerous game of 'cross tig' on the jetty at Kingstown, and conducting club runs to destinations such as Glen of the Downs, Roundwood and the Seven Churches, and club tours to counties Wicklow, Wexford, Waterford, Cork and Kerry.[4] There is no evidence that either of these two clubs was in existence by the early 1880s. Dublin acquired a third bicycle club in November 1875, following an acrimonious split in the County Dublin Bicycle Club. Some of the club members lived in Dublin city and resented what they considered the cliquey behaviour of the Kingstown members, which they believed meant that scarcely anybody but Kingstown residents could get elected to club membership, and there was also 'considerable jealousy' between the Dublin and Kingstown men. Following the committee's refusal on 2 November to move the club's headquarters from Kingstown to Dublin city, Louis Meldon and a prominent racing cyclist, William Persse Blood – the son of William Bindon Blood – decided on the following day to form a club of their own. The new club – the Irish Champion Bicycle Club – whose first general meeting was on 18 November 1875, had committee rooms over Lawrence's on Grafton Street at first, but later changed its headquarters to a premises at Bachelor's Walk.[5] It was instrumental in organising the first Irish cycling championship races in June 1876, which function was taken over in 1882 by the Irish Bicycling Association (whose name was changed to the Irish Cyclists' Association in 1884). A fourth Dublin club, the Dublin University Bicycle Club, was formed in the winter of 1877, with R. Hassard, a well-known racing cyclist, as its first captain,[6] while the Phoenix Cycling Club was established in the capital in 1878.[7] The latter was inaugurated by eight cyclists who met at the Phoenix monument in the Phoenix Park in September 1878. One of these suggested the formation of a club for holding fixed runs in the evenings, which suggestion was accepted by the others present. By September 1881 the Phoenix club, with over fifty members, was the largest cycling club in Dublin.[8]

The 1870s also witnessed the establishment of a number of cycling clubs in other parts of Ireland. The country's second or third club, the Dungarvan Ramblers, was formed in June 1870 by a post office official, R. Edward Brenan, whose house in Devonshire Square was also the club headquarters (the sources do not permit one to state with certainty whether Brenan's club was founded before or after the Earlsfort Terrace Machinery Court Club, which was also formed in 1870). The Ramblers had some twenty-eight members by the end of 1880.[9] As we have already seen, Ulster's first cycling club – the Ariel Bicycle Club – was established in Belfast by Harry Hewitt Griffin in 1874. This was merely

Photograph of members of the Northern Bicycle Club in Ormeau Park, Belfast, *c.*1880. Note the club bugler, third from the right.

one branch of a club that had branches throughout the United Kingdom. In 1874 the Ariel Bicycle Club began to decline when it became known that its prime mover was intimately connected with the company whose machines club members were obliged to ride; this scandal, and also the fact that 'the local riders wanted something more Irish – a club of their own, in fact' – led to the Belfast members of the Ariel club forming the Belfast Bicycle Club in 1875, the name of which was changed to the Northern Bicycling Club in 1877.[10] It numbered some twenty-five members in October 1876.[11] The next Belfast club, 'which for some years displayed great vitality', was the Windsor Bicycle Club, whose head-quarters were at the Queen's Arcade.[12] The first cycling club in Limerick, the Limerick Bicycle Club, emerged in December 1874, when several 'gentlemen' were recorded as learning to cycle in a large room in the city's Masonic Hall – this was also the address of the first recorded bicycle agent in Limerick, Michael Sheehy.[13] In 1877 the County Carlow Wanderers Bicycle Club, which apparently was a short-lived outfit, was established.[14] In 1878 at least two clubs were formed: the Dundalk Cycling Club, membership of which was open to all bicycle and tri-cycle riders residing in Co. Louth 'and surrounding districts', and the Shamrock Bicycle Club of Dublin, which later changed its name to the Eglinton Bicycle Club. The latter club, whose headquarters were at the Burton Hotel on Duke Street, had some thirty-eight members by December 1880.[15] The Tralee Bicycle Club was inaugurated in 1879, as was the Richmond Bicycle Club of Belfast.

The latter club had eighteen members in May 1879; this total rose to thirty-two by June 1881.[16] The first general meet of Irish cycling clubs was held in Dublin's Phoenix Park on 21 June 1879. Reports of the proceedings, consisting of a race (won by R. Hassard), which was followed by a procession of the participating clubs, reinforce the impression that organised cycling (and probably cycling in general) was still, at that stage, largely confined to a small number of urban areas. Dublin clubs dominated the meet – the Dublin University club, with twenty-six or twenty-seven members, led the parade, followed by the Phoenix club (also with twenty-six or twenty-seven members) and the Irish Champion club (with twenty-three or twenty-five members). Two other Dublin clubs are mentioned in the reports – the Ixion, which was based in Inchicore, and the Eglinton. In addition to the previously discussed Dungarvan, Limerick, Belfast and Tralee clubs, the reports also refer to the existence of the Cork Bicycle Club and a Tullamore club. The Cork club had held its first race meeting earlier in the same month.[17] Towards the end of the year, in November 1879, a cycling club was organised in Wexford. According to its captain, R.H. Shaw, who was a future cycling agent, it had a rather humble beginning as its complement of bicycles amounted to only two machines, which were lent to the members in turn. Within a year the club had thirty-six members enrolled.[18]

The following decade saw a noticeable increase in the number of Irish cycling clubs, as the sport gradually spread to more parts of the country. Part of the reason for the increase in cycling's popularity was the wider adoption of the tricycle by women and by 'gentlemen who object to the danger of the bicycle', a trend which was predicted by the *Limerick Chronicle* in March 1879.[19] Indeed, a few tricycle clubs were organised in the 1880s – the first Irish tricycle club was the Belfast-based Ulster Tricycle Club, which was formed in 1884; by March 1885 it had forty-five members, which total increased to over fifty by March 1886.[20] The Dublin City and County Tricycle Club was formed around May 1885,[21] while another tricycle club consisting of five founder members was formed in Newry in April 1886. The latter club had only a single tricycle, which was for use by all of the members – the club rules prohibited members from cycling faster than three miles per hour, which was considerably slower than the eight miles per hour that in 1879 one source estimated a tricycle could cover 'with ease' on a good road.[22] The number of tricyclists increased to such an extent that many clubs that originally had the word 'Bicycle' or 'Bicycling' in their names replaced these with the words 'Cycle' or 'Cycling' instead, in order to accommodate tricyclists. Examples include Dublin's Leinster Bicycle Club and Belfast's Northern Bicycling Club changing their names to the Leinster Cycle Club and Northern Cycling Club, respectively, in 1884.[23] The most significant instance of this trend was the decision by the Irish Bicycle Association (formed after a meeting was convened on 15 April 1882 in the Wicklow Hotel, Dublin, by the Irish Champion Bicycle Club, to establish a national organisation that would hold annual Irish amateur championship races, an annual general meet of Irish cyclists and promote cycling in Ireland) to call itself the Irish Cyclists' Association (ICA) on 2 May 1884.[24] In his review of the 1886 cycling season, R.J. Mecredy stated that the number of cyclists in Ireland had 'increased enormously', with the number of tricycle riders – including women – having doubled in the course of the year. He pointed out that:

> …the principal increase [in the number of tricyclists] has been among the pro-fessional and business classes, and amongst middle-aged and elderly men, who did not before indulge in any kind of vigorous exercise, and who have experi-enced, in almost every case, that a great increase of health resulted, and that the enjoyment and pleasure of life were greatly added to.[25]

While Mecredy was undoubtedly correct in his assertion about the health-pro-moting qualities of tricycle riding, the new pastime was not without its hazards to some elderly riders, as the sixty-year old Dublin doctor Lombe Atthill discovered when he went for a spin on his newly acquired machine in March 1887 and lost control when riding down an incline along the Grand Canal. Atthill ended up being pitched head first into the canal, with his tricycle landing on top of him.[26] In addition to the growing popularity of tricycle riding, the other main factor in cycling's increasing popularity in Ireland in the latter half of the 1880s was the introduction of the safety bicycle – a topic which will be discussed later on in this chapter. For most of the 1880s, however, the Ordinary bicycle was the machine most frequently ridden by Irish cyclists.

The number of cycling clubs increased gradually in the first half of the decade. On 16 January 1880 J.B. Cherry, a solicitor, formed the Waterford Bicycle Club at his house on William Street. Some twelve men, including the Mayor of Waterford, L.A. Ryan, joined the club at this inaugural meeting, and by the year's end some forty-two members had enrolled.[27] The Limerick Amateur Athletic Club formed a bicycle club in April 1880, which initially consisted of some thirteen members,[28] while the Greenisland Bicycle Club, organised on 29 May 1880, had fourteen members by the year's end.[29] Cycling clubs which were begun in Dublin in 1881 included the Clontarf, Palmerstown, Richmond and Atlas Bicycle Clubs, the last of which had almost twenty members in September. The Richmond club recruited members from the Clontarf and Drumcondra districts.[30] A second Waterford club, the Urbs Intacta, was launched around September 1881.[31] At the first North of Ireland cycling meet at Ormeau Park, Belfast, in 1881, some six clubs participated – the Richmond club, with eighteen members, the Windsor club, with fourteen members, the Northern club, with eleven members, and the Greenisland club, with five members, as well as two new clubs – the Rovers club, represented by five members, and the Queen's College club, represented by two members.[32]

" Maria will be furious if I've forgotten anything."

The tricycle was a mixed blessing for some Irish cyclists.

The year 1882 saw the establishment of at least eight clubs, including the Ardbraccan Cycling Club – Meath's first cycling club – and Mullingar's Westmeath Cycling Club in March, and another club in Maryborough in April.[33] Another Limerick club, the Limerick City Bicycle Club, was also instituted in 1882.[34] At least four clubs were organised in Dublin in this year – the Eblana, Leinster, Commercial and Metropolitan clubs, which brought the total number of clubs in the city to eleven.[35] The Metropolitan Bicycle Club was formed at a meeting held in the Portobello Hotel on 28 January, following a split in the Phoenix club, which had been established in 1878. While the causes of the split that led to the formation of the Metropolitan club remain obscure, it is known that '[f]or a considerable time, there remained an unwholesome rivalry between the "Mets" and the Phoenix', which dissipated after a number of years. The Metropolitan started off with twelve members and grew slowly – by the close of the 1886 season it had experienced only a modest growth, to seventeen or eighteen members, and at the end of the 1887 season only nineteen members were on the books and the club was in a bad financial state. A new captain took over in 1887 and turned the club's fortunes around, to the extent that by the end of 1888 it consisted of forty-two members, most of whom were introduced to the club by the new captain, and in 1889 it had more than fifty members.[36] Clubs which were organised in 1883 include the Portadown Bicycle Club (which was, apparently, a short-lived outfit as there was no cycling club in the town in 1888),[37] Dublin's Albion Bicycle Club, which was formed by riders from the South Circular Road district, Belfast's Mossley Bicycle Club and the Portarlington Bicycle Club,[38] while the Omagh Cycling Club, Newry Bicycle Club and the Iona Cycling Club of Dublin were started in 1884.[39] In 1885 the ranks of Irish cycling clubs swelled with the addition of the Londonderry Bicycle Club, consisting of thirty-six members, the Glenageary Cycling Club, with at least thirty members, and Belfast's Western Cycling Club, with twenty members initially, and clubs which were established in Bangor and Newtownards.[40] Other clubs which were in existence in 1885, but whose starting dates have not been ascertained, included the New Ross Bicycle Club[41], the Kerry Bicycle Club, which had more than thirty members in this year,[42] and the Belfast Ramblers Bicycle Club.[43]

The picture that emerges of Irish cycling down to the mid-1880s is that the pastime was sufficiently strongly grounded in urban centres in many parts of the country, with the exception of west of the Shannon, to sustain cycling clubs, with Dublin and Belfast cyclists being particularly fond of associating in clubs. A few areas, such as Limavady, that had an estimated twenty-five or twenty-six cyclists, also had enough riders to form clubs but had not done so by the middle of the decade. An account from Co. Antrim in 1888 stated that 'Cycling as a means of exercise and recreation is progressing in popular estimation. Every town has a respectable number of devotees in what is called "a quiet way"; that is to say, there is not much desire for public display by means of club meetings and affiliation with national organisations'. The Ballymena Cycling Club, established in 1886, was the first cycling club to be formed in Co. Antrim, excluding Belfast.[44] Other clubs started in 1886 included the Cookstown Cycling Club,[45] the Cruisers Cycling Club in Belfast,[46] the Banbridge Cycling Club,[47] the Roscrea Cycling Club, which had around twenty members in June 1886,[48] and a club in Skibbereen. The Skibbereen club acquired its cycles in a unique fashion. An enterprising local coachbuilder bought a consignment of bicycle and tricycle parts, part of the salvaged cargo of an Atlantic steamer which had been shipwrecked off the coast. The rubbers had been lost, but he imported some from England and then assembled an assortment of machines, which he sold to the new club for the very cheap price of from £4 to £6 apiece.[49]

Most cyclists in this period were athletic young men, as they had to be in order to accomplish the tricky feat of riding the Ordinary bicycle. In the latter half of the 1880s, however, increasing numbers of Irish riders took to the roads on a machine which represented the latest advance in cycling technology, the chain-driven safety bicycle with two equal-sized wheels, the first example of which was John Kemp Starley's 'Rover' bicycle, developed in 1884 and launched in 1885. A safety bicycle for women was developed in 1886. The first men's safeties arrived in Ireland in 1886. Perhaps the first recorded instance of the purchase of a safety

The safety bicycle was a much safer ride than the Ordinary bicycle.

bicycle in Ireland occurred in April, when the agent for the Rudge company sold one in Drogheda and also took orders for five more machines.[50] One observer recorded in November that the 'rage' for safeties had reached Dublin and that orders for safeties and enquiries about them were numerous, and Carson Brothers of Bachelor's Walk were reported to be constructing their own machine.[51] Most of the increase in the number of cyclists in the capital was ascribed to tricycle riders and safety riders.[52] R.J. Mecredy recorded that at the close of the 1886 season safeties 'came greatly into vogue', the 'Rover' proving particularly popular, with 'the undoubted safety, lack of vibration, speed and ease over rough roads proving irresistible recommendations'.[53] In the following year a Dublin observer calculated that the number of 'votaries of the wheel' had almost doubled since the previous season, and that such was the 'rage' for rear-driven safeties that the cycling depots had been 'denuded' of them; tricycles were also said to be in keen demand, but there was no demand for Ordinaries.[54] In Cork the Munster Safety Bicycle Club was formed in 1888 'with a nucleus of eighty members',[55] another early indication of how popular the safety bicycle quickly became with many Irish cyclists.

Many Ordinary riders viewed the new machine with disdain, however, and it took a number of years for the safety bicycle to completely replace the Ordinary as the machine of choice of Ireland's 'crack' riders. The fact that the safety bicycle was, as its name suggests, a relatively safe machine to ride actually counted against it in the eyes of many Ordinary riders. It took courage to ride an Ordinary bicycle, especially given the frequently wretched state of Ireland's roads (a subject discussed below). Headers – spectacular accidents in which riders were pitched head-first over the handlebars of Ordinary machines – were common occurrences,[56] and, indeed, were welcomed by some riders;[57] one Wexford cyclist described how he was 'sent flying through the air with that old well-remembered sensation which is one of the most endearing peculiarities of the Ordinary bicycle'.[58] The danger was increased by the fact that Ordinaries were not always equipped with brakes,[59] and even when they were, daredevil riders refused to use them, even when riding down dangerous hills.[60] A Derry cyclist, who went with a colleague on a cycling tour through counties Derry and Donegal in 1884, records the exhilaration of carelessly riding Ordinaries downhill at Druminin: 'We had a fine run down-hill here, legs over, which quite refreshed us, and made us, in fair exuberance of spirits, sing in no gentle voice of the pleasures of the wheel, to the no small alarm of the natives'.[61] The reckless exuberance of young bicycle riders is illustrated vividly by the example of the Coleraine bicyclist who in 1883 rode an Ordinary across the foot-wide arch which connected Dunluce Castle with the mainland, heedless of the precipitous drop on either side; and the Limavady rider, 'a youth upon whose cheeks the silky down has not yet made its first appearance', who, in November 1886, attempted to ride down Lisnakelly Hill with his feet over the handlebars and his arms folded carelessly.

The difficulty of mounting an Ordinary bicycle is illustrated in this sketch.

When his bicycle hit a stone at the bottom of the hill he was pitched over the handlebars and knocked unconscious.[62] The Irish Champion riders who went for a moonlit ride for two miles along the cliff edge at Howth in May 1887 were cut from a similar cloth.[63] The satirical journal, *The Jarvey*, printed a verse which summed up the dangers of riding Ordinary bicycles:

> Melancholy Occurrence.
> He said, 'A bicyclist I'll be',
> We heard his speech with sorrow;
> He bounded on his '53' –
> His funeral's tomorrow.[64]

The glamorous image of the Ordinary bicycle is illustrated by this cartoon of knights on the high-wheeled machine, in an advertisement for a race meeting of 'Ireland versus Creation' to be held at Ballsbridge on 7 July 1888.

To ride an Ordinary, then, was to display bravery and manliness, which helps to explain the patronising view of one Drogheda cyclist in 1886 that:

> ...a man looks ludicrous on any safety. After a good deal of serious thinking, and studying the matter over coolly, I have come to the conclusion that the [O]rdinary bicycle is the best and safest after all; and I will not give up 'my old friend for the new'. The safeties are no doubt very good for the timid, and for those who are not strict teetotallers, and I would certainly recommend them to aged riders, whose lumbar and ventral regions have assumed aldermanic proportions.[65]

One gains further insight into the hostility shown by some Ordinary riders to the safety bicycle, from the opinion of a Kingstown devotee of the Ordinary that the safety bicycle was a 'less dignified mount'.[66]

Another reason why many Ordinary riders declined to ride safety bicycles at first was that the latter were slower than the former. Safety bicycles were initially fitted with solid tyres and, later, with 'cushion' tyres – these were hollow tubes with a bore of about half an inch in diameter, which had the disadvantage that they often cracked at the rims and had to be replaced if they developed even small cracks, making them fairly expensive to use.[67] Ordinary bicycles were faster than the first safeties, as a single revolution of their solid-rubber-tyred front wheel carried riders further, and with less effort, than solid-tyred or cushion-tyred safety bicycles. However, John Boyd Dunlop's development of the pneumatic tyre in Belfast in 1888, spelt the end for solid and cushion tyres, and for tricycles and Ordinary bicycles as well. Dunlop's nine-year-old son, Johnnie, rode a solid-tyred tricycle which he used to race against his friends in the People's Park. It was difficult for Johnnie to ride this machine on Belfast's roads, especially on those covered with stone setts, so his father set himself the task of devising a tyre that would both overcome vibration and be fast on all surfaces. The pneumatic tyre fitted the bill admirably – indeed, young Johnnie was easily able to keep pace with, or even outdistance, adults riding solid-tyred tricycles. The new tyre was brought to the attention of the Irish cycling public on 18 May 1889 when William Hume of the Cruisers Cycle Club (this club, which had its headquarters at the Prince George Hotel, had been formed in May 1886 as an offshoot of the Ulster Tricycle Club) [68] raced on a pneumatic-tyred safety at the Queen's College sports. The new tyres were a source of amusement to the spectators and the other racers, who were riding solid-tyred Ordinaries, but this soon changed when Hume, a moderately successful racer until then, easily beat his opponents. [69] When the 'Irish Brigade' of racing cyclists – B.W. Piggott, K.N. Stadnicki, R.J. Mecredy, F.F. MacCabe, and Arthur and Harvey du Cros – 'swept the boards' in the races in which they competed in England in 1890, once again easily defeating the opposition on their pneumatic-tyred machines, despite the initial hilarity with which the pneumatic tyre was greeted, the tyre's success was assured and 'there was not a racing cyclist left who did not clamour for pneumatic tyres'. [70]

As we shall see below, it took a few years for the supply of pneumatic tyres to meet the demand, and for a number of years Ireland's roads were travelled by cyclists on Ordinaries, tricycles, and solid-tyred and pneumatic-tyred bicycles. For instance, some fourteen of the twenty-three cyclists in Cookstown in October 1889 rode Ordinary bicycles, while eight rode 'R.D.' safeties and one rode a 'Girder' safety. In Armagh in January 1892, where as recently as 1888 a tricycle was considered 'a startling novelty', the Armagh cycling club, comprised of from twenty-five to thirty members, rode 'Premier' safeties 'instead of fifteen-year-old Ordinaries and massive rear-steering tricycles'. All of these machines had solid tyres. [71] The general trend, however, was for established and would-be cyclists alike to opt for pneumatic-tyred safety bicycles. A Dublin resident wrote in September 1889 that:

> The pneumatic fever is the disease of the hour. Anything like the extraordinary run on this machine has never come under my notice; nor that of anybody else I should think. I was in Bowden and Swenys the other day for a short time, and while there the proprietors never ceased answering queries about the machine, and lending it to fellows. It is wonderful. [72]

The fact that the first arrival of the pneumatic-tyred safety bicycle in Newry was reported in the Irish cycling press in April 1890, with similar events recorded for Tralee in July and Athy in August of the same year, and that it was considered newsworthy in September 1890 that the first of this type of bicycle had just been bought in Wexford, also indicates the importance that contemporaries attached to the new machine. [73]

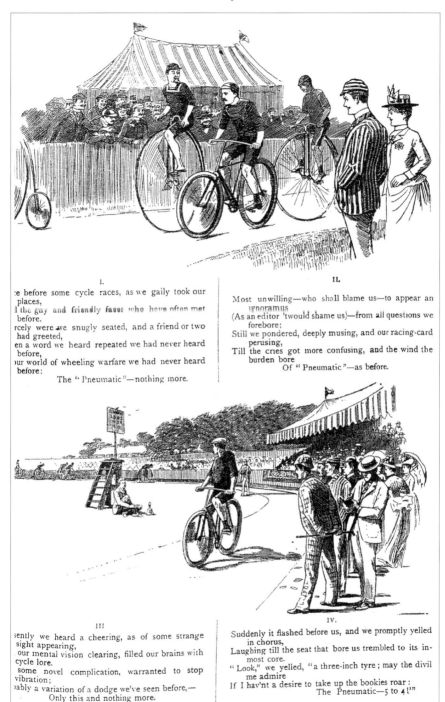

I.

e before some cycle races, as we gaily took our
places,
l the gay and friendly faces who have often met
before.
rcely were we snugly seated, and a friend or two
had greeted,
en a word we heard repeated we had never heard
before,
ur world of wheeling warfare we had never heard
before:
    The " Pneumatic "—nothing more.

II.

Most unwilling—who shall blame us—to appear an
ignoramus
(As an editor 'twould shame us)—from all questions we
forebore;
Still we pondered, deeply musing, and our racing-card
perusing,
Till the cries got more confusing, and the wind the
burden bore
    Of " Pneumatic "—as before.

III

ently we heard a cheering, as of some strange
sight appearing,
our mental vision clearing, filled our brains with
cycle lore.
some novel complication, warranted to stop
vibration;
ably a variation of a dodge we've seen before,—
    Only this and nothing more.

IV.

Suddenly it flashed before us, and we promptly yelled
in chorus,
Laughing till the seat that bore us trembled to its in-
most core.
" Look," we yelled, " a three-inch tyre ; may the divil
me admire
If I hav'nt a desire to take up the bookies roar :
    The Pneumatic—5 to 4 ! '"

The first racers to ride pneumatic-tyred safety bicycles were scoffed at by spectators
and by fellow competitors riding Ordinaries. Their relatively easy victories soon wiped
the smirks from their tormentors' faces.

B. W. PIGOTT   COUNT STADNICKI.   R. J. MECREDY.   F. F. MACCABE.
              AR. DUCROS.   HARVEY DUCROS.

The 'Irish Brigade', who were victorious on English race tracks on their pneumatic-tyred machines in 1890.

A Derry observer commented in July 1890 that 'The pneumatic fever is raging in this city and district, and solid-tyred machines have, in consequence, depreciated in value'.[74] In February of the following year the Irish Cycle Company of Nassau Street and Clare Street, Dublin, reported that solid-tyred bicycles were 'almost unsaleable' and offered their machines for the extremely low price of £5.[75] One gains insight into the profound changes that were occurring in the Irish cycling world at this time through the fact that by the end of April 1891 there was only one rider of the Ordinary in Waterford – this was W.G. Todd, the honorary secretary of the Waterford Bicycle Club.[76] The *Irish Cyclist* reported on 25 March 1891:

> This spring trade has been the best on record for Dublin agents. Trade has been extremely brisk, and orders are pouring in to the various cycle depots. Probably the main factor in this is the immense impetus given to the trade by the intro-duction of the now universally used air tyres.

The newspaper also commented on 'how much the safety has supplanted the tricycle with riders who are comparatively advanced in life' and that in Dublin 'it has become quite common to meet white-haired gentlemen, of grandfa-

"ERIN UP TO DATE."

The harp that once in Tara's Hall
  Played many a lively tune—
For instance, "Clara Nolan's Ball"
  · And "Up in a Balloon;"
Now hangs upon a peg for sale,
  By many a pawn-shop door;
The lovely maids of Innisfail
  Will twang the harp no more.

The strings have all been snapped, they say,
  From lying in the damp;
But this is not the reason they
  Are never heard to "vamp."
The voices which we loved to hear,
  Now echo no refrain,
And goodness only knows, my dear,
  When they will wake again.

And why has Erin ceased to sing
  The thrilling songs of yore?
Why hangs the harp with broken string
  Behind the pawn-shop door?
Fair Erin doesn't care a bit
  For any busted lyre,
For all her "hands" have learned to fit
  The great Pneumatic Tyre.

'Erin Up To Date': a cartoon from 1891 illustrating the revolutionary impact of the pneumatic tyre on the Irish cycling world.

therly aspect, astride the two-wheeler'. The introduction of the pneumatic tyre was undoubtedly a key factor in making the safety bicycle attractive to elderly riders. In April 1893 McGregor and Alexander, cycling agents in Derry, reported that bicycles were also popular with middle-aged men in the Maiden City.[77]

£500 PRIZE) A. MECREDY, CYCLE AGENT. (£500 PRIZE) (£500 PRIZE) A. MECREDY, CYCLE AGENT. (£500 PRIZE)

The Largest Cycle Agency in Ireland, A. MECREDY, Proprietor.

Solid tyres in Dublin appear to have been replaced by pneumatic tyres by April 1893, according to a Kildare observer,[78] while in 1894 the phrase, 'Mean enough to steal a solid-tyred Ordinary', was used to denote 'the lowest form of depravity'[79] – this also shows how far from favour the 'Grand Old Ordinary' had fallen in Irish cyclists' eyes. By May 1894 Ordinaries were so rare a sight on Dublin's streets that one observer considered it newsworthy that he had encountered two on Molesworth Street.[80] In January 1895 it was reported that tricycles in Dublin were 'now nearly obsolete', and that all Dublin cycle agents were selling women's safeties instead.[81] The growing popularity of cycling amongst Irish women in this period is another sign of the revolutionary impact of the pneumatic-tyred safety bicycle on Irish society, a topic which will be discussed in greater detail in chapter four.

Cycling undoubtedly made tremendous strides in Ireland in the ten years from 1885 to 1895, and by the latter end of this period a pronounced cycling 'boom' was under way in the country. In June 1886 the vice chairman of the Irish Cyclists' Association claimed that there were thousands of cyclists in Ireland,[82] while the *Irish Athletic and Cycling News* described cycling as 'our national pastime' in August 1889.[83] The example of Portadown is indicative of the spread of cycling in the late 1880s. There were no more than six bicycles or tricycles in Portadown

Right: An advertisement lauding the qualities of the Dunlop pneumatic tyre.

Opposite: Alexander Mecredy's Irish Cycle Company, Dublin, in 1890.

in 1887, while a year later the number of cyclists in the town amounted to almost a hundred. According to one of these, 'Nor is the art confined to any particular class or age[:] gentle and simple, old and young, fathers, mothers, and children take a like delight in their newly-found pleasure'.[84] In February 1888 the *Irish Cyclist* referred to 'the wonderful increase' in cycling which had occurred in the Dublin district in the previous two years, pointing out that doctors were recommending the pastime and that 'professional men and ladies are taking to it largely, and that it is steadily becoming more popular in every grade of society.'[85] Cycling was allegedly so popular in Ballyclare in 1889 that cricket, 'the favourite summer recreation in the past', was 'almost extinct, as its votaries have taken to the wheel'.[86] At the other end of the country, an Enniscorthy cyclist stated in April 1890 that 'The cycling epidemic is raging fiercely here at present, everything in the shape of a machine being bought up at good figures, and should things continue as they have commenced, we shall eventually have the whole town on wheels'.[87] The *Irish Times* claimed in June 1891 that 'the brotherhood of the wheel has increased a hundred fold within the last two or three years', and that 'the cycling body includes peers, judges, clergymen, barristers, medical men, solicitors, merchants, and other respectable folk, and the cycles are used as much for business and health as for pleasure.'[88]

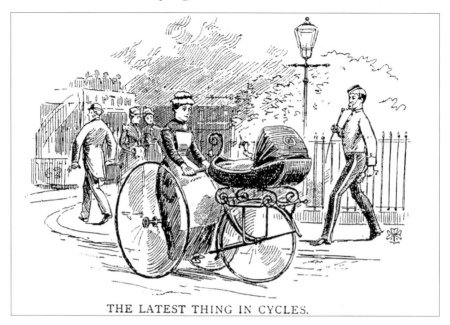

THE LATEST THING IN CYCLES.

It seemed to some Irish observers in the early 1890s that just about everyone was riding a cycle of some sort.

Many of the cyclists in this period were fanatical about their pastime – indeed, according to the coachman of Fr M.J. Murphy, parish priest of Kildare, in 1891 the cyclist clergyman was so enthusiastic about riding his solid-tyred safety bicycle that 'he would ride it up stairs to his bedroom if he could'.[89] A distinguishing feature of this fanaticism was an obsessive cataloguing of distances and routes cycled. As early as July 1870 a Kerry cyclist displayed this trait when he detailed the miles that he had cycled and the places he had visited awheel in Kerry and Limerick over the course of a single weekend – his catalogue was compiled in order to dispel the notion held by many that the bicycle was a 'more toy'.[90] Like-minded enthusiasts included the Limerick tricycle rider who recorded that he had cycled 1,160 miles in twelve months in 1879 and 1880,[91] and the bicyclist and tricyclist who rode some 1,418 miles in Co. Waterford in 1886.[92] Gerald Stoney, a doctor based in Lucan, recorded a precise total of 5,177½ miles cycled in 1886. Dr Austin Meldon estimated in March 1890 that he had ridden some 11,650 miles, mostly in morning rides before breakfast, on his 'Singer' safety bicycle, as well as 3,700 miles on a 'Singer S.S.' tricycle specially built for him in 1886. A veteran Cork cyclist, Robert Jeffers Haynes, aged fifty-eight in 1894, was noted for the fact that he always cycled before breakfast and thought nothing of covering thirty miles before breaking his fast each morning; from the start of 1894 to 25 July of the same year he had cycled 2,924 miles, and was aiming to cycle 5,000 miles before the year's end.[93] One of the most meticulous of these obsessive cyclists was the *Irish Cyclist* editor, R.J. Mecredy, who estimated in January

1895 that he had cycled some 75,000 miles since 1878. He clocked up some 7,013 miles over 307 days in 1894 and 7,053 miles over 300 days in 1895, averaging some twenty-three and a half miles daily; his longest ride in this period was 180 miles.[94] The figure of the fanatical cyclist, for whom the main pleasure of the new pastime lay in notching up personal milestones such as riding a hundred miles in a single day, was lampooned by one Irish newspaper in December 1895:

A Hundred Miles

> He tumbled from his weary wheel,
> And set it by the door;
> Then stood as though he joyed to feel
> His feet on earth once more;
> And as he mopped his rumpled head,
> His face was wreathed in smiles;
> 'A very pretty run,' he said;
> 'I did a hundred miles!'
>
> 'A hundred miles!' I cried. 'Ah, think!
> What beauties you have seen!
> The reedy streams where cattle drink,
> The meadows rich and green.
> Where did you wend your rapid way,
> Through lofty woodland aisles?
> He shook his head. 'I cannot say;
> I did a hundred miles!'
>
> 'What hamlets saw your swift tires spin?
> Ah, how I envy you!
> To lose the city's dust and din
> Beneath the heavens' blue:
> To get a breath of country air;
> To lean o'er rustic stiles!'
> He only said, 'The roads were fair;
> I did a hundred miles!'[95]

Nevertheless, the urge to compile statistics of distances cycled persisted. For example, in January 1896 C.F. Brennan of Kilkenny recorded that he had clocked up some 9,230 miles on a Dunlop-tyred Raleigh racing bicycle, as well as 1,000 miles on a tandem with various partners, while in February 1901 Alex McCormick of Portarlington, who 'practically lives on his bike', claimed to have cycled over a quarter of a million miles in his long cycling career.[96]

The increase in the number of cyclists who participated in organised cycling activity in the form of clubs provides a good measure of cycling's growth from the mid-1880s to the mid-1890s. The ICA experienced a marked expansion in this period. One critic in February 1884 felt that it was ridiculous that this body should use the term 'Irish' to describe itself, as its membership was practically confined to Dublin,[97] but the affiliation of clubs from all parts of Ireland in the succeeding years rendered this criticism of the ICA redundant. By March 1886 the ICA contained some fifteen clubs, including six that were not Dublin-based – these consisted of clubs from Belfast, Derry, Portarlington, Waterford, Wexford and Limerick.[98] The ICA increased to include some forty clubs in 1890 and sixty-one clubs in 1891, with an Ulster regional branch of the organisation being established in the latter year.[99] The establishment of the Ulster branch of the ICA reflects the strength of cycling in the northern province, which was reputedly home to more than one-third of Ireland's cycling clubs in 1893.[100] By 1897 there were some fifty-five Ulster clubs affiliated to the ICA, which had an estimated 10,000 members in this year;[101] by May 1899 there were some seventy-three clubs affiliated to the Ulster Centre of the ICA alone.[102] While the steady growth of the ICA may be taken as a sign of the increased popularity of cycling in Ireland in the late nineteenth century, one should bear in mind that not all clubs joined the ICA. In 1891, when the ICA consisted of some sixty-one clubs, the *Irish Cyclist's* masthead for 15 April shows that some seventy-six cycling clubs had appointed that newspaper as their official organ; furthermore, the newspaper's editor claimed in December 1890 that he could enumerate nearly 100 Irish clubs.[103] Nor should one regard club activity as the only measure

Right: Members of a Belfast cycling club on the road to Ballycastle, July 1886.

Opposite: Members of a cycling club in a public house in 1895. Note the cycling board game on the table.

of cycling's popularity in this period, although it was undoubtedly an important feature of Irish cycling – the *Irish Cyclist* referred in October 1888 to 'the great army of the unattached' when describing those cyclists who did not belong to cycling clubs, while the same newspaper calculated in February 1892 that for every member of a cycling club in Ireland there were approximately fifteen 'unattached' members; this proportion rose to approximately twenty or thirty in Dublin.[104]

Who were Ireland's cyclists in this period? As we shall see, the tricyclists and bicyclists came from all sections of the population, but in general, and especially before the widespread use of pneumatic-tyred safety bicycles, they tended to come from the better-off segments of society. After Ordinaries, tricycles, and solid-tyred bicycles became obsolete in the 1890s, the prices of these machines fell and there is evidence that for a number of years in this decade these machines were increasingly ridden by those who could not afford the up-to-date, pneumatic-tyred bicycles. Before the 1890s, however, new tricycles or bicycles were simply too expensive for most of the population. This was certainly the case for the 'Dublin' tricycle, manufactured by the Singer Company of Coventry, whose three models cost £18, £18 10s and a massive £44 19s, respectively, in 1880. Women could pay an additional £2 for a screen to conceal their feet. The 'Irish Duplex' Ordinary was a more affordable £16,[105] but this was still far beyond the reach of all but the more well-to-do Irish customers. As far as can be ascertained, the cheapest bicycle on the Irish market in the 1880s was probably the 'Lombard Roadster' Ordinary offered for £8 10s by the Belfast ironmongers and bicycle and tricycle dealers Jennings and Osborne of 14 Lombard Street, in 1884.[106]

One did not have to be a club member to enjoy cycling, as this advertisement for the Booth Brothers' 'Singer' cycles in 1887 shows.

This was not typical of the prices on offer in the 1880s, however, as may be gathered from the prices of machines sold by the firm of Fletcher Brothers of Dublin, the sole Irish agents for 'Premier' and 'Sparkbrook' bicycles and tricycles. An advertisement from March 1886 shows that they usually sold second-hand 'Club Premier' Ordinaries for £18 10s. The prices of their new machines ranged from a low of £11 5s for a 50" 'Popular Premier' to £20 15s for a 'D.H.F. Premier'; the prices of 'slightly used' machines varied from £18 to £21 1s, while their 'stockworn' machines cost from £12 12s to £18.[107] In 1888 Walker, Carpenter and Company of 24 Duke Street, Dublin, sold 'Psycho' tricycles for £22 10s. Their safety bicycles were cheaper, at £12 for a Clark 'Cogent' and £14 10s for an Andrews 'Sanspareil'. In the same year Robertson's Cycle Works of Lemon Street, also in Dublin, was selling safety bicycles for either £14 10s or £18. The shop's Ordinary bicycles were offered for £7,[108] a sure indication of the decreasing popularity of the high-wheeled machine with the Irish cycling public. In the following year the Rudge depot at 1 Stephen's Green, Dublin, was selling a Rudge diamond-framed safety bicycle for £14 7s 6d.[109] In 1892 the Napoleon Wheel Company of Rathmines was selling 'Juno' pneumatic-tyred safeties for £12 12s.[110] As late as May 1897 the cycling correspondent of the *Weekly Irish Times* considered bicycles that cost '£12 or thereabouts' as cheap, but recommended spending £20 to secure a good machine.[111] Machines at these and similar prices were clearly aimed at a middle-class and upper-class market. There is some evidence to suggest that cyclists from these classes of society could not always easily afford to pay for new tricycles and bicycles – for instance, when James George Woulfe Flanagan, a thirty-four-year-old Dublin barrister, bought a bicycle in 1898, he had to borrow £18 as he could not afford 'to fork out so much', while Lady Augusta Gregory described the £24 that she paid in April 1897 for a 'Humber Wolverhampton' bicycle as 'a large sum which I can't very well spare'.[112] It is significant that in 1894 R.J. Mecredy wrote about the '[m]any fairly well-to-do young men and women, who have longed for years to enjoy the pleasures of cycling, but cannot raise the necessary sum for a machine'.[113] Even as late as 1907 in Dublin, when the price of a 'reasonable model' of bicycle had dropped to £5, a bicycle was considered 'just about affordable' for a middle-class family.[114]

It is not surprising, then, that cycling in late-Victorian Ireland was mostly an elite pastime, more so than in Britain at the same period. In 1890 the *Irish Cyclist* contrasted Irish cyclists with those in Britain. It explained that in the early years cycling in Ireland was promoted by university academics and doctors 'and such like men of position and standing', so that the pastime was considered 'fashionable':

> …the leading doctors took to it, and recommended it to their patients, especially to their lady patients; barristers, solicitors, clergymen, etc., adopted it in great numbers, and never considered it infra dig to be seen spinning about on wheels, and in fact it became firmly established amongst a class of people who in England prefer cycling in their carriages.

Although the social basis of cycling had expanded in Ireland in recent years, businessmen and professionals still dominated the pastime and there was 'almost an entire absence of the rowdiness inseparable from the mechanic and factory element', unlike in Britain, where the business and professional element was in the minority. The majority of British cyclists consisted of:

> …young riders who indulge in scorching, racing, and other pursuits that bring men together, and cause them to join clubs, and of the latter a proportion do not behave as gentlemen, and cause the sport to stink in the nostrils of the same class of men who support it so strongly in Ireland.[115]

There is plenty of evidence to support the general picture that Irish cycling was dominated by members of the middle and upper classes. An examination of the occupations of the officials of the Westmeath Bicycle Club, which was founded in Mullingar in March 1882, is particularly revealing. The occupations of ten of the twelve officials are known. The club captain was a bank official, as were three of the eight committee members, including one bank manager; the vice-captain was a solicitor, the secretary was an ironmonger, and the treasurer a leather seller and seed merchant. A doctor and two publicans were also on the committee.[116]

MORE TYRANNY.

Orator (*who has an audience of car-drivers*): "Yis—an' not contint wid thavin' ou land from us, the blay-gard Saxins are now thryin' to thave our livelihoods from us

Irish jarveys did not look kindly on the arrival of bicycles and tricycles.

The Drogheda Cycling Club, formed in April 1886, had a magistrate – G.H. Pentland – as president; its vice-captain was the borough surveyor, Mr Green, while D.A. Hall of the Munster and Leinster Bank was the club treasurer.[117] In May 1887 members of the prestigious Fitzwilliam Lawn Tennis Club in Dublin, including Arthur H. Courtenay of the Common Pleas Division of the High Court of Justice, were described as 'all going in for tricycles', prompting one observer to comment that 'The accession of such men, belonging as they do to the upper ten thousand, is calculated to advance the sport here to an enormous degree'.[118] Courtenay was not the only figure in the Irish legal profession to take to cycling in this period – in fact, so many members of the legal profession were cyclists that they had their own cycling club, the Jurists' Cycling Club, by December 1889.[119] A Dublin livery-stable keeper complained to the editor of the *Irish Cyclist* in February 1894 that his trade was suffering considerably due to barristers taking up cycling. He lamented that 'I used to get no end of orders from barristers and so on…they would have a horse sent round every morning for a canter in the park before breakfast, but now nearly all of them have bicycles, and use those instead.'[120] In March 1899 in Belfast, the Independent Order of Foresters Cycling Club was formed 'in connection with the City Courts'.[121]

Irish cycling journals and other newspapers provide enough information about the class or occupational backgrounds of cycling club members and other cyclists to enable one to piece together a social profile of the Irish cycling world in the 1880s and 1890s. Many clubs catered for a select group of cyclists or had patrons from the elite of Irish society, which reinforces the idea of cycling as largely an activity for the well-to-do. In the 1870s, for instance, Lord Lurgan became patron of the Belfast Bicycle Club, while Lord Ardilaun and several other noblemen became patrons of the Leinster Bicycle Club of Dublin in 1884.[122] Lord Londonderry was president of the County Meath Cycling Club, established in Kilmessan towards the end of 1886, and Earl Fingal and Lord Athlumney were among its patrons.[123] The Duke of Abercorn was another of the Irish aristocratic patrons of cycling – he was president of the Strabane Cycling Club, which was established in March 1887.[124] Viscount Massereene was a member of Belfast's Cruisers Cycling Club in 1887.[125] Lord Dunsany was another keen Irish cycling aristocrat. In March 1891 – by which time he had been 'an ardent cyclist for many years', having been a member of the winning team in the first bicycle race between the universities of Oxford and Cambridge – he ordered a 'Hadley' tricycle from Messrs Bowden and Company of Dublin, explaining that every Irishman should order through an Irish dealer when he could. Dunsany became president of Dublin's Elysian Harriers Cycling Club in March 1892.[126] Viscount Carlow of Emo was an enthusiastic member of the Portarlington Cycling Club in 1891 and, after he succeeded to the title of Earl of Portarlington, he won the club's twelve-mile bicycle race in June 1895.[127] Lord Wolsely became president of the Dawson Street Gymnastic and Cycling Club in Dublin, in 1892.[128] Another Irish peer, Viscount Castlereagh, was a keen cyclist and wrote a public letter endorsing the bicycle supplied to him by the Seddon Pneumatic Tyre Company of Dublin, which was equipped with Seddon pneumatic tyres, in June 1893.[129]

The various Irish lords lieutenant in the final decade of the nineteenth century also gave public indications of their support for cycling. For instance, the entertainment in Dublin's Leinster Hall which was organised on 24 March 1890 to boost the funds of the Irish Cyclists' Association – an entertainment which consisted of a display of trick riding by the seven du Cros brothers and a musical concert – was held under the patronage of the lord lieutenant, the Earl of Zetland, as well as Prince Edward of Saxe-Weimar and the officers of the Dublin garrison.[130] In January 1895 the lord lieutenant, Baron Houghton, learned to cycle, although his clumsy efforts 'amused the *habitués* of the Phoenix Park not a little'.[131] His successor, Lord Cadogan, was a much more accomplished cyclist.[132] In January 1897 he and his wife each bought a 'Royal Enfield' bicycle at the Dublin Cycle Show, held at the Royal Dublin Society's grounds in Ballsbridge, from W.R. McTaggart of Grafton Street, Dublin.[133] By May 1897 the viceregal couple owned some twenty bicycles, employing one man whose sole job was to look after these machines.[134]

Not all aristocrats, however, were automatically keen on cycling; as late as March 1893 it was stated that Ulster's upper classes considered cycling to be 'beneath their dignity'.[135] The example of such aristocratic cycling pioneers as

Viscount Massereene, Lord Dunsany and Viscount Castlereagh, and the support given to cycling by various lords lieutenant, were undoubtedly an important factor in helping to break down whatever hostility towards cycling existed amongst elements of the elite of Irish society. The fact that Queen Victoria's daughters and the Prince of Wales took to the wheel [136] was probably also another reason why Ireland's social elite, along with their British counterparts, became avid cyclists between 1895 and 1897 – the years when cycling went beyond being a popular, largely middle-class pastime to assume the form of a 'craze' amongst 'fashionable' society. Aristocratic and other well-to-do observers, who hitherto remained aloof about the new pastime, now took to the wheel with enthusiasm. [137] In January 1895 'The Chef', who wrote the 'Irish Stew' cycling column for the *Irish Wheelman*, provided an intriguing insight into how and why attitudes towards cycling changed amongst many of the well-heeled of Irish society in the mid-1890s:

> I feel that I have scored distinctly over my old-fashioned relatives – especially the females – who regarded my deeply-rooted love of the wheel as a species of madness scarcely tolerable. I remember years ago when the wheel first fascinated me and made me a servile slave. I could scarcely get leave to keep my beautiful Singer's Challenge in the stable. My cycling doings were regarded coldly, and my appearance in cycling costume rendered me unfit for appearance before visitors. In fact I had to do most of my cycling surreptitiously, and say little about it either. If I met with an accident I got no pity. If I won a race I earned no enthusiasm. If I suggested calling upon any relative upon the poor, innocent machine I was regarded with scorn and derision. In fact my early cycling was barely tolerated, and certainly not encouraged. Now *my* time has come! Need I say that I rub it in rather strong. I religiously collect every paragraph I can see relative to the doings of princes, peers, nobles, and notables of all sorts when awheel, and read them out with a sarcastic emphasis which is intended to be very galling. Oh, my turn has come at last. Cycling has received such patronage of late that it cannot longer be decried. [138]

The Irish society magazine *Social Review* stated in November 1895 that cycling had become so popular with its readers that a regular cycling column was 'almost a necessity' – it was written by Beatrice Grimshaw, who wrote under the pseudonym of 'Graphis'; *Irish Society* followed suit with a regular 'Society on Wheels' column in January 1897. [139] The leading Belfast cycle dealer Thomas Edens Osborne numbered 'several distinguished members of the aristocracy' amongst his customers in 1896, [140] an indication of the transformation in attitudes towards the bicycle which had occurred amongst the elite of Ulster society since the early 1890s, while in 1897 W.A. McCrum's Leinster Street depot in Dublin was 'extensively patronised by the upper classes.' [141] One of the features of the Dublin

An advertisement for Thomas Edens Osborne of Belfast.

Cycle Show in the latter year was the sight of 'fashionable dames [who] discussed the merits of the rat-trap pedal and the cyclometer with an eloquence evidently born of knowledge.'[142]

In the mid to late 1890s cycling was incorporated into the social round of the Irish gentry. The exclusive Fitzwilliam Lawn Tennis Club of Dublin – whose members, as we have already seen, began cycling enthusiastically in 1887 – found in 1896 that so many members were neglecting tennis entirely, in favour of cycling, that it was considered necessary to institute bicycling 'at homes' in the summer, in order to revitalise the social life of the tennis club. Kilgobbin Castle was rented as the club house, and at the first bicycling 'at home' there in May 1896 at least one hundred bicycles, most of them ridden by women, were in evidence.[143] Bicycle gymkhanas and paper-chases – 'the quality playing cat and mouse', as the residents of Cappoquin described a bicycle paper-chase organised by Major and Mrs Chearnley of Salterbridge in November 1896[144] – were also popular with the landed gentry during the cycling 'craze'. In June 1896 the *Irish Cyclist* provided a good description of what bicycle gymkhanas entailed:

W.A. McCrum's cycle depot, Leinster Street, Dublin, in 1900.

Bicycle gymkhanas are all the rage at present among society people who enter-
tain. A gymkhana, it may be premised, for the sake of those who are not familiar
with this form of diversion, is a kind of comic athletic sports meeting, when all
kinds of absurd events are programmed, and real exertion is rather at a discount.
In a bicycle gymkhana, there are usually bill-posting races, egg-and-spoon or
parasol races, slow races, and all sorts of fancy competitions such as a cup-of-tea
race, when the competitors stop in the middle of the contest to drink a cup of
tea poured out by a friend of the opposite sex, or a thread-of-the-needle race,
which comprehends a stop to receive a needle and thread from a marshal of the
course, thread the needle, and go on. Fancy riding is almost always introduced
in various forms; figures of eight, and hands-off meanderings in and out of a
flagged course, being the commonest types.[145]

In the same month the Earl of Huntingdon held a gymkhana at his Sharavogue
demesne, in King's County, which included a women's bicycle race in which the
competitors had to ride in and out of a line of bottles without touching them.[146]
The bicycle gymkhana for women was considered to be the highlight of the summer season at Ranelagh in 1896 – the participants had to accomplish a number
of what were considered difficult tasks, such as trundling a hoop or opening and

The cycle show at the Royal Dublin Society, January 1897.

closing a parasol while cycling.[147] The bicycle gymkhana at the Mallow tennis courts in October 1896 opened with a competition parade of women's bicycles decorated with flowers, followed by a fancy dress competition on bicycles. This was followed by a 'bending race in and out of bottles', a race in which competitors had to ride a bicycle and roll a hoop simultaneously, a 'tortoise race' and a potato and spoon race, all of which featured male and female contestants. Two races were confined to male riders – in the first, contestants had to ride to a basin of water 'where after a good deal of splashing and spluttering they did, or did not, pick up an apple and ride again to the starting point'; the second race involved riding with a dummy figure on one's bicycle. The final event was a musical ride on decorated bicycles.[148] The Belfast Royal Irish Constabulary (RIC) sports in June 1897 also included a bicycle gymkhana. It was witnessed by Elizabeth A.M. Priestley of Saintfield, who wrote newspaper articles on cycling under the pseudonym of L.A.M.P.:

> At all events the lady leader of the Gymkhana on Saturday, and those she led seemed equally expert in indicating and executing with an ease and skill that showed neither hesitancy nor doubt, the various manoeuvres and evolutions they performed on wheels. Sixteen cyclists took part in the musical ride – eight

ladies and eight gentlemen – all of whom were attired in white. Six ladies and six men had red ribbons on their handles, with belt and band on hat of the same colour; a corresponding number had white, and the remaining four blue ribbons – a combination of red, white and blue, meant as a subtle little touch of loyalty in this month of [Queen Victoria's] jubilee…The ladies' costumes were white drill coats and skirts. The musical ride was very effective and admirably done, especially the drawing up in line at the end. A hearty burst of applause greeted the performers, as from the solid phalanx the 'thin white line' of cyclists drew out to its full complement in mid-field. The plaiting of the Maypole, which I understand is the most difficult performance, was done by four ladies and four gentlemen. Each rider held a brightly coloured ribbon, and, guiding the machine with the other hand, wound in and out, and round, entwining the ribbons, lifting them over each other's heads, &c. The sudden turns and wheels, the precision and facility required from every rider, showed an absolute mastery of the gentle art of balancing.

At the end of the gymkhana each female participant was presented with a memento of a gold scarf-pin decorated with the harp and crown emblem of the RIC.[149]

The gentry's keenness for cycling during this period is also documented by a report which shows that during the winter of 1895 to 1896 several paper-chases were organised in the Nenagh district, and that the female members of the Derry Castle Hunt had taken to cycling 'in considerable numbers' since the end of the hunting season. The master of the hunt, Colonel G.C. Spaight, organised a 'cycling carnival' in the grounds of his residence, Derry Castle, on the shores of Lough Derg on 2 June 1896, which featured two bicycle races for these women, on a half-mile course. Some sixteen of the twenty-two ladies who put their names forward participated in the races, wearing jockeys' colours. In the first race, for a silver pin box inlaid with ebony, Miss G. Brereton defeated Miss Blanche Poë; in the second race, a consolation competition for a prize of a silver buckle, Miss S. Morton defeated Miss Poë. The 'carnival' was attended by numerous members of the gentry from counties Tipperary, Limerick and Clare – among the guests were the Countess of Dunraven, Lord and Lady Dunalley, the Lord Bishop of Killaloe and Standish O'Grady.[150] Later in the year, a Galway observer commented in November 1896 that 'The pastime [of cycling] had taken the elite by storm, just as it did the bourgeois by hurricane a few years ago. A paper-chase on wheels was organised by the former class last week, and they liked it so well that a few more have been arranged.'[151]

According to one observer of Sligo cycling the following year, women who had taken 'a foremost place in the hunting field' in the previous winter were now prominent in the local cycling community. He added, 'Now paper-chasing on wheels and cycle parties of every kind are all the vogue.' One of these cycling parties, consisting of thirty-eight 'ladies and gentlemen', was organised by officers

Two women on a tandem following a hunt.

of the Sligo garrison; the cyclists rode to Rosses Point, where they played 'a capital game of polo on the strand', and then enjoyed 'a sumptuous tea' supplied by
the military hosts.[152] According to a Waterford commentator in the same month,
'Paper-chasing on wheels is the favourite pastime of the upper classes here this
season. Once a week they hold their runs.'[153] Further evidence of the frequent
overlap between the gentry's hunting and cycling interests during this period
comes from the Clonakilty Cycling Club.

The *Irish Cyclist* stated of this club in October 1897 that 'there is scarcely
any member, either lady or gentleman, who is not equally at home in the pig-
skin, and not a few of the fair members have carried off the brush after many
a hotly-contested gallop with the Carbery Hunt Club.'[154] Many hunt followers
took to cycling after fox hunts rather than riding horses, particularly in Kilkenny
and Clare, and occasionally were 'in at the death'.[155] The development of a
cycling version of that most aristocratic of sports, polo, probably reflected the
growing enthusiasm amongst the landed classes for cycling. The idea of playing polo on bicycles was suggested as early as September 1876 by the Irish
Champion Bicycle Club[156] but the sport did not immediately gain in popularity,
as suggested by the fact that when two American trick cyclists performed an
exhibition bicycle polo match as part of their repertoire in Dublin's Earlsfort
Terrace in 1886, it was described as 'something that has never been seen before'.[157]
The ubiquitous R.J. Mecredy inaugurated the modern sport of bicycle polo with

several of his Ohne Hast clubmates in their Kilternan clubhouse in October 1891, with Mecredy drawing up the rules;[158] by April 1894 the sport was being played by several Dublin clubs and had also been taken up by the Mullingar Cycling Club.[159] Jack B. Yeats, a keen cyclist, witnessed bicycle polo matches between the Ohne Hast, Vagabond and Dublin University clubs at a fête in Ballsbridge in May 1894 and published several amusing cartoons of the contests.[160] The Irish Bicycle Polo Association was formed in Dublin in August 1898, with Mecredy on the committee and, in April 1900, he was elected as the organisation's honorary secretary;[161] by then the sport had not only been taken up by Dublin's exclusive Mount Temple Lawn Tennis and Cycling Club and the Fitzwilliam Tennis Club,[162] a revealing insight into the type of person playing the new sport, but was also being played by clubs in Rathclaren, Belfast (the Commerical Cycling Club), Newtownards, Banbridge, Cork and Enniscorthy.[163]

Beatrice Grimshaw's description of the 'cycle stable of a large country house' in July 1898 speaks volumes about the appeal of cycling to the Irish gentry in the late nineteenth century:

A long range of horse stalls appeared to have been thrown into one, and here, supported by racks, was a tremendous stud of bicycles. In one corner stood two triplets of different make, one rather lighter than the other, and built more

Right: An American trick cyclist at Earlsfort Terrace, Dublin, in 1886.

Opposite: The 'Ramblers' of Clonakilty consisted of members of the local hunt.

decidedly for scorching – the heavier one being used at times for long rides and tours. Three tandems were in another part of the stable. One was dropped behind to carry a lady in skirts; another was a strong diamond-framed road-ster; the third, a light fast road-racer. The number of singles I had not time to count; it was something between twenty and thirty. There was a plain town roadster belonging to the master of the house, his lighter roadster, his speedy featherweight aluminium Humber, brakeless, mudguardless, and high-geared; also two or three average machines of varying make. The lady of the house was the owner of a neat aluminium diamond-framed racer, for riding on good roads in rational dress, and several drop-frame machines of different weight and gear. There were two or three tiny bicycles belonging to the children, and one ridden by their governess. In a corner by themselves were ranked several fine old veterans, released from all active service save the duty of playing polo. On the wall hung a long array of saddles of every make, ranks of lamps stood on the window sills; there were spare tyres stored away, and a whole armoury of wrenches, spanners, turnscrews, etc, hung in a carpenter's rack on the wall. The sight was decidedly an impressive one, and one was astonished to hear that the care of this stud of machines rather more than occupied the entire time of one man.[164]

Left: A Jack B. Yeats cartoon of bicycle polo at Ballsbridge in May 1894.

Opposite: A bicycle polo match between Rathclaren and Ohne Hast at Oakbridge, October 1898.

Members of the landed gentry who were late converts to the wheel in the final years of the nineteenth century included the Earl of Dunraven, who wrote in a nostalgic vein in his memoirs of how he 'thought it "swagger" to ride eighty or one hundred miles in the day',[165] and Lord Ormonde, who in August 1897 became president of the St James's Park Cycling Club, the newly-formed cycling club of the Kilkenny Agricultural Society.[166]

Although the gentry's growing participation was a striking feature of Irish cycling in the late Victorian years, the pastime remained a largely middle-class and, increasingly in the 1890s, a white-collar activity. Prominent middle-class proponents of cycling included Sir Charles Cameron, medical analyst of Dublin city, and Sir Robert Jackson, MD, president of the Bohemian Cycling Club and the Pembroke Cycling Club, respectively, in 1890.[167] In the same year, H.A. Ivatt, an engineer working for the Great Southern and Western Railway, was president of Limerick's Kincora Cycling Club.[168] Well-known land agent John Townsend Trench was elected president of a newly-formed bicycle club in Kenmare in July 1890; the club's deputy vice-president was a bank official, Mr Minhear, and its secretary was Mr McGillycuddy, a petty sessions clerk.[169] The Thomastown Cycling Club was formed in March 1893 by J.J. Flynn, the manager of the Hibernian Bank, who was also the club's first president.[170] There were enough keen journalist cyclists in Dublin to form the Metropolitan Journalists' Cycling Club in 1893, whose name was changed to the Metropolitan Newspapers Cycling Club in 1894.[171] In 1893 Professor Steinberger of University College Galway was president of the Galway Cycling Club – he was also described by one source as 'one

of the most zealous and enthusiastic cyclists west of the Shannon', while later in the decade W.J.M. Starkie, the college president, was also a keen cyclist.[172] When the Dundalk Cycling Club was re-formed on 18 April 1893, those present at the inaugural meeting included R.L. Browne JP, H. Pring, an inland revenue supervisor (who was elected the club treasurer), W. Gorman of the Belfast Bank and J. Mathews of the National Bank, Sergeant Nolan of the RIC and Sergeant Grant of the 15th Hussars, the last two of whom were elected to the club's committee.[173] The Manorhamilton Cycling Club, which was formed in March 1894, was typical of many cycling clubs in this period, as indicated by the fact that both its captain and its treasurer were employees of the Ulster Bank and its secretary was a solicitor, C.P. Wray.[174] In 1895 Belfast's West End Cycling Club, which was formed in 1891, had a solicitor – Frank Kerr – as president; M.R. O'Malley, a doctor and a justice of the peace, was one of the club's vice-presidents, as was another magistrate, David Leahy.[175] The North Kerry Cycling Club was formed after a meeting which was held in Listowel Town Commissioners' Hall in April 1896, under the chairmanship of Mr Mulcahy, of the Bank of Ireland. The meeting selected a magistrate, James D. Crosbie of Gurtenard House, as club president. The vice-presidents included Colonel Trent Stoughton, Kerry High Sheriff; Colonel Harrison; Francis Creagh, a solicitor who also owned a number of race horses; Gerard Pierse of Ballyduff, a doctor; and J.H. Tibbs, a National Schools inspector. The club captain was J. Shannon, a racing cyclist and member of the RIC; the treasurer was Dr Brosnan, who was also a town councillor; and one of the secretaries was T.F. O'Sullivan, a journalist. William Farmer, a business manager, was placed on the committee.[176]

Willie Redmond and his
'Pierce' bicycle, 1899.

The president of the longer-established Tralee Cycling Club was a prominent
businessman and chairman of the Tralee Town Commissioners, St John Henry
Donovan. Stephen B. Roche, an Inland Revenue officer, started the Tralee
club.[177]

The fact that several Irish Members of Parliament were keen cyclists is further testimony to cycling's fashionable status in the late nineteenth century.
Amongst the earliest devotees of the wheel were the Home Rule MP for South
Leitrim, Jasper Tully, who stated in 1898 that he had been a cyclist for the previous fourteen or fifteen years, and James O'Connor, Home Rule MP for West
Wicklow, who stated in the same year that he became a cyclist in 1885.[178] A
number of Home Rule MPs caused a sensation in 1886 by amusing themselves
by riding a tricycle on the terrace of the House of Commons in the interval
between debates – one of these, P.J. O'Brien, MP for North Tipperary, had a
mishap which resulted in a black eye.[179] Prominent Irish MPs who were cyclists
included T.P. O'Connor,[180] Tim Harrington[181] and Tim Healy; Tim Healy was
particularly keen on the pastime.[182] Cyclist MPs who were less well-known
nationally included P.A. Chance, MP for South Kilkenny, and William Field of
Dublin,[183] Samuel Young of East Cavan,[184] Sir James Horner Haslett of North
Belfast,[185] Thomas Russell of South Tyrone,[186] James Alexander Rentoul of East
Down,[187] and Thomas B. Curran of North Donegal.[188] The Home Rule MP

for Wexford, William Redmond, mixed politics with pleasure by having himself photographed with a bicycle built by the Wexford firm Pierce's in July 1899; his brother, John, also rode a Pierce-built machine.[189] Another cyclist parliamentarian, Patrick O'Brien, the Home Rule MP for Kilkenny city, came to the attention of the cycling press for coming in first on the death of a fox which was killed by the Meath Hunt on 3 October 1896. A later advertisement depicted O'Brien, who had been following the hunt on a Marriott bicycle, carrying the fox's brush aloft as he cycled down a country road.[190] In April 1897 O'Brien established the Parliamentary Cycling Club at Westminster,[191] which indicates how popular cycling had become amongst MPs by this time. Apart from the obvious enjoyment which they derived from the pastime, one of the reasons why Irish MPs cycled in London, according to Matthias McDonnell Bodkin, was that it saved them the expense of hiring alternative transport to and from their lodgings.[192] The local profile of a number of MPs benefited from their involvement in Irish cycling clubs. For instance, the North Sligo MP, P.A. McHugh, was president of the Sligo Wanderers Cycling Club in the 1890s. In 1897 another MP, Alderman Nernard Collery, was a vice-president of the club.[193] The MP for Mid Antrim, Robert Torrens O'Neill, was patron of Ballymena's Red Hand Cycling Club in 1897. This was a club that was very attractive to prominent members of the local community, as evidenced by the fact that its vice-presidents included five justices of the peace, one of whom was a doctor, one resident magistrate, five clergymen, two doctors and two solicitors, while the local head constable was on the club committee.[194] Another Ulster club with a similar social profile was Belfast's Shore Cycling Club. In 1899 three MPs – Colonels J.M. McCalmont and Hugh McCalmont and James Gray – were vice-presidents of the club, as were three magistrates, two doctors, one clergyman and one barrister.[195] Members of Parliament were not the only political figures to become involved with Irish cycling clubs in this period. A number of mayors and other prominent municipal politicians also gave their support to local clubs – for instance, the Mayor of Limerick, F.A. O'Keefe, was president of the Limerick Gaelic Bicycle Club in 1887, while Cork's mayor, Daniel Horgan, was president of the Cork Gaelic Cycle Club in 1890.[196] Limerick's mayor in 1893, B. O'Donnell, was a vice-president of the Limerick Commercial Cycling Club; while Sligo's mayor in the same year, Thomas Scanlan, was vice-president of the Sligo Wanderers Cycling Club.[197] In 1897 five aldermen were vice-presidents of the same club.[198] Belfast's mayor in 1899, Otto Jaffé, was elected president of the newly established Castleton Cycling Club, which recruited from the Shore Road district. The club's vice-presidents included two magistrates, two doctors and a clergyman.[199]

As the previous paragraphs demonstrate, such respected and influential members of Irish society as doctors and clergymen frequently featured on the officer rolls of cycling clubs. Seeing men of such respected callings awheel must have considerably increased cycling's popularity in Irish society. As 'Pedal-Pin', an Arklow correspondent to the *Irish Cyclist*, wrote in June 1886 regarding the 'conversion' of a local doctor to cycling, 'the conversion of men in positions such as his does more for our pastime than that of a dozen others'.[200] Perhaps the most high-profile cycling doctor in the late nineteenth century was Dr G.J. Mackesy, JP – not only was he president of the Waterford Bicycle Club in 1891, but he was also president of the Medical Association of Ireland.[201] Doctors were particularly prominent in the Drogheda Cycling Club in 1897 – Dr J. Bellew Kelly, who was also a magistrate, was re-elected club president in that year, while Dr J.V. Byrne and Dr W. Bradley, who was also a magistrate, were elected as vice-presidents.[202] Dr W. Gibson, who was also a magistrate, was president of the Independent Order of Foresters Cycling Club in Belfast in 1899.[203] By 1897 Dublin had 'a host of cycling doctors',[204] and it was common elsewhere for doctors to do their rounds on bicycles.[205] By the turn of the century it was also common for district nurses to be issued with bicycles for visiting their patients.[206]

Clergymen were another collective pillar of Irish society to be drawn to cycling in the late Victorian era. Possibly the first Irish cleric to cycle was Reverend Robert Jervoise of Corofin, who rode a wooden-framed and wooden-wheeled 'Edinburgh' tricycle around the year 1870 – it was the sight of this machine which inspired William Bindon Blood to develop his 'Dublin' tricycle some years later.[207] In November 1880 a rural cleric recommended the tricycle 'as a means of rapid, convenient, and economical locomotion' to clergymen in rural livings. He contrasted the tricycle with the horse in favourable terms:

> From seven to eight miles an hour is my speed, and I can do fifty miles a day. I can ride up any hill almost, and I carry my portmanteau behind me. The tricycle requires no grooming, no corn, and is not taxed nor tolled. You can leave it at the door of a cottage and it wants no one to hold it; and better than all it has done my health – which was shattered abroad – more good than all the physic I have swallowed.[208]

Other pioneering clerical cyclists included Robert William Whelan, the Church of Ireland canon of Maynooth, who bought a 'Royal Mail' tricycle around 1885,[209] and a Cork dean and curate who purchased a Rudge tandem in the same year, which they used for visiting their parishioners. The new machine was a source of considerable embarrassment for the curate when he took a female parishioner for a spin; her dress got caught in the bicycle's chain and she had to undress to free herself, and the curate had to fetch an ulster overcoat for his companion to spare her blushes.[210] Other early cycling clergymen included Reverend T.H. Burkett, a member of the Waterford Bicycle Club, who rode from Dunmore East to Galway in a single day 'in or about the year '85';[211] Reverend Samuel Smart, rector of St Mary's parish in Newry, who suffered a severe injury in June 1886 as a result of

Foxhunting on a bicycle: Patrick O'Brien, MP, in 1896.

being thrown over the handlebars of his bicycle, after he startled 'a spirited young horse' at a steep hill near Drogheda when cycling from Dublin to Newry;[212] and Reverend W.J. Jamison of Kilrea, who stated in December 1890 that he did all of his parochial visits by bicycle instead of by horse, his former method.[213]

According to the *Irish Cyclist* in September 1888, a 'very great number of clergymen in Ireland cycle', but few of this number were priests. In September 1890 a priest wrote to the same journal and predicted that in the future cycling would 'become very general among priests', but clearly this was not the case when he wrote to the newspaper.[214] Amongst the first Catholic clergymen to cycle was the parish priest of Blessington, who bought a 'Premier' tricycle from Messrs Fletcher of Dublin in 1888 because 'The sight of so many cyclists passing through the town was too much for him',[215] and Fr Maher of Bray, who was knocked unconscious for a few hours after he lost control of his tricycle (which he was riding for the first time) when travelling down a hill, and the machine crashed into the embankment at Putland Road, in August 1888.[216] Another unfortunate pioneering cycling priest was Fr John Murray, the curate of Bagenalstown, who suffered a severe wrist fracture when he lost control of his tricycle while travelling down a hill near his residence in June 1890.[217] Not all priests were clumsy cyclists in this period, however; for example, Fr Sheridan of St Peter's College, Wexford, was described as 'an ardent votary of the wheel' in March 1891, and he was reputed to ride more than any other cyclist in Wexford.[218]

The evidence suggests that there was an ambivalence amongst the Catholic clergy towards the idea of clerics cycling. It is also likely that there was a generational split on the issue, with curates – who tended to be younger than parish priests – in general looking more favourably on the pastime than their immediate superiors.

Ballymena's Red Hand Cycling Club in 1897.

As the 1890s progressed, however, it generally became accepted that cycling was an activity that benefited the clergy. The enthusiasm of the students at Maynooth for cycling was noted in August 1894, while the *Irish Cyclist* claimed in January 1895 that there was hardly a parish in Ireland that did not have a cycling parish priest or curate.[219] It is likely that a disproportionate number of these cyclists were curates and younger priests. It is not without relevance that in the work of Canon Patrick Sheehan, an astute observer of Catholic clerical life, riding bicycles was one of the features that distinguished the younger generation of priests from their elders.[220] Another observer in the mid-1890s, the *Weekly Irish Times*'s 'Murty', made the telling observation that it was 'mostly Methodists and curates' who made up Ireland's cycling clergy, and that 'Parish priests of both churches still considers (sic) that the sole of your foot was made for walkin' on heel and toe, not for treadlin' through space.'[221] In 1895 the more conservative members of the hierarchy tabled a motion on the agenda for the Irish bishops' meeting in Maynooth, which criticised as undignified the growing use of bicycles by priests and seminarians. The bishops' views were not unlike those of some of the Protestant laity who had earlier been scandalised by the sight of ministers cycling, particularly on Sundays – such sensitivities had led to Mr Webster, the Methodist minister of Belleek, being forced to resign in 1889 and move to Armagh because his congregation disapproved of his cycling on Sunday, while Canon James Owen Hannay caused similar scandal to his Church of Ireland parishioners in Westport when he cycled on Sundays after his arrival in the hitherto bicycle-less Mayo town in 1892.[222] Unfortunately for those bishops at the Maynooth meeting who wished to curtail the cycling activities of the Catholic clergy, Archbishop William Walsh of Dublin, the primate of Ireland, was an avid cyclist and, aware that the anti-cycling proposal was one of the items up for discussion, he arrived at the meeting on his bicycle, having ridden it from Dublin – Walsh's telling action left 'little room for further discussion' on the matter![223] Those members of the hierarchy who were hostile to priests cycling were possibly unaware that Archbishop Walsh had been a keen cyclist since his youth, having ridden a boneshaker around the grounds of Maynooth College in his seminarian days.[224] Walsh's intervention would undoubtedly have been welcomed by such priests as Fr O'Keiran of Clones, who in February 1895 was thought to be 'one of the most enthusiastic cyclists in that district', riding his machine daily and in all kinds of weather,[225] and the numerous priests in Belfast and the surrounding districts who were described as 'ardent cyclists' in May 1895 – these included Fr Boyle of St Malachy's College, who had participated in the tour to Glendalough which was organised by the *Irish Cyclist* in 1894.[226] According to J. McCormick, who wrote an article on 'Cycling in the North of Ireland' for *The Cycle* in January 1897, the clergy in Ulster had 'by their example and influence done a great deal to influence public opinion as to the benefits of cycling', and 'In many of the outlying districts the Catholic clergy find the wheel a splendid instrument for visiting their flocks'.[227] Although there was still some lingering hostility in the late 1890s amongst elements of the hierarchy towards the idea of priests cycling, as evidenced by the fact that the Archbishop of Tuam in 1897 objected to his clergy using their bicycles outside of their own parishes,[228] there seems to have been a general warming to the pastime by this stage; otherwise it is difficult to see why bicycle races featured in the bazaar which was held in Johnswell, Co. Kilkenny, in aid of the funds of the Church of St John the Baptist in January 1897 or, more tellingly, why 'comic bicycle races' and a 'comic bicycle procession' in Roscommon and the surrounding districts were included in the 'Tir-Na-Nog-Fête' to raise funds for a new church as a memorial to the late Bishop of Elphin.[229]

Irish clergymen cycled for a variety of reasons. For some, such as the curate of Blessington parish in 1891, the parishioners of the little church at Cloughlea were too poor to afford their clergyman's car hire from Blessington, so he purchased a safety bicycle to enable him to attend to their spiritual needs on Sundays.[230] In August 1893 the Parnellite *Leinster Leader* pointed to the economy of cycling, relative to horse riding, when urging Catholic clergy to adopt the former mode of transport. Its advice arose following the case of Fr Buchanan, curate of Summerhill, Co. Meath, who injured himself after falling from a horse:

> It is not edifying for non-Catholics and strangers to see the priests of the poorest people in the world riding the best-blooded horses that money can buy. When the use of such high-class animals has become dangerous to the priests themselves, it is quite time that the bishops should require them for their own

safety – if for no higher motive – to be content with mounts more becoming their vocation, and within their control; otherwise a [horse] riding school will become an indispensable adjunct of Maynooth College.

The newspaper recommended that the clergy use pneumatic-tyred tricycles instead of horses, but its case was rather undermined when it described the recent example of Fr Woods, curate of Kinnegad, who had a 'terrible smash' when cycling from Delvin.[231] Apart from cycling's relative cheapness, some clergymen such as Canon Otway considered it to be a quicker, more efficient and less time-consuming means of transport than travelling by horseback.[232] Reverend Dr Busby, an elderly clergyman who gave one of the opening speeches at the first cycle exhibition to be organised in Ulster, which was held in Belfast in February 1893, recommended both the health-giving benefits of cycling as well as its utility for clergymen. He explained that he often came up with ideas for his sermons when visiting his parishioners in the countryside on his tricycle.[233] A minister of Belfast's Marylebone Presbyterian Church in 1897 recommended cycling in the countryside as a source of inspiration for sermons.[234] Bicycles also helped the clergy to monitor the behaviour of their flocks. For example, Fr Michael Ahern, curate of Ladysbridge parish in Co. Cork, used his bicycle to travel around the neighbourhood and to check whether the country people had gone home after the local fair finished or whether they congregated in the various public houses in the district.[235] Sean O'Casey claimed that the curate of St Margaret's, in Dublin, used his bicycle when suppressing gatherings of young male and female members of the St Margaret's and Drumcondra branches of the Gaelic League, who had assembled together for crossroad dances on summer Sunday evenings.[236] The bicycle also facilitated the closer scrutiny of the parochial clergy themselves by their superiors, as one hapless curate in a rural Dublin parish discovered to his own detriment. The curate was habitually late for saying daily morning Mass in the chapel, which was 'some miles from the city'. When Archbishop Walsh got wind of this he cycled to the church one morning and celebrated Mass in place of the tardy curate, who arrived – horror stricken – just as the primate was finishing, and afterwards received a 'quiet wigging' in the vestry from the archbishop.[237]

Factors such as cycling's relative cheapness and its utility were not the only reasons clergymen cycled in this period. One should also bear in mind the sheer pleasure that riding on tricycles or bicycles accorded to cycling clergymen – as one 'provincial priest' explained in June 1891, 'never before have I enjoyed such vigorous health and strength, and all round well-being'.[238] Reasons of utility do not explain why Fr Murphy of Kildare regularly rode his tricycle from his residence to his church, as these were separated by a distance of less than 200 yards – it was the intense enjoyment of cycling which appealed to the Kildare clergyman, as suggested by the fact that Fr Murphy and six priests who visited him for dinner in June 1891, organised a bicycle race after they had finished their meal, a contest which Fr Murphy won.[239] The sheer joy of cycling also explains why the Protestant clergyman, Reverend F. Townsend of Waterford, 'a mud-plugger of the first order', regularly defied the elements and cycled in inclement weather, wearing 'a light helmet, a Gamage Featherweight Poncho, rubber sea-boots, and oilskin knee-caps constructed to carry the rain over the tops of his boots'.[240] The most extreme example of clerical *joie-de-vivre* while cycling was exhibited by Fr Duffy of Longford, who was killed in July 1897 while 'coasting' with his feet off the pedals of his bicycle – he lost control of his bicycle when he had to swerve suddenly to avoid some children who got in his way, which resulted in a fatal fall for the clergyman.[241] Participation in cycling clubs was a more typical manifestation of clerical enthusiasm for cycling. An early example is the Wardenstown Cycling Club (later renamed the Killucan Ramblers), a 'typically middle class' club formed in March 1893. The local parish priest was the club's president; the dispensary doctor was the secretary, while the local National School teacher and post office clerk were committee members.[242] According to the *Irish Cyclist* in March 1895, the Circular Cycling Club, 'a very energetic private club in Dublin', was 'smiled on by the Church', as its ranks included eight 'parsons'.[243] In April 1896 Dean Finlay was president of the Carlow Cycling Club and Reverend C.K. Blount was vice-president; in May 1896 the Church of Ireland clergyman, Reverend Thomas Joseph Charlton, chaired the meeting in Castleblayney that led to the formation of the Castleblayney Cycling Club, and he was elected the club's vice-president.[244] The president of one of the more unusual cycling-related clubs, the Tralee Cycling and Literary Society, founded in 1897, was the local curate, Fr J. Kirby.[245] In 1898 the Dal Riada Cycling Club, whose headquarters were in cafés in Ballymoney and Coleraine, had a clergyman, T.M. Benson, on its committee and another five clergymen on its membership roll. In the same year Reverend Robert Andrews was captain of the Donaghadee Cycling Club.[246] In May 1900 the Ballymoney Cycling Club had three clergymen as officers; at the other end of the country, Fr Corbett of Mallow founded a cycling club in the latter town the following month.[247]

Members of the clergy were not the only guardians of Irish society's morals to take to cycling in significant numbers – the new pastime also proved attractive to many policemen. The first Irish policeman to cycle was probably Sub-Inspector Samuel Waters of the RIC, who bought a boneshaker in 1866 which a Sligo blacksmith had constructed on a pattern brought back from Paris.[248] In 1876, Oughterard's sub-inspector was another officer cyclist pioneer.[249] Although cycling was a minority pursuit in police ranks in the 1860s and 1870s, by 1883 there was a sufficient number of cyclists in the force for the holding of a bicycle race at the RIC's first annual sports, in Dublin's Phoenix Park on 25 September,[250] and in September 1886 the *Irish Cyclist* stated that many members of the RIC were cyclists.[251] One of these, Constable Thomas John Lowry of Limerick, was a leading figure in the Irish cycling world, winning some five title races at the Munster cycling championship meeting in 1887.[252]

Left: Constable Thomas John Lowry of Limerick, an avid racing cyclist in the 1880s.

Opposite: A constable of the Royal Irish Constabulary cycling through a village.

The evidence suggests that from the late 1880s cycling became more widespread in police ranks, as in the rest of Irish society. The first RIC cycling club was started at the Phoenix Park training depot in 1890, which numbered some 163 members in 1894.[253] A general RIC Cycling Club was established in December 1891.[254] In the following year the inspector-general, Sir Andrew Reed, announced that 'steady' men might receive permission from their county inspectors to keep bicycles on barracks' premises, and also to absent themselves from barracks for up to two hours when not required for duty. Special mileage allowances were also introduced for policemen who used their own bicycles, with permission, on patrols or on other duties that would normally have necessitated car hire.[255] In 1894 Reed ordered that whenever an RIC man wished to participate in cycling sports he was to be allowed every facility to do so, adding that he looked upon cycling as 'a grand adjunct to the life and pleasure of an RIC man'.[256] This official encouragement was one reason why the RIC experienced a cycling boom in the 1890s. A number of flourishing local clubs were established. The Belfast RIC Cycling Club had around one hundred members in September 1891, almost all of whom rode Singer safeties which were supplied by Thomas Ramsay of 105 Donegall Street; by February 1893 there were 125 members in the club. By October 1893 it was the largest individual cycling club in Ulster.[257] The Belfast club's impressive numbers were eclipsed by the even more spectacular growth of the Waterford RIC Cycling Club, which was founded in December 1892 with some twenty members. According to *Sport*, 'All the big wigs in the force in the surrounding district are taking a great interest in the success of the club', whose main organiser was Sergeant (later Head Constable) John Adolphus Carbery, who started cycling in 1884.[258] By March 1893 some 154 RIC men had joined the Waterford club, and by March 1895 it consisted of some 198 members, making

it the largest single cycling club in Ireland at that time.[259] By April 1896 its numbers had increased slightly, to 220 members.[260] The Limerick RIC Cycling Club, which was started in April 1895, enjoyed rapid growth, increasing to some eighty members in just two months.[261] These local examples of flourishing police cycling clubs were some of the more striking examples of the general phenomenon of a marked increase of cycling in the RIC;[262] indeed, according to the *Irish Cyclist* in March 1895, if cycling continued to grow at its current rate in the force the letters 'RIC' would soon stand for 'Royal Irish Cyclists'.[263] This was an understandable comment, considering the fact that there were an estimated 4,700 cyclists in the force in 1895.[264]

It is likely that cycling was indulged in more by single men than married men,[265] as the former would have had more spare cash and time to devote to the pastime than the latter, although married men did not entirely refrain from cycling. In addition to the situation in Waterford, cycling was also particularly encouraged by the RIC officers in Westmeath,[266] Kerry (where County Inspector Waters promoted cycling as an antidote to the monotony of his men's lives)[267] and Clare; by 1898, almost all of the constables, acting-sergeants and sergeants of the latter county were cyclists.[268] It is likely that similar active encouragement was in evidence in Wexford, as the Wexford RIC Cycling Club contained some 450 members in March 1901, making it not only the RIC's largest cycling club, but Ireland's also.[269] One gains clear insight into how ubiquitous cycling had become in the constabulary by the end of the period by the fact that an estimated 1,600 to 2,000 RIC cyclists, including Inspector-General Neville Chamberlain, assembled at the fair green in Athlone on 16 May 1903, prior to holding a sports meeting at Lord Castlemaine's estate near the town – possibly the biggest ever gathering of cyclists in Ireland.[270]

From Photo. by]   COMMITTEE OF R.I.C. C.C., WATERFORD.   [*Poole, Waterford.*

W. Lambert.   J. F. Tyndall.   J. Devlin.

J. Cahill. J. Farrell. P. Byrne. T. Gilbert. P. M Golrick. W. Elders. C. Riordan.

M. J. Collins. P. Duggan. A. Lacey. H. B. Somerville, D.I. A. Gambell, C.I., J.P. Dr. W. R. Connelly. J. A. Carbery. J. Blessing. T. Torsney. P. Tynan.

The committee of the Waterford RIC Cycling Club in 1894.

As well as joining the various official RIC cycling clubs, constabulary members also participated in local civilian cycling clubs, often in a leading capacity. For example, District Inspector T.J. Smith was captain of the Dungannon Cycling Club in 1894. Smith was credited with infusing new life into the club, which comprised of between forty and fifty members. Another district inspector, Alfred Valentine McClelland, was re-elected chairman of the Banagher Bicycle Club in April 1896, and the club members stated that the club would not have existed without his involvement.[271] In August 1896 Head Constable Denis Horgan was described as 'the principal prop' of the Nenagh Cycling Club, which, with some 120 members, was one of Ireland's largest.[272] When Sergeant Boylan of Borrisokane, 'an ardent cyclist', retired in September 1897 the vice-president of Borrisokane Cycling Club stated that 'his efforts to promote the love of the wheel in Lower Ormond largely contributed to the formation and strengthening of the neighbouring clubs'.[273] After his promotion to head constable and transfer to Ballymena, Head Constable Carbery, a leading figure in the Waterford cycling world, became captain of Ballymena's Red Hand Cycling Club and also served as the club's racing secretary.[274] Another constabulary member, Sergeant Dunlop, was captain of Belfast's Shore Cycling Club in 1898 and 1899.[275]

RIC men cycled for recreational purposes, but they also invested in bicycles in the hope that this would improve their crime-fighting ability and thus increase their chances of promotion or of receiving an award from the constabulary reward fund.[276] Instances in which policemen used their bicycles to track down suspects or perform other duties (such as the exciting chase after a rabid dog in the Poyntzpass-Jerretzpass district which was undertaken on bicycles by a Newry sergeant and constable in September 1897)[277] were frequently publicised in the press,[278] and these undoubtedly helped to fuel policemen's desire to purchase machines. The following account from April 1896 is a representative example of the laudatory tone in which these reports were often written:

> Constable Butler, who has been for some years doing cycling duty at Borrisokane, has been transferred to Birdhill. During his service at the former district station he was most successful in securing convictions against tramps for roadside thefts, 'bullying', and assaults. Prior to his time the country around there was infested with a bad type of these rural footpads, who levied blackmail with absolute impunity in the small isolated homesteads. But the vigilance of the cycling constable put a period to their operations, and the nuisance has diminished almost to a vanishing point.[279]

The bicycle's usefulness for police work, when compared to the horse, was noted in a poem, 'Bikes for Bobbies', in December 1889:

> To the District Inspector the constable spoke,
> 'A bistickle, sir, is a wonderful yoke;
> They can go like the wind, and they don't seem to tire,
> In spite of the wind and the mud and the mire.
>
> So sell all your horses and call up your men,
> On bistickles, sir, you can mount them agen,
> Look out the best sort, sir, and soon you will see,
> That we'll catch all the rogues in the vicin-i-tee.
>
> When we hear of an outrage there's always delay
> Before a man mounts on his horse and away;
> But with a machine you'd be off like a shot,
> And get on the trail while the scent is still hot.
>
> Then again, with a horse, when you come in half dead,
> He has got to be groomed ere you take to your bed,
> But you know that your cycle will never take cold,
> Though the mud on its back may be twelve hours old'.[280]

The widespread use of bicycles by members of the RIC was probably one of the main reasons behind the reduction of the constabulary's mounted section from 261 men to 138 men in 1897. Some eighteen counties were left without any mounted police, and in the remainder the mounted men were regarded as unnecessary, except for riot control, due to the number of cyclist policemen who could undertake tasks such as despatch duties, which had previously been the preserve of the force's mounted section.[281] In November of the same year the *Constabulary Gazette* stated that 'we do not think it too much to say that there is no class in the community who use the bicycle so much as the RIC', and it particularly noted the frequent use of bicycles by plain-clothes policemen to counter the ubiquitous offence of Sunday drinking in rural public houses. The speed with which cyclist policemen approached public houses meant that they could swoop before the publicans' scouts could give warning of approaching danger. In one revealing case a defending solicitor lamented that 'it was all due to those blackguard bicycles' that his client had been caught breaking the Sunday licensing laws.[282]

RIC constables, who had been receiving wages of more than £1 per week since 1882, were amongst the elite of Ireland's non-salaried workers, and bicycle dealers directly targeted this potentially lucrative market. In 1891 R.J. Mecredy's brother, Alex (nicknamed 'The Energetic'), who ran a cycle business on Clare Street, Dublin, designed a bicycle – built in England – which he called the 'Energetic'. The 'Energetic' bicycle was 'specially designed to withstand the strain usually put upon their bicycles by the every-day heavy-weight bobby'.[283] There were three

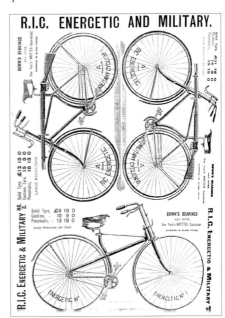

Right: The 'R.I.C. Energetic and Military'
bicycle, 1891.

Opposite: The Swanlinbar RIC station
party with two Ordinary bicycles, *c.*1892.

models of 'Energetic', two of which, the 'RIC Energetic and Military', numbers
one and two, were aimed at members of the RIC. The first model retailed at £12
15s, £15 5s and £16 15s for the solid-tyred, cushioned-tyred and pneumatic-tyred
versions respectively, while the second model retailed at £11 15s for solid-tyred
machines, £14 5s for cushion-tyred machines, and £15 15s for pneumatic-tyred
machines.[284] C. Mannin's Clincher Pneumatic Tyre and Cycle Exchange, which
opened on Great Brunswick Street in early 1892, made a special offer of 'Universal
Rover' bicycles to members of the RIC; solid-tyred machines were available at
£9 or £10, while cushion-tyred machines could be purchased for £10 or £11
10s.[285] In 1893 the Birmingham firm of Guest and Barrow manufactured the 'RIC
Girder Star' bicycle, which it offered at special prices not just to members of the
constabulary but also to prison warders and 'other officials';[286] in the same year the
Dunlop Cycle Company, with branches in Dublin, Belfast and Cork, offered special
terms to RIC members for its machines.[287] Also in 1893 Maxwell and Harding of
Derry were selling the English-made 'Special RIC Royal Sovereign'; the cushion-
tyred version cost £10 10s., while the pneumatic-tyred model cost £18 18s.[288] An
advertisement in District Inspector Dagg's road guide for use by members of the
RIC, published in 1893,[289] illustrates the type of special deal which bicycle agents
and companies were prepared to offer to constabulary cyclists. The Pneumatic Tyre
and Booth's Cycle Agency, based at Oriel House in Westland Row, Dublin, offered
the 'Oriel', 'Our Special RIC Safety Bicycle for [the] 1893 Season', for £12 12s
cash or £15 15s on 'Easy Terms'. RIC men could procure a cushion-tyred 'Oriel'
on easy terms for a £1 deposit and monthly payments of £1 thereafter, and a

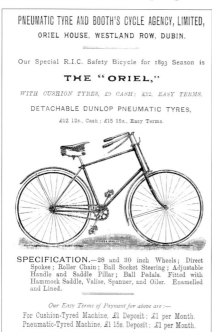

PNEUMATIC TYRE AND BOOTH'S CYCLE AGENCY, LIMITED,
ORIEL HOUSE, WESTLAND ROW, DUBIN.

Our Special R.I.C. Safety Bicycle for 1893 Season is

THE "ORIEL,"

WITH CUSHION TYRES, £9 CASH; £12, EASY TERMS.

DETACHABLE DUNLOP PNEUMATIC TYRES,

£12 12s., Cash; £15 15s., Easy Terms.

SPECIFICATION.—28 and 30 inch Wheels; Direct Spokes; Roller Chain; Ball Socket Steering; Adjustable Handle and Saddle Pillar; Ball Pedals. Fitted with Hammock Saddle, Valise, Spanner, and Oiler. Enamelled and Lined.

Our Easy Terms of Payment for above are :—
For Cushion-Tyred Machine, £1 Deposit ; £1 per Month.
Pneumatic-Tyred Machine, £1 15s. Deposit ; £1 per Month.

Left: The 'Oriel', a bicycle aimed specifically at RIC customers.

Opposite: Not all Irish cycle agents were enamoured of easy payment schemes.

pneumatic-tyred machine for a £1 15s deposit and monthly payments of £1.[290] Some ten years later the *Constabulary Gazette* took the unusual step of endorsing the 'Star' bicycles sold by R.W. Stevens of 8 Aston's Quay, Dublin, as the 'the best value ever offered to us'; the bicycles, which were guaranteed to carry the weight of a twenty-stone rider, were offered to RIC members for monthly payments of 12s. The arrest of a fugitive from the Glasgow police by Constable Maugham of Garrison, who succeeded in capturing the suspect after riding nine and a half miles on his 'Star' bicycle, was offered as proof of 'the necessity of having "Star" bicycles in the RIC.'[291,]

Cycle agents also specifically targeted members of the Dublin Metropolitan Police (DMP), whose cycling club affiliated to the ICA in 1893.[292] DMP constables were paid even higher wages than their RIC colleagues, so it is understandable that cycle agents should have regarded them as prime potential customers. One of the most successful providers of bicycles to the DMP was W.R. McTaggart of Grafton Street, who also sold to the RIC; indeed, he was made an honorary member of the RIC Depot Cycling Club in 1897 in recognition of the good service which he provided to RIC cyclists.[293] The fact that McTaggart had many DMP men on his books as hire purchase customers, and that he never pressed constables or sergeants who fell behind in their payments, came in handy when he inadvertently blundered into Ireland's first police speed trap for motorists, on the Dublin to Stillorgan road. Mistaking it for a speed test and cheered on by an appreciative crowd, he proceeded to beat the times set by previous motorists. The DMP sergeant in charge

No More Tick.

" I've quit selling bicycles on the instalment plan.

" Why's that ? "

"Our machine is of such a superior quality that we are never able to catch the fellows that owe us."

of the speed trap allowed McTaggart to proceed without charge when the cycle dealer informed him of his customer-friendly business dealings with members of the force.[294] One advertisement for McTaggart's bicycles depicted a twenty-three-stone DMP constable holding a 'McTaggart Royal' machine.[295] R.W. Stevens also supplied bicycles to DMP members. Stevens's depot received a lot of publicity from having supplied a 'Star' bicycle to Constable Maurice Wolfe, for whom the machine was especially built. Wolfe stood at six foot six inches tall and weighed some twenty-one stone, and his bicycle was reportedly the biggest bicycle ever made in Ireland. Wolfe achieved fame when he was stopped in the street by the lord lieutenant, Lord Dudley, who asked him to appear before him on his newly-built machine, which had caused a public stir when it was exhibited in Stevens's shop window.[296] Another Dublin cycle agent, John O'Neill of 14 South King Street – maker of the 'Lucania' bicycle – offered his machine to RIC and DMP members at the attractive price of just 3s per week, while special terms were offered to wives of policemen who wished to buy the women's 'Lucania No.2' model.[297]

The sheer number of constabulary cyclists, and the fact that they were scattered in towns and villages throughout Ireland, probably made members of the RIC the most visible Irish cyclists in the late nineteenth century. However they were not the only occupational group to take to cycling in significant numbers. The civil service was another body keen on cycling. The Civil Service Sports Club was founded in 1867 and confined its membership to the 'gentleman class', which included civil servants, army and naval

officers, the learned professions and gentlemen of independent means.[298] Bicycle races featured at the club's annual races from at least as early as 1877,[299] and a separate cycling club – the Irish Civil Service Cycling Club – which was open to civil servants and their sons, was established in Dublin in 1887.[300] Michael McCarthy's perceptive account of life in *fin-de-siècle* Ireland noted that tennis or cycling parties formed part of the comfortable summer routine of what he termed the 'Civil Service Class' of Dublin.[301] The staff of a number of post offices also formed cycling clubs. These included the Electric Cycling Club, the club of the Waterford General Post Office, which was formed in 1890. It apparently went into decline, as it was revived in 1900, with an additional 'ladies' section'. Kindred clubs included the Belfast Postal Cycling Club formed in 1892, the Hawk Cycling Club, started in 1896 by employees of Dublin's General Post Office, and the club started by employees of the Cork General Post Office in 1900.[302] It is likely that these Post Office cycling clubs were similar in ethos and membership to the Civil Service club, as suggested by the fact that the Belfast Civil Service and Post Office cycling clubs amalgamated in March 1893, adopting the title of the former club.[303]

University students came from similar social backgrounds to those of civil servants, and they also featured prominently in the Irish cycling world. P. McGreer, a correspondent for the *Irish Cyclist*, commented in June 1886 that cycling was ideal for 'the toil[er]s in brain work, the sedentary student, [and] the city man or city clerk' who could not afford a horse.[304] University students do not appear to have had difficulty in affording bicycles, and the Dublin University Bicycle Club annual races at Trinity College formed an important part of the social calendar of the Irish elite in the 1880s and 1890s.[305] Well-known Trinity student cyclists included R.J. Mecredy, a successful competitor in cycling races in the 1880s, especially on tricycles;[306] Count K.N. Stadnicki, a Polish student who also performed well in

Right: P.P. Kilkelly and his Ordinary bicycle in May 1891.

Opposite: Photograph of Dublin University Bicycle Club races, June 1890.

tricycle races in the 1880s;[307] P.P. Kilkelly, a medical student who won the Irish five-mile bicycle championship title in 1888;[308] Oliver St John Gogarty, another successful racer while studying medicine in the 1890s;[309] and John Millington Synge, who loved to cycle round Co. Wicklow,[310] including 'coasting' down-hill with his feet over his bicycle's handlebars.[311] When revising for the Trinity entrance examination Synge would read books while cycling, and after passing the examination he cycled to Trinity from Greystones, wearing knickerbockers while attending his lectures.[312] A cycling club was formed at Queen's College, Cork in 1891, but it does not appear to have met with the complete approval of the college authorities, as cycling on the campus grounds was banned later in the 1890s by the college council, despite the protests of Marcus Hartog, professor of zoology.[313] In Queen's College, Belfast, cycling was popular with the students and some of the staff, and cycle races featured in the college annual sports in the 1880s and 1890s. A cycling club was active there in the 1880s and the early 1890s, but did not survive into the twentieth century.[314]

University students and academic staff who cycled came from the more advantaged spectrum of the scholarly world. Although National School teachers were less well off than their third-level colleagues, nevertheless growing numbers of the more humble layer of the teaching profession also took to cycling in the late 1880s and the 1890s, either for travelling to and from work or for pleasure.[315] Teachers were paid less than policemen, but they had permanent work and, therefore, a steady income, and perhaps on account of this they were attractive targets to Irish cycle dealers. In 1890 the Fletchers of 4 Nassau Street, Dublin, advertised their 'Premier' and 'Sparkbrook' bicycles 'on the easy payment system on exceptionally easy terms to teachers' in the *Irish Teachers' Journal*. These bicycles, which normally cost a lump sum of £12 12s, could not be afforded

THE PLEASURES OF COASTING.

The pleasures of coasting.

by many, indeed most teachers, hence the journal's endorsement of the Fletchers' 'easy payment system' of monthly or quarterly instalments. Similar arrangements for teachers were available from most dealers, according to the journal.[316] Firms which extended easy payment schemes to teachers included the Pneumatic Tyre and Booth's Cycle Agency of Dublin, which sold new safeties at prices ranging from £8 to £25, and second-hand safeties at prices ranging from £6 to £15. The Irish Cycle Company of Clare Street, Dublin, sold 'Sparkbrook', 'Northern' and 'Adams' bicycles to teachers for £11 on the easy payment system.[317] There is evidence that these special deals enabled numerous teachers to purchase bicycles in the 1890s, and many of them were also able to afford cycling tours during their summer holidays.[318] Cycling clubs in which teachers played a prominent role included Listowel's North Kerry Cycling Club, founded in 1896, the mainstay of which were the local teachers and members of the RIC,[319] and the Abbeyfeale Cycling Club, established in 1901, whose first captain was a National School teacher, Jeremiah McCarthy.[320]

Another club with important teacher participation was the Draperstown Cycling Club, whose headquarters were at the Great Northern Cycle Company. This was the grandiose title of a firm run by two colourful National School teachers, Masters Connolly and Byrne. These two rogues divided their time between what could be loosely termed as teaching, allegedly manufacturing and selling poteen, and from 1893, pursuing a profitable sideline as cycle agents of dubious honesty. Master Byrne attended Bancran National School wearing 'full cycling costume' and on one occasion, in late August 1894, absented himself to participate in a twenty-five-mile road race in Co. Antrim which was organised by the West End Cycling Club. Complaints that Byrne's commercial interests were having a negative effect on his teaching prompted a visit by a schools inspector to investigate the complaints. He reported that Byrne had two bicycles at Bancran school, one for common use in the yard and the other a racer which was kept in the schoolroom, covered with a map to protect it from dust; it was, the inspector acidly commented, the only object in the room that showed any evidence of having been cared for. The inspector recommended that Byrne 'be called upon to elect between the occupation of public teacher and cycle agent'. Master Connolly claimed rather lamely that the bundle of bicycle catalogues found by the inspector on his desk had been sent to him, without his having requested them, by the John Griffiths Cycle Corporation of Derry, and that he was merely keeping them in the school for use as toilet paper. The teachers were involved in manufacturing bicycles at Byrne's home at Sixtowns, Draperstown, and selling them at bargain prices. These were examples of what Irish newspapers termed 'gas-pipe' machines – bicycles of inferior quality which were assembled from parts acquired from various companies, and passed off as machines of superior quality. Beginning in March 1896, the two teachers even had the audacity to advertise their wares in the Irish teaching profession's organ, the *Irish Teachers' Journal*, as the 'fastest, soundest, best and cheapest cycles in the kingdom'. Although the two teachers successfully resisted all attempts to remove them from their teaching posts, their luck as 'gas-pipe' manufacturers ran out in 1897, when the Rudge Whitworth Company took legal action against the Great Northern Cycle Company after discovering that it was offering bicycles, purporting to be built by Rudge Whitworth, at £12 each, which was only half of the normal price for their machines. The Draperstown bicycles were fakes – their only genuine article was the machines' Rudge Whitworth badge. Judgement and costs were given against Masters Byrne and Connolly, leaving them to fall back on their teachers' salaries as their sole source of income.[321]

Other salaried workers who used bicycles in their jobs in this period included county surveyors;[322] Board of Works engineers such as Percy French, who, while working in Cavan from 1887 to 1892, increased his income considerably by cycling almost everywhere he went and pocketing the 9*d* per mile travelling expenses normally paid out to engineers;[323] landlords' agents, including the Ulster agent who sent a message to would-be 'moonlighters' in his district by setting up targets in his avenue and firing at them with his revolver while he sped by on his bicycle at racing speed each morning, and never missing his mark;[324] and geologists, including Grenville Cole, Chair of Geology at the Royal College of Science from 1890 to 1924 and, from 1905, director of the Geological Society of Ireland. Most of Cole's surveying trips were done on bicycle.[325] Employees of the Congested Districts Board, which was formed in 1891, used bicycles in their work. These included the gentleman bee-keeping enthusiast in the west of Ireland who, according to Stephen Gwynn, travelled by bicycle 'preaching the gospel of bee-keeping…carrying a magic-lantern in little bits, and a queen bee in each pocket'. There were reports that this individual conveyed a swarm of bees about with him by this method.[326] The middle-class organisers of the Irish Agricultural

Organisation Society (IAOS), established in 1894, also found that the bicycle was important for their work in spreading the cooperative principle amongst Irish farmers.[327] George William Russell ('Æ') was a particularly keen cyclist and made good use of his bicycle in his IAOS work from 1897 to 1905.[328]

Workers at a number of business establishments also either used tricycles or bicycles which were supplied by their employers for use at their work, or they formed cycling clubs to promote convivial and recreational association with work colleagues. As early as 1884 the proprietor of the *Dublin Evening Telegraph* introduced tricycles for the purpose of conveying his publication to Dublin's suburbs each evening.[329] By June 1885 delivery boys delivering evening newspapers to the suburbs by tricycle were a common sight in Dublin.[330] By the late 1880s the *Freeman's Journal* was holding an annual sports meeting that featured cycling races, and by August 1889 the staff at the newspaper had their own cycling club.[331] In February 1891 it placed an order for fifty 'Raleigh' safeties from Messrs Pim of South Great George's Street,[332] which gives a good idea of how widespread cycling was amongst the newspaper's employees. By January 1895 almost all employees of the *Independent* group of newspapers in Dublin were also cyclists.[333] Other cycling clubs connected with Dublin businesses in this period included that which was formed by some twenty-five to thirty of the employees of Messrs Pim, the exclusive general retailers, in 1886,[334] the Abbey Athletic and Cycling Club which was established in June 1888 by the staff of Eason's bookshop,[335] and the Powerscourt Cycling Club, a 'semi-private' association formed early in 1890 by employees of the firm of Alexander Ferrier and James Pollock, a wholesale warehouse company based at 59 William Street, the former town house of Lord Powerscourt.[336] Around the same time employees of the Great Southern and Western Railway Company, based at Inchicore, founded the Ivy Cycling Club, the name of which derived from the fact that most members rode 'Ivy' safety bicycles. By December 1892 there were around one hundred members in the club.[337] In April 1892 the employees of Crowe, Wilson and Company, a wholesale woollen, silk, footwear, clothing and trimming warehouse at 26 Lower Bridge Street, formed the Magenta Athletic and Cycling Club,[338] while in the following month the owners of the Pneumatic Tyre Company, based at Oriel House in Westland Row, started a club called the Oriel Cycling Club, membership of which was confined to the firm's employees.[339] In 1897 the employees of John C. Parkes's hardware establishment at the Coombe formed the Eclipse Cycling Club.[340] By the end of the 1890s the Dublin United Tramways Cycling Club was also in existence.[341] In 1900 the employees of the fashionable Mary Street hosiery and drapery establishment of Todd and Burns, whose annual sports meeting had featured bicycle races from 1889, started a cycling club which they called the New Century Cycling Club.[342] Perhaps the most unusual works-based cycling club in Dublin was the Hengler's Circus Cycling Club. Hengler's Circus toured throughout the United Kingdom, spending several weeks in Dublin each year and appointing the *Irish Cyclist* as its cycling club's official organ.[343] All of the club members rode 'Humber' bicycles in 1892 and switched to 'Nelsons' in 1893, by which latter year there were more than thirty members enrolled in the club. A friendly rivalry existed between the Hengler's Circus Cycling Club and the cycling club of Wulff's Circus, a German outfit that also visited Dublin, with races – which were closed to members of the public – being held between the two clubs. It was claimed that at the Hengler's sports at Ballsbridge in 1892 one of the races featured a lion competing on a tricycle![344] Evidence of works-based cycling clubs in the rest of the country is scarce, but at least one such club was organised in Belfast – this was the Arcade Cycling Club, formed in early 1897 by the employees of James Lindsay's Ulster Arcade drapery establishment.[345] In the same year it was reported that all of the young men working at the Commercial Cable Company of Waterville were cyclists,[346] although it is not clear if they had a cycling club at this stage.

In addition to works-based clubs, a number of cycling clubs for shop workers in general, as well as related occupations, were established in Dublin. The first of these, the Grocers' and Vintners' Assistants' Cycling Club, with an initial membership of thirty-four, affiliated to the ICA in May 1887.[347] It changed its name to the Tally-ho Cycling Club in February 1890.[348] Cycling races featured at the Pawnbrokers' Assistants' Association annual sports in the Phoenix Park in 1889 and 1890,[349] and a cycling club for pawnbrokers' assistants, which was in existence from as early as July 1890, became affiliated to the ICA in the following month.[350] The Purveyors' Assistants' Cycling Club was formed with more than twenty members in March 1893,[351] while a cycling club in connection with the Capel Street Trades Hall was started in July of the same year.[352] Bicycle races featured at the inaugural Dublin Hotel and Club Assistants' races in September 1894.[353] A few months later, in April 1895, the Dublin Drapers' Club formed the Commercial Cycling Club.[354] There is also evidence of shop workers and similar non-manual workers cycling in other parts of the country. For instance, the Tralee Cycling Club decided in May 1886 to admit 'young men engaged in mercantile pursuits' as associate members, for an annual subscription of 10s.[355] A Mullingar observer noted in July 1890 that 'A noticeable feature in and around the town lately has been the scudding along the road of bycylces [sic] and tricycles by young men, who are engaged in the commercial houses of the town'.[356] In Maryborough in 1892, employees in 'professional offices or business houses' were allowed a half-holiday every Saturday, which enabled many to participate in the Maryborough Cycling Club's activities.[357] In nearby Abbeyleix, shop assistants were also favourably treated by their employers in 1893, as the early hours at which 'business houses' were closed facilitated their efforts at 'becoming adepts in the manipulation of the steeds of steel'.[358] It is likely that a similar pattern was evident in other areas of Ireland. In Clonakilty in 1896 a member of the Board of Guardians, who looked on cyclists as nuisances who were likely to frighten children and horses, considered that bicycles 'were principally owned by drapers' and attorneys' clerks, who were not worth a straw'.[359] Some postmen – or 'letter carriers', as they were frequently described – also used

Left: An advertisement for Pim Brothers of Dublin, January 1886.

Opposite: The Dublin Tramways Cycling Club in 1899.

tricycles or bicycles to deliver letters and parcels,[360] but this was not as common a feature of the postal system in Dublin, or in Ireland generally, as it was in Britain in the late nineteenth century.[361]

Commenting on the ubiquity of cyclists from below the ranks of the aristocracy and middle classes in Dublin's Phoenix Park in 1897, 'Murty' of the *Weekly Irish Times* complained that:

> …you can't walk now on a footway but you're screeched and wheeled off of it by a girl and her lover that sells bacon and Cork butter in Francis [S]treet when they're not careerin' in front of the lord lieutenant's parlour windy; they're by no means civil to a poor fellow that has no other locomotion than his brogues; they seem to think that the modern world was made for Dunlops; they're geared up to the nines, and display their lumpy feet amazin'ly; they roam all over the place, and I'd be long sorry to utter the poetic word, nuisance, but truth will out!…[C]ooks on Grapplers, housemaids on Humbers, and 'kids' on Singers, ought to keep the roads outside the walk that is for humanity, and take their chance of bein' run over by mineral-water carts and 'Larries' carryin' the quality to dinner with Royalty![362]

How does one account for the evidence of cycling by workers who were not particularly well paid in this period? It is probable that postmen were supplied with their tricycles or bicycles by the Royal Mail, but what about the other occupational

THE DUBLIN TRAMWAYS CYCLING CLUB.

TAKEN AT GLENDALOUGH ON THE OCCASION OF THE INAUGURAL DINNER.

groups mentioned in the previous paragraph? How could they have afforded to cycle, given the fact that, as we have seen, middle-class riders sometimes struggled to pay for cycles and that the *Irish Cyclist* stated in March 1892 that the price of a new pneumatic-tyred bicycle 'makes a considerable hole in any salary that is under three figures for the year'?[363] Some cyclists of modest circumstances could have purchased relatively cheap second-hand machines that were advertised in newspapers such as the *Freeman's Journal* in the late 1880s and early 1890s. Particular bargains included a 50" 'Special Club' Ordinary which cost £20 new, offered for £4 in June 1888 as its owner had bought a safety bicycle; a 50" Ordinary offered for £1 in July 1888; a tricycle offered for £3 10s in July 1889; a 48" Ordinary which was too tall for its owner and ridden less than ten miles, offered for £4 10s in July 1890, and a similar-sized bicycle offered in the same month for £2, which was being sold as it was too small for its owner; and a 52" Ordinary offered for £3 in August 1890, as its owner had purchased a pneumatic-tyred bicycle.[364] It is not known whether the 52" 'Special Club' Ordinary, offered for sale in July 1890 for £5 'owing to death of owner', had any buyer.[365] The firm of Browne and Beck of Donegall Street, Belfast, was a notable source of cheap cycles, including pneumatic-tyred machines, some of which were offered at the exceptionally low price of £4 10s in 1893.[366] Later in the decade McCowen's of Denny Street, Tralee, sold inexpensive second-hand machines, including a solid-tyred tricycle for £1 10s.[367] Cheap machines could also be procured when pawnbrokers sold off bicycles that were unredeemed pledges.[368] Some aspiring cyclists were so eager to acquire

cheap machines that they were easy prey for unscrupulous dealers and manufacturers who sold shoddy cycles which they pretended were of decent quality.[369]
The most elaborate swindle of gullible cyclists seeking cheap mounts occurred in
Belfast in 1899, when several hundred bargain hunters paid 15s 6d each for what
the Glasgow and New York Manufacturing Company of Great Eastern Street,
Glasgow, advertised as 'new model bicycles'. These 'model' bicycles were indeed
models – they were nine-inch-long, five-inch-high brass miniatures![370]

   The *Freeman's Journal* advertising columns show that the best bargains were
for Ordinaries, as experienced cyclists deserted the once-favourite machine to
buy safety bicycles and well-off, first-time buyers preferred to purchase safeties
rather than Ordinaries. The price of Ordinaries collapsed, making them much
more affordable than hitherto for prospective cyclists of relatively humble means.
By October 1891, according to the *Irish Cyclist*, only die-hard enthusiasts for the
Ordinary, as well as juveniles and the 'impecunious', 'to whom the initial outlay
on a safety is a consideration when compared with the cheap Ordinaries that can
be picked up', rode the older machines.[371] Beatrice Grimshaw stated in March
1892 that 'a very decent [O]rdinary is anywhere procurable now for thirty shil-
lings or so'.[372] Second-hand Ordinaries could be purchased for even less than this
at the Central Cycle Showrooms on Fleet Street, Dublin, where they were on sale
for prices which started from 10s.[373] It was not only Ordinaries which suddenly
became affordable for cyclists of relatively modest means. By 1892 solid-tyred and
cushion-tyred machines were also 'dirt cheap' because of the pneumatic boom,
according to the *Irish Cyclist*.[374] In Ulster in 1893, the season's cycle trade was
marked by provincial riders snapping up the now cheap solid-tyred and cushion-tyred cycles, while in the following year there was a 'phenomenal demand'
amongst rural cyclists for such machines from Belfast agents.[375] A Dubliner commented in 1894, 'To the eyes of a metropolitan rider there is something very odd
about the constant stream of starved-looking, solid-tyred machines to be met with
in country districts', and added that 'one of the pleasant results of this plenitude of
solids is the admiration received by the up-to-date cyclist on his '94 machine. He
is nobody at home, where all his friends are as well mounted as himself, but away
in the lonely country place, where rattling ordinaries and side-steering tricycles
still crawl about the footpaths, he is quite the hero of the hour'.[376]

   As well as purchasing cheap machines which had been superseded by the
advent of the pneumatic-tyred safety bicycle, poorer cyclists also took part in
the new pastime by hiring bicycles by the hour or for a day's ride, at rates which
were probably affordable for all except the most destitute of prospective riders.
For instance, the Dublin Bicycle and Tricycle Depot, opened at Infirmary Road
in April 1888, hired out machines for a mere 6d per hour or for 3s per week.
It opened for business on Sundays, which meant that working-class customers
could avail of the cheap rates to go cycling on their day of rest.[377] Some ten
years later one of Ireland's largest cycle dealers, Thomas Edens Osborne's of 1

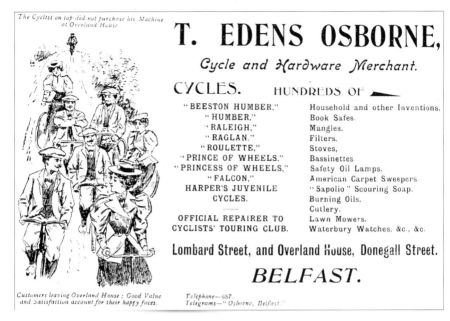

An advertisement for Thomas Edens Osborne in June 1898.

Donegall Street, Belfast, was hiring bicycles for 10s per week or 35s per month, while learners could hire machines for 7s 6d weekly or 30s monthly.[378] It was also common around this time for Belfast dealers to hire out bicycles for 10s per week to customers going on cycling holidays to Connemara or elsewhere, so long as they produced two local references.[379] Hiring tricycles or bicycles was clearly an attractive option for many who could not afford to purchase these machines. As early as June 1888 the *Irish Cyclist*, in its description of cyclists in Dublin's Phoenix Park, stated that 'amongst the cyclists present [was] a considerable percentage of the "great unwashed", for the most part, we presume, riders of hired machines'. One of these riders, 'dressed in ragged garments, came sailing by on an ancient crock'.[380] In September 1888 the newspaper's editor was aghast to learn that in one public house customers were asked whether they preferred the *Irish Cyclist* or another cycling journal, and a running score of the responses was kept on a printed card. 'How nice to have the merits of the paper discussed by Johnny the shoeblack, on his hired crock, or the messenger boy from the grocer's up the road', was Mecredy's disdainful comment.[381] Mecredy's poor opinion of the type of person who hired bicycles was probably not improved by the case of a Dublin tram conductor named William Mackey, who hired a tricycle during his holiday in June 1889 and rode it to Lucan, a popular resort with Dublin cyclists. According to one source he 'imbibed freely' on the outward and return journey, so that the latter 'was a very zigzag one'. At Carsis stream, two miles from Lucan, he lost control of his tricycle and fell

under the Dublin steam tram, which killed him instantly.[382] Some years later the
Irish News identified 'scorching' road hogs as riders who hired bicycles for weekends. According to this source, 'the "Saturday to Monday" wheelman…believes
in going the pace, and does so, until he rushes madly into a pedestrian, gets sum-
moned, and the payment of a fine cools his ardour until sufficient money has
been acquired to hire another bike, and terrorise the country again'.[383]

The hiring system provided opportunities to some thieves of easily purloin-
ing expensive tricycles and bicycles and pawning them.[384] One came unstuck in
March 1902 when he pretended to be an Inland Revenue officer from Dublin
when hiring a bicycle from a dealer in Cahir and, instead of returning it, tried
to pawn it to a Clonmel pawnbroker, to whom he pretended he had lost all of
his money playing cards – unfortunately for the thief he referred to his 'Humber'
bicycle as a 'Hudson', prompting the suspicious pawnbroker to alert the constabulary.[385] Most illegally acquired machines were stolen directly from private owners;
bicycle thefts were so common by September 1892 that *Sport* urged every owner
to purchase a padlock and chain to protect their property.[386] Such thefts were
particularly common in Dublin and Belfast,[387] but also occurred elsewhere. One
crime which probably did not prove particularly taxing for the police to solve
was that of the theft of a bank official's bicycle from a hallway on George Street,
Limerick, in April 1897 – the tramp who stole it must have been rather conspicuous as he cycled it on the road to Ennis.[388]

The availability of machines for hire at cheap prices, as well as the bargain prices
for Ordinaries, tricycles and solid-tyred and cushion-tyred bicycles meant that,
for a number of years in the late 1880s and 1890s, Ireland's roads were travelled
by a motley collection of cyclists and cycles. This is illustrated by the comments
of a visitor to Portarlington in April 1894, who wrote that 'Here the cyclists are

Right: Cyclists came in all shapes and sizes. A rural scene some ten miles from Dublin, May 1891.

Opposite: Bicyclists and tricyclists in Dublin, February 1890.

drawn from every class from the doctor, who does not consider it *infra dig* to visit his patients on wheels, though his postman may deliver his letters by the same means of locomotion, to the labourer, who rides with evident satisfaction a relic of an [O]rdinary'.[389] According to a Galway witness in July 1896, 'Galway never had so many of its inhabitants awheel since the introduction of the bicycle as this season. Peasants, police, solicitors, priests, ministers, lords, ladies, clerks, butchers, bakers, grocers, merchants, are all cyclists, and as for Her Gracious Majesty's army, it's awheel to a man here'.[390] An observer of Dublin's streets on one Saturday afternoon in March 1898 commented that 'all the crocks of the last half century would seem to be out for a holiday. Every class of bike, from the boneshaker to the latest and most up-to-date machine, was in evidence everywhere'.[391] Cyclists from the lower classes in this period included Robert Bell, a servant of Mr A. Watt of Thornhill, Co. Derry, who was seriously injured when he crashed his bicycle at Buncrana in September 1896; a disabled maker of fancy wickerwork from Lisnaskea who sold his wares by travelling from town to town on his 'complete wreck' of a tricycle; a young farm labourer named Tooney who accidentally killed an old man named Daniel Carlin when he collided with him on his bicycle at Portaferry in July 1899; and a sixty-seven-year-old bill-poster from Castlewellan named William Carlisle, who used a tricycle when carrying on his trade.[392] One fortunate servant girl was given her mistress's old bicycle as a present, which she then had repaired and hired it out to her friends for learning purposes as well as for general riding. She bought herself a bicycle with the proceeds.[393]

The eagerness with which some members of the lower classes viewed the prospect of cycling may be gauged from an incident in March 1891, when a Kilkenny collier offered to swap his donkey for an Ordinary bicycle.[394] Others used more dishonest means to satisfy their curiosity about the new pastime, as discovered by the irate Meath cyclist whose bicycle was damaged when sent to him by rail from Dublin in July 1893. It had evidently been damaged by a porter riding it without his permission, leading him to fulminate against 'the audacity of railway clerks, porters, and others, using and abusing machines lying at stations awaiting their owners or being sent by the trains'.[395] In June 1896 Constable Gallagher of Reaghstown station successfully sued the Great Northern Railway Company for £10 damages at Dundalk Quarter Sessions, the damage having been caused by a railway clerk who took the locks off the constable's bicycle when it was being conveyed by rail and borrowed the machine for a ride, damaging the back wheel in the process. Mr Kisbey, QC, awarded the £10 against the company in the hope that it would teach railway porters and clerks not to interfere with other people's property.[396] In June 1895 the *Irish Cyclist* wrote an interesting article on the frequency of unauthorised borrowing of bicycles:

> This evil practice is undoubtedly on the increase, the reason, in all probability, lying in the fact that so many men of the unmoneyed classes are anxious to learn how to ride, so as to have the power of utilising any opportunity for a spin that may turn up. It is generally for learning purposes that cycles are secretly borrowed, and many a light machine that the owner himself feared to learn on has been put to this very work by his gardener or knife-and-boot man, or even by some stray friend of the cook's. If 'the master' is away for a day or two his bicycle is likely enough to be lent out, unless the servants are unusually honest; and if the machine is habitually kept in a stable or outhouse that can be reached by strangers (and many country riders give their mounts no better care than this), it is more than likely that some morning will discover dents and scratches and traces of mud that cannot be accounted for by legitimate use. Cycle *stealing* is another matter, and mostly affects people who leave machines standing in the street. Cycle *borrowing* is usually a trick of country people.[397]

According to Beatrice Grimshaw, unauthorised borrowing at night was a particular problem in country hotels, with hall porters being the main culprits.[398] In an interesting case in November 1897, Dr John Yorke of Longford took legal proceedings against Maud Kennedy, keeper of the railway hotel at Athenry, to recover £20, the alleged amount of the damage caused to his bicycle when it was crashed by the hotel 'boots', Patrick Duffy, when ridden without Yorke's permission. The doctor was awarded damages and costs totalling £8 8s, after it was discovered that his bicycle, a 'Regal Raglan' built by Robert Raglan, a manufacturer of bicycles in Galway, had only cost £17 10s when bought two months previously, and Raglan estimated that the damage would have cost just 7s 6d to repair.[399] These cases of unauthorised borrowing show that not all members of the lower classes were able to afford cycles, even the numerous obsolete or second-hand machines that were available in the 1890s. While many people of modest means participated in the cycling boom at the end of the nineteenth century, the pastime still remained a largely middle-class and upper-class activity. Edward O'Malley, who was born in Owenwee, Westport, in 1904, records that as late as 1911 only policemen had bicycles in his native area (one of whom, when taking the census in 1911, cycled around the district with a small ink bottle hooked to the front of his tunic).[400] Patrick Kavanagh, who was also born in 1904, provides evidence regarding the rarity of bicycles when he was growing up in Co. Monaghan. He records that when he went on pilgrimage to Lady's Well, a holy well that attracted pilgrims from Monaghan, Cavan and Louth, a solitary cyclist who passed Kavanagh's party of pilgrims caused comment, such was the rarity of bicycles in the district at that time.[401]

Most of the details described so far have concerned adult cyclists, particularly men. The topic of women and cycling will be explored in the next chapter. The remainder of this chapter will focus on the subject of children and juveniles as cyclists, as they also constituted a significant element of the Irish cycling world. Children were often caught up in a similar kind of enthusiasm for cycling as their elders – R.J. Mecredy, who was born in 1861, remembered 'the longing desire for a velocipede which sprang up in our youthful breast when, at the age of seven, a gentleman who had returned from London told us of the wonderful iron horses' which he had seen in the British capital.[402] His heart's desire was finally fulfilled when, as a pupil at Portora Royal School, he bought a 'Singer Challenge' Ordinary bicycle with ten guineas which he had won as a school prize. On Good Friday, 1879, he attempted to ride the 105 miles to Dublin before he had learnt to dismount with confidence, but had to abandon the attempt and take a train at Navan, having been misdirected along the way. Undaunted, Mecredy accomplished the return journey from Dublin 'at ease' in eleven hours.[403] The joy of boyhood cycling was recorded by Percy French in a poem, 'A-sailin' through the spring', of which the following are a few representative stanzas:

'Twas a crock, if e'er there was one, and second-hand at that,
And the only rigid portion was the saddle where you sat;
It was tight about the bearings, it was loose about the nuts,
With a singular facility for running into ruts.
But it seemed to me to swoop around like swallow on the wing,
When a boy upon a bicycle, a-sailin' through the spring.

It *was* a fearful instrument – it's lumber long ago,
The up-to-date young jackanapes would sneer at it, I know.
The brake was out of order, and it bucked up at a stone,
But oh, the pride of pedalling a cycle of one's own.
If he chanced to meet a welkin he made that welkin ring,
Did the boy upon a bicycle, a-sailin' through the spring.[404]

Joss Pearson recalled that when he first began cycling, as an eleven-year old in
Newry in 1884, on a 52" Ordinary bicycle, he suffered numerous falls 'as cycling
consisted of gymnastics as well as riding'[405] – this mirrored the experience of
many adult Ordinary riders. Boys who 'scorched' also copied the behaviour of
many older cyclists.[406] Others imitated their elders by forming their own clubs.
These included eight Dublin boys who formed their own club, the Rovers,
'bound together by the closest ties of friendship, by a common love for all kinds
of sport, and by a common desire to get away from the smoke of a large city'.
The boys, who owned either bicycles or tricycles, loved to go on camping holidays in the Dublin and Wicklow mountains.[407] Some Kilkenny juveniles started a
club in May 1892, riding to Danesfort on their first club run; the Treaty Cycling
Club, whose membership was 'confined to the teens', was formed in Limerick in
1894; while the Iolanthe Cycling Club for juveniles was established in Dublin in
1895.[408] Some clubs, such as the Limerick Commercial Bicycle Club and Cork
Cycling Club in 1892, introduced half-price membership fees for youths under
the age of eighteen.[409]

Several schools inculcated a love of cycling in their pupils. Probably the
earliest school to do so was Portora Royal School, whose boys began cycling
around 1878.[410] The Rathmines School Bicycling Club was established in
1881.[411] By May 1887 there were enough schoolboy cyclists in Ulster for the
inclusion of a half-mile bicycle race, confined to pupils of public schools, in
the Queen's College sports programme: amongst the competitors were pupils
from Ballymena School, St Malachy's College, Belfast, and the Royal Belfast

Right: Malcolm P.
Robertson on his
bicycle, 1898.

Opposite: Belmont
Ladies' College fête,
Knock, Belfast, in 1898.

Academical Institution. The race was won by W.S. Knowles of Ballymena, 'the flying schoolboy', riding an Ordinary; he later raced as a pupil at the Royal Belfast Academical Institution.[412]

In 1889 there were around twenty bicycles at Clongoweswood College, and bicycle polo was a popular recreation with the pupils there. Amongst those who sped around the school's gravel track in the 1890s were Oliver St John Gogarty and Tom Kettle.[413] Ex-pupils of Clongoweswood formed the Al Fresco Cycling Club in 1891, which consisted of nearly eighty members in October 1891 and over one hundred in December 1896.[414] Other institutions where cycling constituted a significant part of school life by the late 1880s included Castleknock College, where a cycle track was laid down in 1889, and pupils were permitted to go on cycling trips to such places as Bray, Tara, Maynooth and St Vincent's College, where cycling was so popular in 1889 that the school authorities decided to lay down a cinder cycling track.[415] In August 1890 the *Irish Cyclist* was the official organ of the Coleraine Academical Cycling Club, the High School Bicycle Club and the Leeson School Cycling Club; by April 1892 the Coleraine club, consisting of some forty-six members, was considered 'one of the largest and most influential in the north of Ireland'.[416] Cycling was promoted in Blackrock College in the early 1890s by the construction of a 'velo-drome' gravel path; bicycles were at first hired and later purchased for use by the pupils, who paid a modest fee for their use. John Dunlop, Jnr, enrolled at the school in 1892 and cycled around the velodrome on his tricycle; Eamon de Valera, who enrolled in the college in the late 1890s, was a keen cyclist while

An advertisement for children's tricycles and bicycles as Christmas presents, 1888.

studying at Blackrock.[417] Rockwell College was another school that promoted cycling and in 1893 a cycling track was laid down around its large cricket field.[418] Cycling become part of the regular routine at St Mary's College, Dundalk, by 1896.[419] Some girls' schools also promoted cycling. For example, in April 1894 a cycling club was founded at Alexandra College, Dublin, for past and present pupils and teachers.[420] In June 1896 some forty pupils cycled to the Scalp, in Co. Wicklow, where they had tea and visited 'their favourite haunts'.[421] The annual fête of the Ladies' Collegiate School, Kingstown, took the form of a cycling gymkhana in 1897.[422] In the following year cycling, as well as cricket and tennis, were 'vigorously pursued' by the girls of Victoria College, Belfast.[423] At the May fête of the Belmont Ladies' College in Knock, Belfast, in 1898, the pupils participated in a number of cycling events, including bicycle chequers, a ladies' chain, bicycle polo and a 'cyclorama', the last of which involved the pupils completing a number of graceful evolutions on their machines.[424]

C.S. Andrews records that his father, a Dublin auctioneer, was able to procure a bicycle for him for 'little or nothing' in his auction sale rooms.[425] Four-year-old Malcolm Robertson of Belfast, described in 1898 as Ireland's youngest racing cyclist after he cycled round the track at Ballynafeigh on Easter Saturday, received a present of a miniature bicycle which his father, Tom – inventor of a bicycle valve – built for him.[426] Most middle-class parents who gave their children presents of tricycles or bicycles, obtained them from the growing number of cycle deal-

An advertisement for children's bicycles, 1897.

ers who included children's machines as part of their stock. In November 1885 Walter Carson's cycle business in Dublin was offering children's tricycles from £3 10s.[427] Booth Brothers of Dublin, aiming at the Christmas market in 1888, offered miniature tricycles from £3 10s to £10 10s, miniature Ordinary bicycles from £4 10s to £9 9s, miniature safety bicycles from £6 to £8 8s and miniature tandems from £10 10s to £12 10s.[428] One lucky possessor of a tricycle around this time was the seven-year-old James Joyce, who rode on his machine from Dublin to Bray to visit a nurse, causing his parents to search frantically for him.[429] In 1895 the Humber company designed 'a sweet little Dunlop-Tyred Safety for Youths of nine to twelve years'; to encourage parents to buy this machine for their offspring, Humber's sole Belfast agent, Thomas Edens Osborne, offered the £15 bicycle at a net price of just £11.[430] Better prices were available from the John Griffiths Corporation depots in Dublin and Derry in 1897, which were selling children's safety bicycles at prices of £8 8s for 'Ariel Midget' and £9 9s for 'Juvenile' machines, respectively.[431] The prices that were being sought for miniature tricycles and bicycles shows that these enthusiastically-received presents[432] were, like the machines aimed at the adult market, mainly the preserve of the middle class and comfortably-off sections of Irish society.

4

'In a Sort of Social Churn':[1] Irish Women and Cycling

In May 1882 a tricyclist named Maguire, while cycling outside the viceregal lodge in Dublin's Phoenix Park, was the first person to come across the bodies of Lord Frederick Cavendish, the recently arrived Chief Secretary for Ireland, and his under-secretary, Thomas Burke, assassination victims of the Invincibles.[2] In 1899, 'Skin-the-Goat' (whose real name was James Fitzharris), one of the cab drivers who drove the assassins to the park, was, on his release from Kilmainham Jail, reportedly 'fairly paralysed at the changes in Dublin since he went to prison seventeen years ago, and especially at the number of cyclists'. The London-based Irish cycling journalist, E.J. O'Reilly, was not surprised at the released prisoner's amazement. O'Reilly visited the Phoenix Park one night and found that:

> …the roads were alive with cyclists, chiefly girls. They were there in groups and singly, with young men and without them. Most of them, I presume, were girls who had been working hard all day. A few years ago every cyclist you saw in the park was a male, and, numerically, they were not in it with the present lot. The change was amazing, and was the most remarkable thing that came under my notice during my visit. I could not help thinking what a grand institution the cycle must be to have wrought such a change, and how thankful the girls ought to be to us – the other fellows and myself – who were the leaders in a movement that has given woman more health and liberty than she ever knew before, and that has made it possible for a woman to say, as one did the other day, that since she had taken to cycling there were two souls in her breast instead of one.[3]

This remarkable change in the profile of Dublin's cyclists was mirrored in the rest of the country. 'Portia', the cycling columnist of the women's society journal, *Irish Society*, summed up the transformation which had occurred in Irish cycling when she exulted in May 1897, 'We are all cyclists now'.[4] As this chapter shows,

The Phoenix Park murders: a tricyclist discovers the bodies of Cavendish and Burke.

this profound change came about in the face of much opposition from the male-dominated Irish cycling world, as well as from Irish society in general.

The earliest recorded instance of an Irish woman cycling dates to around 1870, when Miss Jervoise, the daughter of Reverend Robert Jervoise of Corofin, used to ride her father's cumbersome 'Edindurgh' tricycle.[5] The next recorded instance of an Irishwoman awheel dates from the mid to late 1870s, when an unidentified woman rode a 'Dublin' tricycle from Galway to Spiddal and back in a single afternoon.[6] William Bindon Blood's sister-in-law, a Miss Persse, also rode one of these tricycles, which was equipped with a frame apron to prevent her ankles from coming under public view as she pedalled the machine;[7] this was probably in the same period. The paucity of information concerning these pioneering cyclists reflects the fact that cycling in Ireland was, at first, an overwhelmingly male affair. However, the new pastime gradually gained in popularity with Irish women and, accordingly, references to their cycling activity became more common in the cycling press. The first female cyclists all rode tricycles, as neither velocipedes nor Ordinaries could be ridden while wearing the long dresses of the period.[8] As early as 1881 at least three Meath sisters named Hopkins reputedly went on runs of seventy to eighty miles on solid-tyred tricycles of 'enormous weight'.[9] The *Wheel World* reported in July 1881 that tricycling was becoming popular in Dublin's southern suburbs, with 'a fair sprinkling of the fair sex' included among the new cyclists. Another source claimed that the number of 'lady riders' in the Dublin area more than doubled in 1886 alone, and that 'Wherever one goes they are to be met riding in parties of five or six, in pairs, singly, or with escort'.[10]

Miss Persse rides a
'Dublin' tricycle, late
1870s to early 1880s.

One of these was probably R.J. Mecredy's wife, who first took to cycling in 1883.[11]
The Sandymount area of Dublin was said to be 'simply swarming with cyclists,
especially of the fair sex', in June 1887, while an English visitor to the capital in
April 1888 recorded his impression that 'Tricycling is very extensively practiced
by ladies in Dublin, proportionately to the population'.[12] The pastime was also
popular with women in Co. Antrim by the late 1880s. One observer wrote of that
county in 1888 that 'Tricycling is gaining in respect among the gentler sex. It is
no longer a rare sight to find young ladies pegging away at [a] good round pace
along country roads'.[13] It was observed in Armagh in 1888 that 'the ladies have
taken to the tricycle with a show of enthusiasm'.[14]

Female cyclists were rather less common sights in other parts of the country, as
suggested by the fact that a Waterford witness considered it newsworthy to record
in June 1886 that 'Three of the fair sex passed through here, on Friday last, mounted
on tricycles', while a Newry witness stated in September of the same year that
'Lady cyclists are now showing themselves. No less than three were out *at the same
time* one day last week – Record'.[15] According to 'Hylas', a Cork correspondent for
the *Irish Cyclist*, there was only 'a small number of lady riders' in the southern city
in May 1888; a situation that had changed little by February 1894, when another
Corkonian stated that 'A lady cycling [in Cork] causes comment from its very rarity'.[16] A Belfast writer recorded in March 1889 that he was 'rather surprised' to
have encountered a woman on a tricycle in the northern city, and that 'It is seldom
we have the pleasure of seeing a lady cycling in Belfast'; in April 1890 'Zona' of

MAIDEN'S SPHERE.
By Mrs. She-man.

As this cartoon
makes clear,
women would
have been objects
of ridicule if they
had attempted
to ride Ordinary
bicycles.

Wexford wrote that 'We had one lady cyclist last season', adding that 'I trust more of
the fair sex will follow her example this season and not mind what people *will* say'.[17]
Despite the thriving cycling scene in Clonmel, which had a cycling club that was
founded on 2 May 1888 and which contained hundreds of male cyclists 'from the
middle-aged gentleman to the boy of ten years' in 1891, there wasn't a single female
cyclist in the Munster town in the latter year.[18]

When one considers contemporaries' reactions to their first sight of women
riding tricycles, it is surprising that female tricycling caught on even to the limited extent that it did. These reactions varied, but often consisted of outright
hostility that only gradually gave way to mere astonishment. This mixed reception speaks volumes about contemporary notions about women's participation
in strenuous sports, as well as the extent to which cycling was perceived as an
essentially masculine activity.[19] Beatrice Grimshaw, in her overview of the history
of women's cycling in Ireland, written in 1897, recorded the numerous obstacles with which the pioneering tricyclists had to contend as they propelled 'their
metal monsters......persecuted by the relentless ridicule of nine-tenths of the
whole community':

> 'She rides a tricycle' – or sometimes even 'a velocipede', for the word had not yet
> died down in those archaic times – was considered the last word descriptive of
> general fastness and unfemininity; and yells, hoots, prayers, and curses followed
> after the daring pioneers of feminine wheeling wherever they appeared.[20]

Beatrice Grimshaw and her *Irish Cyclist* colleagues, June 1893.

As we shall see, the first female bicyclist in Dublin was a shocking sight to many, but according to Lillias Campbell Davison, the leading English cycling journalist, the first female tricyclists had an even greater impact on public opinion in the Irish capital.[21] The *Irish Cyclist*'s editor, after detailing several advances made in the new sport in Ireland during the 1885 season, made the revealing comment that 'Lady riders are becoming more numerous, and are no longer looked upon as strong-minded or masculine, but, at the worst, are considered, perhaps, a little eccentric and apt to be carried away by their enthusiasm for a harmless and healthful amusement':[22] clearly both of the undesirable characteristics of strong-mindedness and masculinity had been attributed to female tricyclists before 1885.

As time passed hostility to tricycling women gave way to mere astonishment by the mid-1880s. A woman from Kerry, writing under the pseudonym of 'Big Sister', wrote a brief account of a twenty-mile tricycle trip that she and her two sisters undertook to Killarney in May 1885:

> We had any amount of prophecies before starting of 'insults on the road', 'accidents', etc, but never a one came to mar the serenity of our little expedition, and we arrived at our destination in a little less than three hours, delighted with ourselves, our tricycles, and the roads – though I must say we caused no little excitement amongst the *very* country people by the wayside, who exclaimed in terror at the idea of seeing three women – they wouldn't

condescend to calling us 'ladies' – riding on 'maschines'. I heard one old dame speculating on the probable end of the world; I suppose she thought it would be hastened by such a proceeding as ours!

'Big Sister' added that, 'We had, of course, to bear any amount of comments on our appearance and dress; but as we took very good care not to make ourselves more conspicuous than need be, we hope that as the novelty of the thing dies out, so will comments'.[23] More evidence of the surprise produced by female tricyclists comes from accounts of a tour of the west of Ireland carried out by another three sisters in 1885. The trio found that the landlords of the various hostelries in which they stayed 'always wanted us to "move on" quickly, not from a dislike to our presence in their houses, but because lady tricyclists being such a novelty to them, they were most anxious to see how we managed to progress in this unusual fashion'. On their homeward journey the landlord of their hotel in Longford insisted on their stabling their tricycles in his adjacent grocery store, probably to draw custom to his shop as tricycles 'appeared to be quite a novelty in Longford'. In a revealing detail, one of the sisters recorded that they later found out that the locals believed that the three tricyclists were American women[24]: presumably the idea of Irish women cycling was still inconceivable in that part of the country. The astonishment the cycling sisters created may be guessed at from the fact that when they passed through Moycullen 'the whole town – men, women, and children – had turned out, and that the fame of their exploit had spread far and wide'. According to a Galway jarvey, 'the three ladies on the velocipedes were the most wonderful sight ever seen in the town of Galway'.[25] Jack White, a Dubliner, who went on a cycling tour in the West in 1886, found in Leenane, where there was a Cyclists' Touring Club hotel, that 'The three lady tourists about whose prowess I was continually hearing tales all along my route, appear to have made a great impression here. The *employés* were full of them, and could hardly talk of anything else'.[26] Their amazement was matched by the man from Morley's Bridge who simply refused to believe a woman's account that she had travelled all the way from Macroom to 'a little beyond Kenmare' on her tricycle in one day, 17 June 1886.[27]

In September 1886 the *Irish Cyclist* reported on two sisters-in-law from Sandymount who were:

> …traversing the whole country on a Crescent Tandem. Everywhere they seem to have caused quite an impression. The I[rish] C[hampion] C[ycling] C[lub] met them at the Scalp the Saturday before last. They are frequently to be seen at Dalkey, Glenageary, Kingstown, and, not content with these shorter spins, they seem to venture boldly on more ambitious runs – for, on Saturday, we heard that they had been seen passing through Woodenbridge, en route – goodness knows where.[28]

The following account from July 1889 shows that it was not only people in Dublin and Wicklow who were amazed at the sight of female tricyclists:

> Through a distant town in the south-west of Ireland there passed a member of the Ladies' C[ycling] C[lub], and the good people, unaccustomed to such a sight, rushed to their doors and windows, and stared with all the stare in their power. Now, it so happened, that in the same town there was a circus, and the clown was proceeding through the streets like the Pied Piper of Hamelin drawing the crowd after him, when, as the Fates decreed, the fair tricyclist got into that crowd, and quickly became the cynosure of all eyes, and it was not until she had gone some distance that she perceived that she had ousted the clown, the people evidently believing that she belonged to the circus also, and that she was much the most interesting object to follow[;] and then might have been seen the crowd breaking right and left, and leaving a passage to the pavement, and the form of a young damsel fleeing wildly towards the sheltering portals of a chemist and there the damsel remained until the crowd had dispersed, when she timidly ventured forth and fled into the unknown.[29]

In another revealing incident, a Dublin woman who paid a visit to Birr in April 1890 brought her tricycle with her and went riding around the town on it, much to the consternation of at least one of the town's residents. The tricyclist's friend overheard the bemused observer inform a local shopkeeper 'in terms of holy horror' that he had just seen 'the most haynous sight ever wore: a lady dressed in a red shirt bestraddling a cicycle'.[30] Even in the late 1880s, it would appear, the sight of a female tricyclist could still cause a sensation in some parts of the country.

The early hostility and astonishment towards female cyclists arose partly from the mere fact that these women were participating in what was perceived as an essentially masculine activity, and, furthermore, that they were thereby challenging (either consciously or unconsciously) conventional opinion on what constituted appropriate women's behaviour outside of the domestic sphere, as well as ideas about the limits of women's physical endurance. It is interesting to note that tricycles were actually considerably heavier than bicycles and that it took greater physical exertion to propel the three-wheeled machines.[31] Nevertheless, Irish women frequently cycled astonishing distances on their tricycles, particularly considering the restrictive nature of the dresses that they wore and also the deplorable condition of roads throughout much of the country.[32] The *Irish Cyclist* noted on 3 June 1885 that 'Many ladies are able to take runs of forty and fifty miles in the day, and some even undertake tours of several days' duration'. Not only did the Hopkins sisters of Meath travel for seventy to eighty miles on their tricycles, but one of them also succeeded in cycling up the hill from Killiney railway station, 'a feat remarkable even for a man'.[33] In September 1886 a woman succeeded in the daunting task of cycling up the steep hill on the Dublin road out of Newry, a feat which made R.J. Mecredy, editor of the *Irish Cyclist*, 'feel small'. Mecredy also knew several women who rode almost 2,000 miles in the 1885-1886 cycling season.[34] Despite the evidence that women were able to perform quite impressively on tricycles, and in an effort to maintain conventional notions of women's frailty, the tricycle came to be regarded and written about by many men as a machine that was suitable mainly for women, old men and male cyclists who were unwilling or unable to mount Ordinaries – and this was also in spite of the fact that there were annual Irish tricycling championships for male racers in the 1880s. The dismissive attitude towards the tricycle was summed up in July 1886 by 'Cyclo', a male cyclist from Newry, who wrote that 'I have always maintained that the tricycle is not the mount for a man', and he advocated reducing one of his club's officers to the ranks after the latter rode 'one of these go-carts' on a club run.[35] It is a telling detail that women were bracketed in the same category as 'aged and infirm' men by the DMP when it came to cycling, as the Dublin police were instructed to turn a blind eye when they rode tricycles on footpaths.[36] Not only were women's cycling accomplishments and the difficulties inherent in riding tricycles disregarded by many male cyclists, but female cyclists were warned in the cycling press about the dangers of overexerting themselves on their machines.[37] Female tricyclists in Ireland pursued their hobby in a social atmosphere that was frequently either hostile at worst, or dismissive or condescending at best.

Another reason for much of the public consternation at female cyclists is that they often rode alone or in all-female groups. This was at a time when it was considered 'fast' for lone women or even women in pairs to travel in Dublin on outside cars, and 'fast' was, according to Beatrice Grimshaw, 'a word at which everyone trembled'.[38] Middle-class women were expected to travel in the company of a male relative or a chaperone, hence the adoption of tandem tricycles by married couples in some parts of the country by the mid-1880s.[39] The tricycle was built to be ridden by one person and – as we shall see later – the bicycle accorded middle-class women unprecedented opportunities of physical emancipation. The unaccustomed sight of such women travelling freely through the streets of Irish towns and cities and on the roads of rural Ireland, prompted much of the adverse reaction that they received.

Unsurprisingly, given contemporary attitudes towards female cyclists, most Irish cycling clubs were initially reluctant to accept female members. The first recorded instance of a softening in this stance came when the Newry Cycling Club elected a woman as a member in November 1885; this was followed by the Tralee Bicycling Club in May 1886, which allowed women to join for the reduced annual fee of 7s 6d.[40] The first Dublin club with female members was the Ohne Hast Club, formed in late 1886. This was an unusual club in that its membership was a mixed one of men and women from the very beginning. According to one member:

THE WHEEL OF MISS FORTUNE.

WHILST A YOUNG Dublin lady and her companion were cycling up hill recently in front of a regiment of soldiers, the lady slipped a pedal and ran back on the astonished soldiers, scattering them in all directions.— IRISH CYCLIST.

Only a tricycle going up hill,
Only a lady devoid of skill,
Only a youth (for her love he pined),
Only some soldiers, who followed behind.

Only a pedal she slipped, alack !
Only a tricycle running back,
Running right back on that steep incline,
Running right back on " the thin red line.'

Only a moment of awful doubts :
"Britons ! stand firm !" the Colonel shouts ;
Then lady and lover, and Colonel and line,
Are piled in a heap on that steep incline.

Women's cycling misfortunes attracted humorous comment in the Irish press.

A bicycle built for two: a Rudge-Whitworth 'Companion', 1897.

> To encourage the appreciation of scenery, and especially of mountain scenery, is the main object of the Ohne Hast (literally, 'without hurry'), and in their pleasant excursions among the Wicklow, and other mountains, it is the rule of the Ohne Hast members to take it easy, walk wherever walking seems pleasanter than riding uphill, stop and admire the scenery to their hearts' content, and never lose sight of the idea that 'pleasure is to be measured by the hour, not by the mile'.[41]

The male Ohne Hast members often towed their female colleagues' tricycles up steep hills, and according to Lillias Campbell Davidson, the practice of towing female cyclists was much more common in Ireland than in Britain.[42] By January 1890 over one-third of the Ohne Hast members were women.[43] The Sandymount and Pembroke Cycling clubs, which were established in either late May or early June 1887, followed the example of the Ohne Hast club in admitting both male and female members from their inception.[44] In April 1890 Frena Lacey became the first woman to be elected a member of the Waterford Bicycle Club, just a few days after she had learned to ride a tricycle; exactly a year later the first two female members were elected to the Wexford Cycling Club.[45] The Leinster Cycling Club decided to admit female members in March 1892.[46] The progress towards clubs' opening their doors to female members was not entirely smooth, however.

THE GENTLE ART OF TOWING.

Towing female cyclists.

For instance, when a club in Dublin's northern suburbs elected six female members in January 1891 (until that point, women had been allowed to participate in its club runs, but only if they were related to a male member), a minority of the clubmen were displeased with the decision, leading one newspaper to print a tongue-in-cheek account that drew parallels between the discord wrought in the cycling club and Eve's destruction of the harmony that had once prevailed in the Garden of Eden.[47] In the following month W.F. Barry, captain of the Kilkenny Cycling Club, argued strenuously against the proposal to grant women club membership, arguing 'that he would not captain a ladies' club' and threatened to resign if the proposal were accepted. Interestingly, not only did the club vote to accept female membership, it also refused to accept Barry's resignation and resolved that the new female members would have to ride immediately behind the captain on club runs![48]

Rather than waiting for the gradual or grudging emergence of mixed-sex clubs, in May 1888 some Irish female cycling pioneers took the bold step of forming their own clubs,[49] the first all-female cycling clubs in the United Kingdom. The first of these was the Nenagh Ladies' Cycling Club. Apparently it was a short-lived outfit, as its existence is documented only by two letters from one of its members to the *Nenagh Guardian*.[50] During its brief existence, its tricycle-riding members 'caused a sensation' when passing through the Tipperary village of Puckawn on their way to Johnstown, during the club's second outing. Its first outing consisted of a trip to the River Shannon, where the cyclists had a picnic tea. According to one of the participants, the women enjoyed themselves tremendously during the picnic, with 'jokes and laughter being the order of the evening'. Her account of the trip pointed out that:

> There is a general belief that ladies can never thoroughly enjoy themselves when together without the society of the sterner sex, but any one listening to the peals of laughter and the witticisms of our party, would change their minds at once, and for ever. It may not be 'good for man to be alone', but the same thing does not hold good for his sisters, his cousins, and his aunts.

Her description of the club's two outings is remarkably similar to accounts of runs written by the secretaries of male cycling clubs. It even includes a tale of how one of the women lost control of her machine and how she careered dangerously down a steep hill, frantically ringing her bell and scattering donkeys that were in her path. Similar incidents involving livestock on country roads occur in male-authored letters to cycling journals. Despite – or possibly because of – these similarities, one male reader of the *Nenagh Guardian* wrote a caustic letter in response to the newspaper's publicising the Nenagh women's activities. He commented sarcastically that 'Captain Burnaby's ride to Khiva dwindled into utter insignificance' in comparison with their ride to the Shannon, and suggested that their picnic tea 'contained some French colouring, judging by the loud peals of laughter that succeeded the imbibing thereof'. In his opinion, drunkenness also explained the runaway tricycle incident and the laughter and chaffing that occurred on the journey home.[51]

The Dublin-based Ladies' Cycling Club, established by Mrs Ross, 'a lady of considerable literary attainments' who once 'lectured successfully at a leading girl college', and who was the widow of G.L.G. Ross, secretary of the Irish Cycle Company,[52] also met with a mixed response, although it succeeded in maintaining a longer-lasting presence than the Nenagh club. The Ladies' Cycling Club went on two runs per week and thought nothing of covering sixty or seventy miles in a day,[53] and many of them were also members of the Ohne Hast club.[54] Its existence was a source of considerable amusement to the male cycling establishment, who frequently poked fun at the women's activities. The women's club was small – when it went on a run to Lucan in September 1890, some thirteen members were recorded as having participated, although over forty members and friends attended the club's annual picnic at the Salmon Leap, Leixlip, in June 1892.[55] However, rather than offering encouragement to the fledgling outfit, the official organ of the ICA scoffed at it. Its small membership roll evinced the following observation from the newspaper: 'The Ladies' C.C. has been much exercised over the annual election of officials. What between captain, sub-captain, hon. sec., assistant hon. sec., treasurer, and committee, nearly every member has an official capacity'[56]; while a regular contributor, 'An Old File', wrote in September 1890, 'I understand that the Ladies' C.C. rode to Howth a few days ago. I congratulate her upon the achievement'.[57]

After the Ladies' Cycling Club successfully applied for membership of the ICA in July 1889, the ICA council was divided over the prospect of the women actually sending a delegate to attend its meetings in future. The council members were reassured that this was an unlikely eventuality, as delegates had to supply the council secretary with details of their names, addresses and ages: the women's supposed vanity would mean that the final requirement would preclude their attendance![58] In a similar vein, the *Irish Cyclist* featured a comical sketch by Percy French of an imaginary ICA meeting chaired by 'Miss Rubber-Tyre' and attended by several Ladies' Cycling Club delegates. During the course of this meeting 'Miss Footrest' proposed, and 'Miss Spoonbrake' seconded, a motion that men (preferably young ones) be encouraged to participate in the runs of the latter club, particularly so that they could push the women's tricycles up steep hills. 'Miss Backpedal' and 'Miss Carrie R. Luggage' gave speeches in support of the motion. A 'Miss Crank' proposed a motion 'That smoking be prohibited on all occasions', while 'Miss Loo Screw', commenting on how much easier it was to cycle downhill, recommended that the ICA's Road Improvement Committee should substitute descents for ascents on all existing roads and should supervise the construction of all new roads, ensuring that these should all run downhill![59]

While the members of the Ladies' Cycling Club and other female tricyclists, were struggling to be taken seriously by male cyclists and other commentators, there was another – and, in the long term, more serious – challenge to the masculine domination of Irish cycling in the form of the development of the woman's safety bicycle. The first of these, Dan Albone's 'Anfield Ivel', was developed in 1886 and launched in 1887.[60] As early as June 1888 the *Irish Cyclist* reported the presence of a female bicyclist in Blackrock, her existence having been confirmed by an informant who spied on her as she practiced riding her safety bicycle in her garden.[61] This pioneer bicyclist received only a passing mention, as she confined her cycling to the supposed privacy of her garden. This was a far cry from the impact caused by the first public appearance of a female bicyclist, Pearl Hillas, on the streets of Dublin in the same year. According to Beatrice Grimshaw:

Miss Pearl Hillas was the first Irish lady to appear on the safety machine; and it is not too much to say that she and her machine were *the* sensation of the year 1888 in Dublin. Small, wiry and muscular, clad in a severely plain skirt and a coat of mannish cut, at a time when 'draped' skirts were all the fashion, and ladies' coats almost unknown – and wearing a cricket cap on her close-cropped head, pretty Miss Hillas was a remarkable enough figure on foot; but when she mounted on her bicycle, a fire engine was not in it with her in the matter

The initial sight of female bicyclists often caused consternation on Ireland's roads.

of creating a sensation. She rode constantly through the town in the crowded hours of the afternoon, and evidently enjoyed the excitement created by her appearance. So great was the anger and horror aroused by this daring departure, that many a paterfamilias, whose daughters are cyclomaniacs of the most determined type today, was heard to say that the girl's father must be a fool not to lock her up in her own room, and throw the beastly thing into the Liffey![62]

A year later a male witness recorded the impression created by a female bicyclist, possibly Pearl Hillas, in Dublin:

> I had never seen a lady cyclist before, and I was bewildered. I did not know what to do, but as a precautionary measure I told everyone I met, and thus gave vent to some of the fiery excitement that was consuming me and driving me into the Wicklow [Hotel] for cooling drinks. Several ladies whom I told said, 'Horribly forward', 'Perfectly shocking', 'I don't know how any girl could go through town in such a way', and so on.[63]

Also in 1889 the *Irish Cyclist* reported that a husband and wife were to be seen cycling together on safety bicycles in Dublin, the latter on a 'Rudge' machine, while the first woman to suffer a 'cropper' on a safety bicycle – an incident which occurred in Kingstown – was mentioned briefly by the newspaper.[64] Female bicyclists were still a rare sight in the Dublin area in 1890, as may be inferred from an incident in October. A brother and sister who were wheeling a tricycle and a safety bicycle, respectively, in Blackrock were followed by an expectant crowd who wished to see the woman riding the bicycle, which they mistakenly took to be her machine as she was pushing it along (in fact, the man was pushing the tricycle as it was too difficult for his sister to push it). The crowd was disappointed when the pair eventually exchanged machines and rode off on their customary cycles.[65] Female bicyclists were also rare in other parts of Ireland at this stage. For instance, a Belfast correspondent recorded in July 1889 that the northern city had 'at least' two female safety riders; apparently, if there were other women riding safeties in Belfast at that time, they were not numerous.[66]

The adverse reaction with which the pioneering female bicyclists were met helps to explain the safety bicycle's slow growth in popularity with Irish women. Nevertheless, the new machine gradually overtook the tricycle in female cyclists' affections, especially when pneumatic-tyred bicycles became more numerous on the market in the early 1890s. Beatrice Grimshaw charted the progress of women's bicycling in Dublin:

> By 1890, one could ride a bicycle about Dublin without being actually mobbed; by 1891, curses and strong epithets were only heard occasionally in the streets, although [S]ociety still totally ignored the existence of the pastime, and society with a small 's' thought it 'very fast and vulgar'. 1892 and 1893 saw an increase, though not a very marked one, in the number of ladies' safeties; in 1894, the world of Society began to cast sheep's eyes at the pastime which it had so long stigmatised as 'impossible', and a few daring *grandes dames* mounted the wheel, in strict privacy. In 1895 came the cycling boom, 'Society' at last took the plunge on the verge of which it had so long been hesitating, and bicycling all at once became 'the thing'.[67]

Grimshaw's assertion of an increase in the number of women's safeties in 1892 is partly supported by 'Ixion', *Sport's* cycling correspondent, who reported in November that the Wayte brothers' workshop on Lemon Street was 'quite alive with business'. The Waytes were engaged in making women's bicycles, and, according to 'Ixion', 'the firm can hardly turn out machines to meet the demand of the dear little girls, most of whom insist on an Xmas box of a Wayte cycle'.[68] Although some Dublin cycle agents were catering for female bicyclists in 1892, the sight of women on bicycles was still novel enough in 1893 for urchins to run behind them in the streets.[69] By 1894 the trend in women's cycling in Dublin was pronouncedly in favour of bicycling: in February one Dublin woman stated that 'every girl of her acquaintance who does not possess a bicycle is at present engaged in teasing her parents, guardian, or relative to buy her one. The amount of Dublin young ladies who are yearning for the joys of the wheel is something phenomenal, and must in due time bring forth a tremendous crop of riders'.[70] In April the tricycle was declared 'nearly extinct now in Dublin as a lady's machine';

WHAT WE USED TO SUFFER.

An old woman's first sight of a female bicyclist.

in July of the following year, 'Vera' of the *Weekly Irish Times* declared that 'the girls in town here are having the bicycle fever pretty badly – they are teasing their fathers and mothers and husbands and brothers to buy them a pneumatic steed, and those who have learned to ride, and some who haven't, may be seen whizzing in all directions about town'.[71]

Dublin women set the fashion for female bicycle-riding in Ireland. In 1893 the marked difference in the popularity of bicycles with women in Ireland's two largest cities was commented upon – while a number of Dublin women thought nothing of bicycling one hundred miles in a day on bad roads, and continued cycling throughout the winter, most of Belfast's female cyclists stuck to the tricycle and put their machines away for the winter.[72] Although the tricycle remained the most popular women's machine in Belfast in 1893, it was reported in September that there was a slow trend towards bicycling, and in September 1894 it was predicted that Belfast agents would need to make women's bicycles 'a considerable portion of their stock', as the demand for hired machines had far exceeded the supply in the previous month.[73] It was reported in April 1894 that the first 'lady safetiest' had made their appearance on the streets of Limerick, and that other women there were learning to ride the safety bicycle and would appear in public when they were more proficient in its use.[74] Two years later, Limerick horse dealers were complaining that it was impossible to sell ponies 'since bicycles have become so general', with women preferring to shop using their bicycles rather than driving into town, and paying visits by the same means.[75] In May 1895 it was asserted that 'cycling has quite ousted tennis with the fair sex' in Miltown Malbay.[76] We have already seen above that even as late as 1894 female cyclists were rare in Cork,[77] a situation that persisted until early in 1896. Then women in Cork also caught the 'bicycling craze', as recorded by a contemporary:

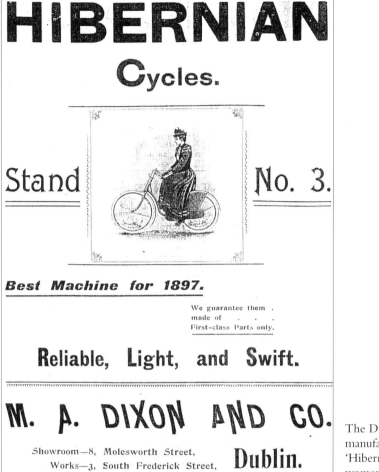

The Dublin-manufactured 'Hibernian' women's bicycle.

Perhaps outside the great metropolis there has been no place in the United Kingdom where the gentler sex have caught on to the cycling mania more than in Cork city and Cork [county]. A few months ago the few female votaries of the wheel in this district were looked upon with unenviable eyes, but suddenly there was a wild, weird, frantic rush to obtain machines, and now the scene is changed. Everywhere, in every street, in every part of the county, ladies on their cycles can be seen pedalling merrily along, sometimes alone, but more often with a party of friends. Those who drove before to their friends' house now go on wheels. Everything – shopping, picnicking, promenading is now done on wheels.[78]

These developments in Cork in 1896 were observed gloomily by 'Shandon', an *Irish Cyclist* correspondent:

> The principal feature of this season's cycling here is the great number of ladies who have taken to the sport. The fine weather seems to have brought them out like bees, and every evening numbers of the fair creatures can be seen pedalling over our suburban roads. Some of them ride remarkably well, and send their mounts along to a tune which would make some of us sit up. This is all very nice in one way, but the disastrous consequences which result from this female invasion are most momentous. The first and most important result was the non-fitness of our racing men for the Easter's racing. They, instead of training, spent their time in teaching females the art and pastime, and when their pupils had attained proficiency in accompanying them on their evening spins.[79]

R.J. Mecredy also viewed women's growing enthusiasm for bicycles with a jaundiced eye:

> Woman makes a craze and overdoes it to death. When a lady cannot make a call six doors down without getting there on a cycle; when she tortures herself into going into town to 'shop' on her cycle, and flutters nervously home with a pile of parcels, and tries to persuade herself that she has gained the tram-fare; when she tries to go every place possible and impossible, riding, pushing, or carrying her cycle; it can't last long. A cycle is not so handy a pet as a pug-dog, or as cheap as an errand boy. The best we can hope is that these cycle maniacs will settle down into ordinary enthusiasts.[80]

Despite occasional negative male comments, women's bicycling gathered apace. In September 1896 a Drogheda cyclist, J. Harbinson, graphically described the transformation that occurred in the world of Irish cycling as unprecedented numbers of Irish women took to the bicycle:

Cycling Song

Oh, many outdoor sports there be
Folk joyfully partake in,
But tennis, golf, and boating now
Alike we see forsaken;
For shady glens and sunny paths
Fresh beauties are revealing,
To those who in these latter days
Go wheeling, wheeling, wheeling.

The elite once called cycling 'low'
And spoke of 'cads on castors',
But now you see them all on wheels,
Of which they're scarcely masters;
The talk is all of nuts and gears,
And tyres most to the liking
Of those who now can daily speak
Of naught but 'biking, biking'.

Once spinsters prim stood quite aghast,
In utter consternation,
As girls on wheels before them passed,
They cried in indignation –
'Is this the forward movement, pray?
Are these the newest women?
They surely must have gone quite 'fey',
Such mannish airs assuming?'

But now e'en these have joined the crowd,
And in all parks and places
Their frightened eyes and rigid hands
And quite too rosy faces,
Are tokens to the looker-on
They don't yet share the feeling
Of pleasure that most people have
Who go a-wheeling, wheeling.

And should this rage go on apace
We'll have perpetual motion
And who'll housekeep in any sense
I've not the slightest notion;
Since old and young and grave and gay
Confess to have a liking
For speedy rushing through the air
And go a-biking, biking.[81]

Evidence from as far afield as Tralee, where there was a 'truly marvellous' number of female cyclists,[82] and Belfast and Enniscorthy, whose cycle agents found it impossible to cope with the demand for women's bicycles,[83] supports the general impression of a bicycling craze amongst Irish women in 1896. Indeed, according to the *Irish Wheelman*, Irish women took to cycling in far greater numbers than

Irish men in this year.[84] A survey of several Dublin cycle agents' sales in 1896 revealed the importance of female cyclists to the trade:

Table 1: Women's bicycles as a proportion of overall sales in selected Dublin companies in 1896[85]

Name of company	Women's bicycles as proportion of overall sales
William McTaggart (Grafton Street)	30% to 35%
William Bown (Bachelor's Walk)	40%
J.J. Keating (Lower Abbey Street)	45%
Shamrock Cycles (Great Brunswick Street)	50%
John Griffiths Corporation (Westland Row)	50%
Rudge Whitworth (Stephen's Green)	50%
Richardson Brothers (Stephen's Green)	50%
J.H. Naylor (Dawson Street)	56%
William McCrum (Leinster Street)	70%
New Howe Company (Bachelor's Walk)	75% to 80%
W.F. McCourt (Duke Street)	80%

By the following year female cyclists reportedly outnumbered male cyclists in Clonmel,[86] and, on some days, there were allegedly more female cyclists on Dublin's streets than male cyclists;[87] in February 1897 a Belfast witness estimated that in another month or so the number of female cyclists would almost equal that of males.[88] While this is only impressionistic evidence, clearly the Irish cycling world had been altered beyond recognition in the space of a few years by the introduction of the pneumatic-tyred safety bicycle. Irish cycling was no longer a largely male preserve.

The fact that the women's cycling clubs founded in the 1890s were met with a better reception than the pioneering tricycling clubs of the 1880s, illustrates how Irish society had grown accustomed to the concept of the female cyclist. The case of the women's cycling club that was started in Bandon in February 1897 is particularly indicative of the shift in attitudes that had occurred. A few years previously, according to the *Irish Cyclist*, 'from a lady's point of view, Bandon was a most abandoned centre, and the ladies who took up the accursed thing were looked upon as suspicious characters', and indignant letters of protest were written to Bandon's Methodist minister after his daughter bought a bicycle. The clergyman showed his support for his daughter, and his scorn for public opinion, by accompanying her as she wheeled her bicycle through the town's streets. The fact that an all-female bicycling club could be started in Bandon some years later, illustrates the remarkable turnaround in public attitudes to women's cycling.[89] Other women's cycling clubs established in the later 1890s included the Belfast Ladies'

Cycling Club, founded in March 1897, with its headquarters at Mountpottinger, and the Ulster Wheel Club, established on 11 May 1897. Members of the Belfast Otter Ladies' Amateur Swimming Club at the Templemore Avenue baths were the founding members of the former cycling club, whose president was the Lady Mayoress of Belfast – an indication that it was considered respectable to be a member. Nevertheless, the club captain, Lucy Kingan, still felt it necessary to write a public letter to deny rumours that the women would soon be invading the ultimate male sanctum, the public house – apparently some Belfast men still looked askance at women indulging in the supposedly masculine activity of bicycling.[90] Although membership of the Ulster Wheel Club was nominally open to men as well as women, it was intended primarily as a women's club. The Marchioness of Dufferin and Ava formally opened the club, and was also a member, while the Lady Mayoress of Belfast was president, in addition to being president of the Belfast Ladies' Cycling Club. The Ulster Wheel Club's captain was Miss Bottomley, the daughter of H.H. Bottomley, the under sheriff for Co. Antrim. She conceived the idea of a centrally located Belfast club for women (its headquarters were on Adelaide Street) after attending a bicycle gymkhana at the Ulster Hall in December 1896. The club's premises were intended as a place where fashionable female cyclists could leave their machines in safety and also participate in conversation and avail of tea and light refreshments. The annual fees were £1 1s for the first 150 members, after which the fees were £2 2s – in other words, the club was intended for a well-to-do membership.[91] Belfast's Phoenix Cycling Club, a Catholic club founded in August 1893,[92] established a female branch – the Ladies' Phoenix Cycling Club – in May 1898, which consisted of some forty members initially, rising to almost one hundred by April 1900.[93] Two siblings, Dan and Nellie McCann, were captain of the male and female branches of the Phoenix club, respectively.[94] A women's cycling club was also formed in Cork in 1898 – the Cork Ladies' Cycling Club – whose captain, Miss A. Ryan, came to public notice after cycling approximately 105 miles from Cork to Mount Melleray and back in eight and a half hours in August of that year.[95]

As well as forming cycling clubs of their own in the 1890s, women also joined what had hitherto been male-only clubs in increasing numbers.[96] Some of the largest Cork clubs announced in April 1896 that they were going to admit women as members, prompting 'Shandon' to dread a future in which 'our roadmen, instead of taking their usual hard runs with the fast divisions of their clubs, will limit their work to an afternoon crawl with their Sunday girls'.[97] Another commentator claimed in 1899 that the countryside was being denuded of dog roses due to 'foolish fellows' picking them for young women on mixed club runs.[98] Although some contemporaries did not warmly welcome the increasing emergence of the mixed club, the main development in club life was for men and women to join together for sociable cycling.[99] The influx of women into cycling clubs revitalised club life which had, according to many observers, been undergoing a decline in the early to mid-1890s, as members concentrated more on training for races rather than par-ticipating in club runs and social gatherings.[100] The Waterford Bicycle Club was an early beneficiary – in 1894 this club, one of Ireland's largest, had many female members, a circumstance which gave it its reputation for being the most hospitable and cordial Irish cycling club.[101] By June 1897 almost every Dublin club admitted women, which, according to one observer, led to a marked strengthening of 'the social side of cycling'.[102] By the end of the decade all clubs in Belfast, whether they had female members or not, set aside special days when women could participate in their runs.[103] The men and women of the Phoenix clubs were particularly fond of mixed runs,[104] and around 160 members rode to Helen's Bay in June 1899;[105] in August 1899 almost seventy riders, half of them women, participated in the first mixed run to Belfast's Bloomfield Cycling Club.[106] Such numbers dwarfed those of club runs in the 1880s, when a run of twenty riders was considered 'a monster turn out'.[107]

One of the main reasons why female cyclists were accepted by public opinion in the 1890s was that most of them conformed to contemporary expectations of what constituted proper female behaviour. In particular, newspaper columnists and other commentators cautioned that female cyclists who appeared unseemly, whether in dress or by 'scorching' (riding at a rapid pace) or overexerting them-selves, would prejudice society against them. *Sport* argued that:

> As long as girls cycle for cycling's sake nobody can say a word against them. Of course, if young ladies commenced to 'shape' on wheels, and damsels acquired a habit of pedalling through the streets in a 'look at me now' fashion, their more sedate sisters would, rather than be reckoned amongst the frivolous ones, aban-don the wheel altogether.[108]

The *Irish Cyclist* offered a similar opinion in September 1893, stating that 'Any woman who cannot remain feminine in nature and behaviour when on a cycle would do well not to mount one at all, if cycling for ladies is to become popular'. It urged Irish women to 'Take warning by the unseemly pranks of English "lady scorchers", and keep the name of an Irish lady rider what it is at present – synony-mous for a gentlewoman'. '[R]owdy behaviour on the road' and 'masculine dress and manners' were to be avoided in particular.[109] Female cyclists didn't always heed these injunctions, as illustrated by the fact that the DMP started a clampdown on speeding cyclists in 1896 following an incident in which Chief Commissioner Harrel, convalescing from a bout of typhoid fever, was knocked down by a speed-ing female tricyclist when he went for a walk on the Stillorgan road.[110] There was an ill-founded rumour in August 1896 that the DMP were about to form a squad of 'expert pneumatic record-breakers to chase and arrest scorchers, especially pet-ticoated specimens of over-speed'.[111] Female scorchers appear to have been in the minority, however, to judge from the paucity of reports of female over-speeding in

the press, although some certainly succumbed to the thrill of 'coasting' downhill at high speed.[112] Most appear to have agreed that moderation was the best policy. Ettie Palmer, from Kerry, who edited the *Wheelwoman*, stressed the point:

> Overstrain is what perforce must be avoided if we wish to make the exercise a pleasure and a benefit. And remember, please, that in this matter we have not only ourselves to consider, for notwithstanding the present rage for cycling, the pursuit is yet in its infancy – on its probation. A bad accident, or an illness, the result of overstrain, is a powerful weapon indeed in the hands of an opponent, and may do much to deter our sisters from learning what would no doubt prove of great profit and delight to them.[113]

Some felt that, in addition to accidents and illness, women who cycled too much might develop a deformity known as 'bicycle hand', in which the hand 'becomes flattened, bulges out at the sides, gets lumpy and out of shape, and the fingers all become crooked'.[114] Mary Butler, the prominent Gaelic League organiser, was one of those who considered cycling unsuitable for women because she believed that it led to their developing overly large feet and hands.[115]

Considerable emphasis was placed on appearance – hence Beatrice Grimshaw's attack on the 'very ugly effects' that arose when stout women wore tight dresses while cycling,[116] and the *Weekly Irish Times*'s satire on the woman who strained herself so much while cycling that she looked like she was in a harness and working a mangle.[117] Female cyclists were given advice on the proper knee and ankle

Right: A typical 'feminine' cycling costume
supplied by Messrs McBirney of Dublin.

Opposite: Waterford Bicycle Club in July 1894

action to use,[118] how to mount a bicycle gracefully,[119] the most attractive form of
hat to wear when cycling,[120] as well as on the necessity of having the height of
their machines adjusted to prevent their presenting a 'hump-backed, bow-legged,
or crooked' appearance when mounted on their bicycles.[121] The ideal of graceful,
decorative riding was also promoted by such means as floral parades – competitions in which women decorated their bicycles with flowers – such as that held
by the Coleraine Cycling Club in July 1896 and the Ulster Cricket Club at their
Easter Monday sports day in April 1897;[122] contests to determine who were the
most stylish female bicycle riders, such as were held at Strabane in 1896 and
1897;[123] and competitions to find the most photogenic woman on a bicycle, such
as was held at the Dublin Cycle and Motor Show at Ballsbridge in January 1897
for the prize of a gold watch, and the competition organised by a Dublin pho-
tographer, M. Glover of 124 Stephen's Green, in the months of July, August and
September 1897, for the prize of a 'McTaggart Royal' bicycle.[124] A competition
was also held at the Ballsbridge show for the makers of the best female cycling
costume, which over twenty businesses entered.[125]

Irish cycle agents were careful to heighten the attractive and graceful features
of their wares when trying to attract female custom. For instance, in January
1897 the New Howe Machine Company of 29 Bachelor's Walk, Dublin, claimed
that its women's safeties were 'the lightest, prettiest, and daintiest machines on
the market'.[126] An advertisement from July 1896 for the John Griffiths Cycle
Corporation, which was aimed at women, claimed that cycling promoted
beauty,[127] while its advertisement in *Irish Society* in May 1897 featured a female

'Coasting' at thirty miles per hour.

bicyclist gliding effortlessly along on her bicycle.[128] The idea that cycling
required little physical effort on the part of women featured frequently in advertisements aimed at the Irish market, including an advertisement for Thornton's
of Belfast in 1898,[129] Glacken's of Navan in 1899[130] and Pierce's of Wexford in
1900, respectively.[131] Perhaps the most evocative of this type of advertisement
was that depicting 'Sally on a Raleigh' in April 1897. The advertisement contained a rhyme in which Sally and her beau are described as being about to
'ride o'er hill & valley' on 'the choicest Tandem in the Land', the '"number 15"
Raleigh'.[132] Other advertisements depicted female cyclists in elegant dresses or
cycling outfits, thereby strengthening the idea that one could cycle and look
attractively feminine at the same time.[133] In 1897 the John Griffiths company's
Westmoreland Street depot in Dublin broke new ground by allotting a room
for the display of women's bicycles exclusively, which was 'handsomely fur-
nished with plush hangings and ornamental stands for the machines'. At one
end of the room there was a large mirror where female customers could admire
themselves on the bicycles and see themselves as others would see them when
they cycled.[134] The Coventry Plating Company of 179 Great Brunswick Street,
Dublin, advertised its bicycle enamelling service with an eye to women who
were concerned about the appearance that they would make awheel, by stating
that they could easily select a shade of enamel to match the colour of their hair,
eyes or dress.[135]

Floral parade of Coleraine Cycling Club, July 1896.

To protect novice riders from the embarrassment of falling from their machines in public, a danger which was accentuated by the long dresses that they wore, [136] a number of enterprising cycling agents in Belfast, Cork and Dublin established learning schools where beginners – the majority of them women – paid for lessons on how to mount and ride bicycles.[137] A visitor to McTaggart's riding school in Dublin in March 1896, found it 'well crowded with beginners mostly belonging to the "upper ten"'.[138] 'Maev' paid a visit to one school in 1896:

There is no such place for studying the many sides of human nature nowadays as at a cycling school. I visited one recently, where the prices are high and the clientele select, and noted some average types. There is to be seen the young lady spinning round nicely to the admiration of her mother and the numerous friends she has invited to witness the display. Presently elation puts her off her guard, and she bites the dust with a twinkle of little feet in the air, and a clatter of bejewelled little hands upon the wooden floor. Her friends surround her, half-laughing, half-crying; she crawls off in deepest mortification, and returns no more. There is the damsel who is doing fancy bicycling in the middle of the floor, and who together with her machine, presently climbs up the back of her more lymphatic neighbour, to the evident discomfort of that individual. There is the lean and elderly spinster who objects to the instructor's arm about her waist, or even in the vicinity thereof, at the end of a strap, because she has 'never allowed young men to embrace her, and does not think it proper even under the circumstances'; there is the hysterical female who giggles when the instructor puts out his hands to save her from a lumbering fall, and the lady who assures her teacher that she would ride much better if her skirts weren't so frightfully long and wide, 'but, you know', she explains, 'it may be foolish of me, but I am *so* essentially feminine: I shall never be able to wear rationals!' Close by her, awaiting her turn, is the stout woman in knicker[bockers]s, accompanied by her husband. 'John insisted that I should wear them', is her remark, 'because he was so afraid of my "silly" skirt catching in the wheels'. On a bench by the platform is the sweet young thing who declares that

Left: This advertisement for the John Griffiths Cycle Corporation emphasises the graceful and attractive nature of cycling for women.

Opposite: Cycling with ease: an advertisement for Glacken's of Navan in 1899.

nothing would ever persuade her into learning, and who persuades herself before the end of the afternoon; opposite is another who loudly assures everybody in the neighbourhood that she has already taken lessons with George in the garden and is 'such an expert', and who requires two instructors to hold her in the saddle when her half-hour's lesson arrives. One just wants to learn enough about wheeling to keep in fashion; another declares that she mustn't be bothered with preliminaries, as she intends to scorch, and so on. An occasional man looks timidly in for a lesson, but as a rule men prefer to learn outside a school…[139]

The learning schools were popular as they allowed women to preserve their dignity while they mastered the art of cycling and thereby saved them from becoming the objects of public ridicule.[140]

The bicycling women who courted most controversy by going against accepted norms of female behaviour were those who wore supposedly masculine 'rational clothes', so-called 'bloomers' or knickerbockers, often with a short tunic as well. In late-nineteenth-century Britain, the United States of America and elsewhere, the knickerbocker-clad woman on a bicycle symbolised the independent and utterly unconventional 'New Woman', who was generally met with a mixture of horror, hostility and ridicule. Imputations of 'mannishness' were frequently levelled against the brave individuals who defied convention by appearing in public in rational clothes.[141] The situation was no different in Ireland, even though 'rationalists' were comparatively rare in the country. In February 1894 R.J. Mecredy, the *Irish Cyclist* editor, declared himself to be in favour of female bicyclists wearing rational clothes as, in his opinion, the outfit gave greater freedom of movement than the long skirts and tight-fitting blouses or jackets worn by most female cyclists. However, he considered that the innovation was one reform too far for Irish public opinion to stomach:

We do not recommend Irish ladies to adopt it at once, for the simple reason that the time is not ripe, and such action would do irreparable harm to the cause. Cycling for ladies is fighting its way into Ireland. As it is, many who ride do so with the strongest disapproval of their friends and relatives, and we know for a fact that the introduction of the rational dress would render it absolutely necessary for many to give up the pastime altogether from the action of their friends, while great numbers of possible recruits would be prevented from starting.

Mecredy added that:

The opposition…would come mainly from the aristocracy – the so-called better class – who, with a thin veneer of refinement and culture, will swallow the camel of immodesty in ball-dresses and strain at the gnat of unconventionality in the seemly and becoming, rational costume. In no section of the community do hypocrisy, immorality, and scandal-mongering hold more sway. They would absolutely do anything to be in the fashion, and would countenance ball-dresses half as scanty again were it the thing, but to them cycling is vulgar under all circumstances, and the rational dress has not received the hallmark of fashion, and is, therefore, immodest and unseemly.[142]

While Mecredy was correct in his summary of the aristocracy's attitude to rational dress, hostility towards the innovation was not confined to the upper class. The first 'rationalist' in the Dublin area appeared in late March or early April 1894, to considerable public excitement. According to Arthur du Cros, this young woman 'rocked the city' by her action, and he added: 'To say that tongues wagged and heads were shaken would be an understatement: for it was universally assumed that the perpetrator of this enormity had condemned her-

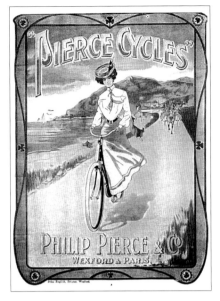

Above left: Cycling with ease: an advertisement for Pierce's of Wexford, *c.*1900.

Above right: Cycling with ease: Sally on a Raleigh.

The Rudge-Whitworth cycling school at Earlsfort Terrace, Dublin, in March 1897.

self to a lonely existence, if not life-long spinsterhood'.[143] Beatrice Grimshaw records that when she cycled in rational clothes in Dublin, she was blamed by a startled beggar woman for having robbed the 'decent poor' of their bread, as 'her audacity and wickedness' had called down a curse on the whole country![144] A rational-clad bicyclist 'created a good deal of sensation in Dublin by doing her shopping awheel, and dismounting to walk about without any alteration in her attire' in April 1895, while the residents of Marlborough Road were 'much exercised by the vision of a lady clad in "bloomers"' who cycled down their street as the middle rider of a triple-seater cycle in the following month.[145] A DMP constable regulating traffic at the junction of Grafton, Suffolk and Nassau Streets on one day in April 1896, was so flabbergasted at the sight of a female bicyclist wearing knickerbockers on Grafton Street that he was rendered immobile and left gaping after her, with an astonished look on his face, while the traffic passed by him unheeded.[146] Unfortunately, information is sketchy about 'rationalists' in other parts of the country; it is known, however, that Derry's first 'rationalist' appeared in April 1894,[147] while a number of 'ladies in bloomers' who cycled through Sligo in August 1895 'excited quite a sensation amongst the staid mammas' in the town.[148] One did not actually have to see 'ladies in bloomers' to be alarmed at what they represented, as indicated by the example of the prisoner in an unidentified prison (possibly Kilmainham) in April 1898, who was frightened by the thought of 'new women' riding bicycles in men's clothes and with 'a cigarette between their teeth'.[149]

Observers frequently ridiculed these adventurous women, particularly by questioning their sexuality – the press contained numerous jokes to the effect that these women who wore 'trousers' were, in effect, 'mannish' women or unsexed females,[150] or published cartoons showing children who were unable to distinguish their mother from their father, due to the former wearing 'masculine' rational clothes.[151] The *Derry Journal* published a verse with a similar theme of gender confusion in July 1896:

> A biker asked a farmer,
> 'Has a lady wheeled this way?'
> And the farmer told the biker,
> 'It's mighty hard to say,
> From the costumes they are wearing,
> From the mountains to the sea,
> If the biker is a she one,
> Or a biker is a he!'[152]

Even children taunted the women, with newspaper boys in Dublin chasing after one 'rationalist' bicyclist with incessant cries of 'All the sporting news, sir!' on one day in January 1895.[153]

THE WHEEL WAS INNOCENT.

Bicycling——: I am sorry, sir, that you have been the victim of an accident, but what else can you expect, when, at this date of the nineteenth century, you ride a horse that scares at a bicycle?.

Victim of Accident (dryly): Madam, it was not the bicycle the horse scared at.

A depiction of a 'mannish' cyclist in bloomers, April 1895.

There was sometimes a stronger reaction towards 'rationalist' cyclists than mere ridicule in print, however. For example, in March 1896 one *Irish Cyclist* correspondent described 'three ladies of position in Kingstown', who were reportedly planning on wearing rational clothes, as 'among the case-hardened who have reached the vanishing point, and whose down-grade education has been completed – society ladies whose cheeks have ceased to crimson with a blush of shame'.[154] The same man described an incident which he witnessed from a tram where a 'rationalist' was cycling down the Rathmines Road:

> There was a gentle breeze blowing at the time, and as the balmy air inflated every garment, ballooning out tunic and knickerbockers and sleeves, a spectacle was presented which I thought was somewhat painful to witness, subjecting this female…to the jokes and laughter of all the out-siders, and the amazed and surprised gaze of all the passing traffic – cabbies, jarvies, messenger boys, etc.

The incident strengthened him in his determination 'to resist the intrusion into this country of the immodest fashions of a dissolute society'.[155] Another revealing incident on the Rathmines Road in October 1894 involved two 'rationalists' on bicycles. When they reached Leinster Square the first rider's bicycle skidded on the greasy setts, causing her to crash and fall off her machine, and her companion rode into her prostrate form and also fell off her bicycle:

The 'gender bending' 'New Woman' cyclist.

THE SON AND HEIR *(gone out to welcome his parents home)*.
"Daddy ! Mammy ! Which is 'oo ?"

...a crowd gathered around to view the show, but none of the bystanders offered any assistance. Indeed, upon the contrary, the crowd amused themselves by firing off remarks of a most uncomplimentary nature anent the costume of the unfortunate ladies, who were struggling with more haste than elegance of motion to rescue their machines.

Eventually one of the women managed to disentangle her machine and rode off; the other bicycle was too badly damaged for riding, and its owner wheeled it away 'amidst the laughter and jeers of the assembled multitude'.[156] One can further guess the extent of the hostility towards females in rational clothing from an incident in 1895 when a girl who attended a cycle show at Dublin's Rotundo wearing rational dress, was dismissed from her position as a monitor in a Clontarf school and her sister was expelled.[157] In August 1899 in the most serious manifestation of public hostility towards women wearing rational clothes, two knickerbocker-clad cyclist tourists in Cork were followed by an abusive crowd who hooted, hissed and yelled abusive epithets at them and pelted them with mud and rubbish. There is conflicting evidence about the make-up of the crowd: the *Irish Cyclist* described the hooligans as 'a crowd of gamins...the scum of the city', while the *Cork Constitution* described the hostile Corkonians as 'rather well-dressed people'; [158] whichever source was correct, it is clear that rational clothes were completely unacceptable to many people in Ireland.

Three girls wearing 'bloomers' at a bicycle show at the Rotundo, Dublin, in January 1895.

Although the *Irish Cyclist* supported rational clothes for cycling women,[159] as did the *Irish Weekly Independent*'s cycling correspondent, 'Old Crock',[160] and a number of 'rationalists' penned passionate defences of the innovatory dress (including one who had been planning on becoming a missionary in China or India before ill health intervened, who advanced biblical-based arguments in favour of the controversial clothing),[161] it is not surprising that most Irish female cyclists conformed to society's expectations of what was considered appropriate women's clothing: in the case of cycling, this meant wearing an ankle-length skirt, a blouse, and a coat or jacket that was not 'masculine' in appearance. Beatrice Grimshaw claimed that nine-tenths of women also wore a corset when cycling.[162] In the opinion of 'The Scorcher', an *Irish Cyclist* columnist, female cyclists in Ireland and Britain were 'compelled by cant and custom to the thraldom of the skirt'. In spite of the greater freedom afforded by rational clothes, most cycling women persisted with the skirt, 'a form of coercion that must be almost as irritating and unpleasant as the red-hot pincers of Torquemada undoubtedly were to the persons upon whom they were used'.[163]

Women's participation in cycle races was another controversial feature of Irish cycling in the 1890s, although this did not arouse the same amount of ire as women wearing rational clothes. The idea of women's races was first mooted by a *Daily Express* journalist who attended the Trinity College Dublin sports in 1890, and who recommended the holding of women's tricycle races on the grounds that 'Tricycling is a graceful amusement, almost specially adapted for ladies, and it is not more distressing than many other athletic performances, such as cricket and lawn tennis, into which they enter with spirit'. The *Irish Cyclist* voiced its opposition through a poem:

> Do you see the racing cyclists, O, my sisters!
> As they bend above the whirling wheel.
> Are you anxious for the bruises and the blisters
> And the sorrows that the victims feel [?]
>
> 'Oh! no', reply the maidens, 'we look bonnie,
> Standing idly in the shade is what we like,
> And we'd often miss a prize in matrimony,
> If we took to flying round upon a trike'.[164]

When the organisers of a race meeting in Omagh in September 1893 went one step further and actually planned on holding a women's bicycle race, stronger words were called for: the editor claimed that women's bicycle races 'are bad enough on the Continent, but it will be ten times worse, and ten times more likely to kill cycling among gentlewomen the whole country over, if such things are to take place in Ireland'. In the event the three 'lady cyclists' who intended to compete, one from Derry and two from Belfast, pulled out of the competition as a result of criticisms in the press. Instead, several youths dressed in women's clothing ran a spoof race[165] – hardly a sign that the women's race had been taken seriously by the organisers in the first place. In August 1893 Beatrice Grimshaw argued that women should boycott any sports meeting where women's bicycle races were held; *Sport* added its voice in opposition in September 1894, arguing that 'no right-thinking man should encourage the fair sex to enter into a new sphere which needs must turn them into ridicule before the (*sane*) world', and stating that 'abuses' such as women's races would 'establish a stronger prejudice than that which existed some years ago, when any woman observed awheel was considered a *brazen hussy*, and leave the lady cyclists open to the buffoonery and jibes of those of the unrefined class who would undoubtedly flock to see them make fools of themselves'.[166]

Despite the conservative rearguard action fought by Grimshaw and other prominent figures in the Irish cycling world, small numbers of women *did* take part in bicycle races – a development which was predicted in October 1893 by one female cyclist who viewed cycling in general, and racing in particular, as a means of demonstrating women's equality with men.[167] The first women's races were held in 1896, including contests at the RIC sports meetings held in Derry and Cork and at general sports meetings in Tuam and Athboy.[168] R.J. Mecredy wrote a critical account of the Athboy race, which was won by a married woman who had been 'received with great suspicion' when she started cycling

Mrs Pardo Kirk of Dublin wearing conventional cycling clothing.

some years previously, and whose runner-up 'belonged to one of the leading county families, whose married sister had been most severe in her strictures on ladies cycling at all'. He noted that the runner-up 'almost fell off with exhaustion at the finish', adding that, although 'From every possible point of view cycle racing for ladies is undesirable', it was likely to gain favour in future.[169] Because of their novelty value, women's races were, indeed, popular attractions for spectators and, therefore, also for many sports promoters, especially at rural sports meetings.[170] Not everyone looked favourably on these contests, however; even the pioneering Cork RIC sports committee in 1896 had been deeply divided on the issue of whether or not to organise a bicycle race for women.[171]

The most strident attacks on women's bicycle races were made by Canon Thomas Doyle, parish priest of Ramsgrange, Co. Wexford, in June and July 1897. The clergyman's ire was raised by a local doctor's praise of cycling as a form of exercise for women, as well as a proposal to hold a bicycle race for women at New Ross. Canon Doyle's response was to attack not only bicycle races, but cycling itself, if women were involved:

> The comparatively few not called upon to perform physical exercises and manual labour have abundant means of supplying the deficit by one of the very best exercises – walking, and by other suitable recreations. Hence, since the creation down to the present day, we have splendid specimens of men and women – heroes and

Conventional cycling costume sold
by Messrs Todd Burns of Mary Street,
Dublin, in 1897.

heroines the world over. David, Jonathan, and Judith required no cycle for their
'physical development'. The heroes of Clontarf, who swept the Danes into the
sea, never saw a bicycle, neither did the magnificent men who held the bridge of
Athlone. The glorious men and women, too, who held the breach of Limerick
never wobbled on wheels. Where were your wheels when an almost unarmed
peasantry, under Father John Murphy, annihilated the brutal North Cork on Oulart
Hill? when under the gallant John Kelly, they swept the myrmidons of English
tyranny like chaff before them over the bridge of New Ross? when, led by Father
Kearns, they routed the red-coats and ruffian yeomanry from the Duffrey Gate,
across the bridge at Enniscorthy, and chased those who escaped the vengeance of
the pikemen in their pell-mell flight to Wexford? The heroine of Bree in '98, who
wrested the bayonet from the wretch who would dishonour her, and pierced him
through the heart, required no 'wheel' to develop her muscular strength. The mus-
cles of that humble peasant woman had been developed by honest labour, and her
love of holy purity strengthened her to avenge the honour of her sex.

The clergyman continued:

There is not a girl or woman in Ireland who does not feel in her conscience
that the use of the cycle is unbecoming, indelicate, and dangerous for females.
Conscience is overborne by bad example and temptation. There are thousands

and tens of thousands, ay millions, who will never degrade themselves nor dishonour their sex by yielding to the temptation. They should be fortified in their
resolution by denouncing those miserable creatures who degrade themselves
and disgrace their sex. An Irish gentleman who was in Paris last summer told
me he went to see one of those great bicycle displays in one of the fine parks
adjacent to that city. He said it was disgusting. So far as dress was concerned, you
could not know a lady from a gentleman. As Paris leads the way in fashions, that
must be the perfection of cycling. Is that what we are about to introduce, at the
instigation of some fribbles, amongst the chaste daughters of holy Ireland? Oh,
but there is Miss So-and-So, a nice modest, virtuous girl, and she rides a cycle. I
don't know Miss So-and-So, but I do know that neither virtue nor modesty nor
chastity ever inspired her to ride a bicycle. The poor weak creature was induced
by bad example, eccentricity, vanity or some other frailty to adopt a practice
which her conscience and all the noble instincts of her sex condemn, but which
her pride and other passions prompt her to continue. I observe that the New
Ross Sports Committee are about to organise a 'ladies' cycle race'. Ladies! save
the mark. Should they attempt such an atrocity, every decent man and woman
should boycott the sports. Should any vile things in the shape of girls dare to
exhibit themselves let the roughs and corner-boys of the town chase them off
the field, and give them a dip in the slob below the bridge. Though we are per-
secuted and poor, let us still be able to say 'On our side is virtue and Erin'. But
there is Mrs Such-a-one, and she is becoming too fat. What is she to do? Let her,
like Solomon's 'valiant woman', attend to her household duties. Let her apply
herself to cottage gardening, which will occupy her the year round, and supply
her house with a variety of the choicest fruits and vegetables. Let her amuse
herself occasionally with her flower beds. Let her live more abstemiously, sleep
less, and work more. Let her train her daughters to go and do likewise, and not
make tomboys of themselves, gadding about the roads on wheels, to the shame
of all virtuous and modest women, and to the disgust of all sensible men.[172]

Canon Doyle's diatribe provoked a torrent of denunciatory letters from female
and male correspondents, including one from a Dublin priest.[173] Only one correspondent offered support to the clergyman, on the grounds that cycling women
presaged the coming of the Antichrist.[174]

Canon Doyle's animosity towards women's bicycle races was unusual in its
violence. Although no figures in the Irish cycling world displayed such intense
antagonism in public, nevertheless there was widespread (if impossible to quan-
tify) unease in the ICA about such races. In August 1898 the ICA decreed that
women's races should be held under the same conditions as men's contests – in
other words, that only members of affiliated clubs could participate, who held an
annual certificate from the organisation's registration committee.[175] One opponent
of women's races expressed the hope that these measures would prove an insuper-

able obstacle for would-be competitors[176] – certainly the introduction of the ICA's registration scheme in March 1894 had resulted in a falling-off in the number of male athletes competing in races under ICA auspices, including some of the best-known racers.[177] In Ulster, where women's bicycle races appear to have been more common than elsewhere,[178] clubs evaded the ostensible obstacle to women's races by electing intending competitors as members or honorary members,[179] as was done successfully by the North Down Cycling Club for eleven contestants in Killyleagh in September 1898.[180] In March 1900 the *Irish Wheelman* condemned 'the honorary-club-member sham', whereby women were simultaneously members of several clubs and thus entitled to participate in their races.[181] Not all clubs successfully pulled the wool over the eyes of ICA officers, however; for example, the Ulster Cricket Club was suspended from ICA membership in October 1899, for organising a women's bicycle race in Easter which included contestants whom the ICA correctly regarded as bogus members of the host club.[182] By the end of the decade there was a marked regional split in the ICA over women's races: most delegates outside of Ulster were 'dead against such events', while Ulster delegates were more or less evenly split on the issue – a motion in the Ulster Centre to prohibit women's races was lost by just one vote in March 1900, but was carried by thirty votes to eighteen in April. After this, women's races were prohibited by the ICA.[183] Opinion had hardened against the women's contests, partly because the exhaustion of many contestants confirmed men's preconceived beliefs concerning women's incapacity for engaging in such strenuous physical activity as bicycle races,[184] and partly because of the unseemly merriment of spectators and the coarse comments which they often directed at the racers. Although there is no evidence that the contestants themselves took offence at spectators' remarks, the middle-class men who controlled the ICA felt that women's races should be ended to protect the respectable image of their sport.[185]

Most women who cycled neither wore 'bloomers' nor raced, but kept their cycling activity within the bounds of what society considered respectable behaviour. Few challenged conventional notions of women's frailty in the way that Beatrice Grimshaw did in 1893, by setting a world record for a twenty-four-hour ride by a woman; carrying luggage and provisions, she covered some 212 miles on a 'Rover' bicycle, beating the previous record by some five miles.[186] Grimshaw was also the first Irish woman to cycle one hundred miles in a non-stop ride, in 1892; by 1897 such feats were common, thanks to the pneumatic-tyred bicycle.[187] One Irish woman cycled the extraordinary total of 4,000 miles in 1896.[188] Most female cyclists clocked up less impressive mileage tallies, but still derived undeniable pleasure and benefits from the new pastime. The supposed medical benefits of cycling for women ranged from preventing one's nose from turning red, due to the improved circulation of the blood which resulted from tricycling,[189] curing headaches and improving digestion and sleep,[190] to banishing 'the depression incident to sedentary monotony'[191] and 'hysterical nervousness', to which women were supposedly especially prone,[192] as well as lowering the incidence of tuberculosis.[193] It was also believed that old women were rejuvenated by bicycling.[194] The idea of cycling as a panacea for women's health problems was best expressed by the *Lady's Herald* in January 1896:

> The ills of woman take a front place in our social life; but if looked into, ninety per cent of them are functional ailments, begotten of ennui and lack of opportunity of some means of working off their superfluous, muscular, nervous, and organic energy. The effect of cycling, within the physical capacity of a woman, acts like a charm for gout, rheumatism, and indigestion. Sleeplessness, so-called 'nerves', and all those petty miseries, for which the 'liver' is so often made the scapegoat, disappear in the most extraordinary way with the fresh air inhaled, and with the tissue destruction and reconstruction effected by exercise and exhilaration…Already thousands of women, qualifying for general invalidism, have been rescued by cycling. Women are very suspect to varicose veins in the legs. Cycling often rids them of this trouble. A girl who has had to stand for hours and hours behind a counter gets relief untold from an evening spin on her 'bike'. Her circulation has been improved, and the aches and pains which would have shortly made an old woman of her have gone, and a sense of exhilaration and relief have taken their place.

Such views on cycling's positive medical impact on women's lives were echoed by the press in other countries.[195]

Apart from medical and physical benefits, Irish women derived a profound and unprecedented sense of liberation from cycling. The sense of mental well-being and physical emancipation that cycling brought to thousands of Irish people, but particularly to middle-class and upper-class Irish women, was probably the most important result of the introduction of the tricycle and bicycle to late-nineteenth-century Ireland – as the *Irish Cyclist* stated in April 1890, cycling 'has burst open the doors of stuffy rooms where the young girl of the old style spent the weary afternoons, listlessly staring through the windows with a half-read novel or partially knitted antimacassar on her lap'.[196] An anonymous female contributor to the same newspaper outlined the benefits which riding tricycles and bicycles had brought to her:

> I am perfectly independent of any other's cooperation. I find that my wheel gives [me] the ability to digest tacks if I found it necessary to subsist on them. I sleep without waking from the time my head is fairly on the pillow. My working hours are long, but I find myself easily able to stand them and enjoy life. I don't feel cross any more. I am prepared to find friends on all sides, instead of that dreadful 'nobody-loves-me' feeling; and, thanks to my wheel, I am as strong and well a woman, I confidently assert, as there is.[197]

Elizabeth A.M. Priestley also gave eloquent testimony of the emancipatory role of the bicycle:

> To glide along at one's sweet will; to feel the delight in rapid motion that is the result of our consciously exerted strength; to skim like a low-flying bird through the panorama of an ever-varying landscape; to know a new-born spirit of independence – that ignores railway time-tables, and is never afraid of tiring (no pun intended) one's steed – to return from a country spin with a healthy appetite, a clearer brain, and an altogether happier sense of life – an altogether unaccountable freshness of spirit; this is to experience something of the joys of cycling, and in so doing to rejoice that such a good gift has fallen to modern woman as the safety bicycle.[198]

It is not surprising that cycling should have appealed to Irish women, whether they were feminists such as Hanna Sheehy, who went on unchaperoned bicycle rides when she and Francis Skeffington were courting (the newly married Sheehy Skeffingtons also went on a bicycling honeymoon),[199] or more conventional individuals such as the 'busy housemother' who wrote that 'I am not a very good rider, and cannot ride a bit after dark, or on muddy roads, but, still, it does me so much good; when I go out walking, my worries walk with me, but, on my bicycle, I seem to ride away from them all, and after an hour or two's ride I come home another woman'.[200] The last word on the subject should probably be left to 'Tadpole', an *Irish Cyclist* correspondent:

> Often when out having a spin along good roads on a perfect summer day, with every growing thing looking its very best; or on a calm bright moonlit evening, and not a care on one's mind – for when out cycling under such circumstances whose mind could retain a care? I congratulate myself, and feel most truly thankful that I live in the present enlightened age of cycles (and pneumatic tyres!) and not fifty years ago; when the greatest diversion appeared to be a quiet stroll round a walled-in garden, under the escort of a foot-man or page – for, of course, no girl with *any* sense of her position would even dream of going about alone and unescorted!
>
> What a change has come over the world since then! Now, no-one thinks it anything at all strange or out of the common to see girls cycling here and there all over the country – often alone, without even a female companion. Truly the 'bad young times' are to be preferred to the 'good old' ones! I often wonder when people refer to the 'good old times' if they *really* mean what they say, and whether they have not all the time in a secret corner of their hearts a strong conviction, that things as they are now are decidedly very much jollier altogether.[201]

5

Cycling's Heyday

Cycling encouraged sociability in Victorian Ireland: whether it was engaged in by clubs, or by cyclists riding together in family groups[1] or as friends, cycling's enjoyment was heightened when it was undertaken by groups. As discussed earlier, employees at particular shops or members of certain professions were fond of organising cycling on a collective basis. Other clubs emerged which allowed people with distinctive leisure time interests to enjoy cycling, or were organised on a denominational or political basis. It is perhaps not surprising that, in a country with deep sectarian divisions, cycling clubs should have emerged whose membership was confined to men or women of a particular religious persuasion. In Birr, for instance, where segregation between Protestants and Catholics was particularly marked, two clubs were formed in 1888, each of which drew membership from one side of the community only. The names of the clubs reflected their politico-religious make-up, with the Parsonstown Cycling Club catering for Unionists and Protestants, and the Birr Cycling Club – whose president was John Powell, editor of the *Midland Tribune* – enrolling Catholics and Nationalists.[2] For a number of years Enniscorthy cyclists were similarly divided, with Protestants enrolling in a club associated with the Protestant Young Men's Association, and young Catholic men forming their own club; in 1890 they were 'both in a very degenerate and a very backward state of organisation'. On 14 May 1891 they amalgamated as the Enniscorthy United Cycling Club, 'an unsectarian non-political cycling club for the town and neighbourhood', after coming to the conclusion that Enniscorthy was too small to enable two separate clubs to sustain a vibrant existence. By September 1896 the club had some sixty-seven members, including eight women.[3] A similar process occurred in 1894 in Wexford. When the Wexford Cycling Club ceased to exist in 1893 'through want of support', there were two cycling clubs left in the town, the Catholic Young Men's Cycling Club and the Protestant Young Men's Cycling Club, but neither of these were strong enough

Lee's 'Central Cycle Depot & Repairing Workshop', one of four cycle shops in Birr in 1898.

on their own to do much to promote cycling in the town. Representatives of the two clubs, feeling embarrassed that the town possessed a splendid cycling track while organised cycling was in a shambles, held a successful meeting in February 1894 to form a new, nonsectarian Wexford Cycling Club which was affiliated to the ICA.[4] The Sligo United Cycling Club, established in 1890 in connection with the Sligo United Young Men's Christian Association (YMCA), was at first confined to YMCA members only, but over time it accepted any cyclist who wished to join, and reaped the benefits accordingly – by August 1896 it numbered some eighty-seven members, and club runs mustered an average of forty riders.[5]

Other towns and cities were more successful in maintaining clubs whose membership was confined to either Protestants or Catholics. YMCA members were particularly keen on establishing such clubs. The Dawson Street YMCA in Dublin started a gymnastic and cycling club towards the end of 1890. By April 1891 this club, which was noted for its abstemious habits on its outings, had fifty cycling members.[6] The Belfast YMCA Cycling Club was formed in February 1891, rising to a membership of eighty-eight by the end of 1891.[7] The Derry YMCA Cycling Club, launched in March 1892, had the respectable number of over forty people on its membership roll, while the Cork YMCA Cycling Club, which was started in March 1890, was the largest single cycling club in the southern city by March 1892. Some sixty-one members set off on one of its runs in April 1896.[8]

Sligo United Cycling Club, 1896.

The Athlone YMCA started a cycling club early in 1894, followed by the Tralee YMCA in April, the same month in which the Fermoy Young Men's Protestant Association Cycling Club was formed.[9] The Mountpottinger YMCA Cycling Club, started in Belfast in 1898, had some 130 members by December 1899.[10] There was even a cycling club associated with the Orange Hall of Rutland Square, Dublin; formed in 1895, it was named the Erne Cycling Club after its patron, Lord Erne.[11] In addition to the YMCA clubs and the Erne club, whose membership was open to Protestants of all denominations, there were also some that were restricted to particular Protestant denominations, such as Belfast's Clarence Cycling Club, formed in early 1891, which consisted of members of the Church of Ireland,[12] and the Central Presbyterian Association's Cycling Club, which decided in April 1897 to admit women as honorary members.[13]

Clubs which only Catholics could join included the Pathfinders Cycling Club, started in 1890 – this was the cycling branch of the Catholic Commercial Club in Dublin[14] – as well as a number of clubs established by various branches of the Catholic Young Men's Society, which included clubs organised in Athlone, Kilkenny and Clonakilty in 1896, 1898 and 1900, respectively,[15] as well as one in Cork.[16] The National Cycling Club, founded in Dublin in 1888, was, in effect, a Catholic and Nationalist outfit.[17] There were three large Belfast clubs in the 1890s which enrolled Catholics only. The West End Cycling Club, established in 1891, quickly became Belfast's largest civilian cycling club under the presidency of Frank Kerr, a solicitor.[18] Its annual excursion was a spectacular affair, the most impressive of all cycling club events in the 1890s, in which an estimated 1,700 to 1,800 Catholic day-trippers (including some eleven priests in 1897) went on a pleasure cruise to the Isle of Man on the *Mona's Isle* paddle steamer.[19] Members of another Belfast Catholic cycling club, the Phoenix, established in August 1893 – which, as we have already seen, had a large female contingent by the end of the decade – also participated in these trips to the Isle of Man.[20] Another Catholic cycling club was established in connection with the Central Catholic Association

(CCA). The CCA was launched in 1896 by the Bishop of Down and Connor, Dr Henry Henry, to provide the Catholic 'commercial class' with a 'bulwark of defence against the strong hostile influences with which they find themselves confronted in many ways'. It was led by priests and funded by 'the upper echelon of the Catholic professional and business elite', and offered its members bars, entertainment and classes in languages and commerce.[21] The CCA's Central Cycling Club was formed in February 1897, under the presidency of Alexander Dempsey, a doctor and magistrate. It was an umbrella organisation for Belfast's Catholic cyclists, with most of its members also belonging to other local clubs before joining it as well – the Central club's members tended to undertake most of their cycling activity under the auspices of their other clubs, and joining in occasionally on Central Cycling Club activities.[22]

A number of clubs emerged which enabled individuals with distinctive leisure-time pursuits to engage in cycling, such as the Kingstown Literary and Debating Society Cycling Club, formed in April 1891,[23] and the National and Literary Cycling Club, started in 1900 under the presidency of James A. Power, high sheriff for the city of Dublin.[24] The Fingal Cycling Club, established in April 1890, consisted of riders who used cycling to further their interest in the history of Co. Dublin. According to one contemporary:

> This new club has been formed for enabling its members to explore systematically the ruins of castles, churches, and ancient monuments in and around the borders of Fingal, so rich in antiquarian lore; for gathering specimens and classifying the rare plants and flowers; for, in fact, carrying out the work of a Naturalist's Field Club; and lastly, for photographing the various places of interest along the routes.[25]

The Antiquarian Cyclist Society of Ireland, which was affiliated to the Gaelic League in 1902,[26] probably had similar interests to the Fingal club. Some groups who had already organised sports clubs for their leisure activity also established cycling branches, or combined cycling with their core sporting activity, as athletes, many of whom had initially looked askance at cycling, accepted that it would not only not detrimentally affect their core athletic pursuits, but would enhance them.[27] Examples include Limerick's Kincora Football Club, who set up a cycling branch with twenty members in 1887;[28] the Ulster Cricket Club, which established a cycling club of over forty members in May 1890, which included 'almost every racing man in Belfast';[29] the Carrickmacross Cycling and Cricket Club, which was founded in the summer of 1890;[30] and Dublin's Elysian Harriers and Haddington Harriers, which formed cycling clubs in January 1891 and May 1892, respectively.[31] Many members of the Gaelic Athletic Association (GAA) were also keen cyclists; not only did large numbers cycle to watch football and hurling matches,[32] but some GAA members also formed their own 'Gaelic' cycling clubs. Initially, relations between the GAA and the

The Newmarket-on-Fergus Cycling Club visit a historic site in November 1897.

ICA were hostile, mainly because the latter resented the GAA's decision in February 1885 to ban athletes who had competed under any laws other than those of the GAA, from participating at its sports meetings, leading RJ Mecredy to call for a united front amongst Irish athletes to 'quash' the GAA.[33] ICA men who competed in bicycle races under GAA rules at Kilkenny and Monastrevan were suspended in September 1885 as members of the cycling organisation,[34] as the ICA supported the anti-GAA campaign of a new national (but not Nationalist) sporting body, the Irish Amateur Athletic Association (IAAA), which was formed in February 1885.[35] The row continued to fester until February 1886, when Archbishop William Croke brokered a deal in which the GAA and IAAA removed their mutual bans.[36] The mutual hostility between the GAA and ICA ceased when the GAA agreed in March that, when cycling races were held at GAA sports meetings thereafter, they should always be held under ICA rules.[37] A.J. Wilson was an enthusiastic fan of bicycle races at the Wexford GAA sports meeting of August 1888:

A concourse of many thousands, swarming all over the place, diving under the railings, bivouac[k]ing on the track three or four deep, with apple-women and other vendors of cheap and nourishing provender walking inside on the track, plying their trade during the races. Such was the scene that greeted our astonished gaze. People who had paid for admission into the reserved enclosure were completely shut out by the mob who wandered over the course. Bicyclists, racing, had to be continually on the *qui vive* to steer out of the way of a hat, or an apple-woman, or a shillelagh, or a baby. When a flat race was run everybody swarmed into the centre, and formed a narrow defile for the sprinters to thread. It was an exhilarating spectacle. Every now and then some irascible old man would come into open conflict with a juvenile sportsman, and the mob would close around whilst the cyclists eased up and cautiously crept past. All the same, there was a terrific amount of enthusiasm displayed, and a closely-contested wheel race provoked demonstrations of excitement that were almost ludicrous to witness.[38]

Cycling races were undoubtedly popular at GAA sports meetings,[39] and the surprising presence of military or RIC bands sometimes added to the entertainment of these occasions.[40] GAA members also showed their enthusiasm for cycling by forming a number of cycling clubs. The first of these, the Limerick Gaelic Cycling Club, was formed in 1885, with Limerick's mayor, Stephen O'Meara, as its president. It was one of the first Irish clubs to supply members with a machine, free of charge, with which they could learn to cycle. The club was particularly fond of weekly spins to 'the historic spots of Limerick and adjoining parts of Clare'.[41] The second club established by GAA members was the Cork Gaelic Cycle Club, founded in 1886 by members of the Cork Cycling Club who were disgruntled with the latter club's insistence that all of its members should join the Cyclists' Touring Club. The secessionists were unhappy with having to join the CTC as their occupations 'over office books or behind a counter for six days of the week' prevented them from touring and benefiting from CTC membership. The Gaelic club – which had more than forty members in June 1888 – went on Sunday runs instead, deriving its entire funds from the shilling it charged each participant on these occasions.[42] The next cycling club founded by GAA members was the Sarsfield Gaelic Cycle Club, formed in 1888 following an argument among the officers of the Limerick Gaelic Cycling Club.[43]

Of all the groups that took to cycling in this period, the Gaelic League was one of the most evangelical in its promotion of the pastime. In 1893, the year of the League's foundation, there was no word in the Irish language for the English word, 'bicycle';[45] by 1896 not only had Irish words been coined for the bicycle and its various parts by Fr Peadar Ó Laoghaire, but the bicycle was being promoted as a powerful instrument for future use by the defenders of the Irish language. The *Gaelic Journal* urged its readers to purchase their bicycles from W.R. McTaggart's depots in Cork and Dublin, on the grounds that he was a native Irish speaker who had spoken only Irish until he was fifteen years old. 'Grappler' tyres were recommended as they were made in Ireland by Irishmen.[45] The Grappler tyre factory was the second pneumatic tyre factory to be established in Dublin. The first, the Pneumatic Tyre and Booth's Cycle Agency, bought out the Booth brothers' establishment at 66 Upper Stephen's Street in November 1889 (one of the brothers remained as a director in the new company) and began manufacturing pneumatic tyres there, as well as selling bicycles and tricycles; it relocated to 33 Westland Row in 1890, giving employment to over one hundred workers at these premises.

Left: An 'Oirish' advertisement for
Dunlop tyres, showing 'Paddy' and his
pig. It is unlikely to have found favour
with Gaelic League cyclists.

Opposite: Another 'Oirish' advertisement,
this time for 'Valkyrie' bicycles.

However, the company, whose factory evaporated between twenty to thirty
hundredweight of a solution of rubber in coal-tar naphtha weekly when manufacturing the new tyres, was prosecuted by Dublin Corporation in June 1891 for
running 'a noxious trade', following complaints from residents in the Westland
Row and Merrion Square areas, as well as from the governors of the Royal
Academy of Music. Although the company won the case, Dublin Corporation
decided to appeal against the judgement and the company's directors decided to
remove their concern to Coventry instead, partly to avoid the hassle of litigation
but also to be nearer the centre of the British cycling industry. The Grappler Tyre
Company, learning from the travails of its predecessor, set up its factory in 1894
in Fairview, on the County Dublin side of the River Tolka, 'just far removed from
town to get from under the harrowing restrictions of the Dublin Corporation'.[46]

In June 1897 the Gaelic League established a cycling association, Cumann na
Cuarta, in Dublin, membership of which was open to Gaelic League members
throughout Ireland; its first run was to Howth. Margaret O'Reilly and Michael
O'Casey were the secretaries, with the latter also serving as captain. They explained
that 'The objects of the association are to utilise the bicycle in spreading the
movement, and to counteract the growing evil which is being wrought by the
constantly increasing numbers of non-Irish-speaking tourists who penetrate into
remote districts where Irish is almost exclusively spoken'. Irish was compulsory at
all Cumann na Cuarta runs and meetings and in correspondence between members.[47] The bicycle assumed such importance for supporters of the Gaelic League

HURROO !!!
VALKYRIES TO THE FRONT
IN OULD OIRLAND.

1st in One Mile Handicap, I.C.A. Meeting, Dublin.
1st in Five Miles ,, ,, ,, ,,

Send for Catalogue and Order without delay.

LONDON DEPOT—38, SHAFTESBURY AVENUE, W

AGENCIES:

Ennis—Kennedy & Co.
Ulster—J. Alexander, 58, Royal Avenue.
Belfast—J. and J. Crean, 136, Donegal St.
Dublin—Maxwell, Harding and Co., Ltd., 5, Eden Quay.

Dublin—North West European Cycle Co., 12, Nassau Street.
Cork—B. B. Baker St. King st.
Limerick—J. D. Cussen, 49, George St.
Newry—J. Wright, Water st.

Springfield Cycle Co., Ltd., Sandiacre, near Nottingham.

that 'Our Gaelic Class', the Irish-language lessons written by Patrick Kangley in the *All Ireland Review*, Standish O'Grady's Gaelic-League-supporting journal, frequently dealt with cycling themes. In these lessons the patriotic, Irish-speaking cyclist was contrasted with the man who opposed the League 'and everything which pertains to our country'.[48] The League's itinerant teachers, the *timirí*, made effective use of bicycles in spreading enthusiasm for the Irish language in the 1890s and the early twentieth century.[49] Their devotion, and the bicycle's integral role in their work, was evoked vividly in a poem by League member Alice Milligan:

The Man on the Wheel

A man goes by on a wheel with the rain on his face,
Against the way of the wind and he not caring,
Goes on through the winter night, towards a distant lonesome place,
For his heart is hot with the glow of the ancient hero daring.

He slows on the slant of the hill, and must walk the higher road,
For he knows of an eager crowd that waits in a lighted hall;
The blast is sharp from the north, on the mountain breast it has snowed,
And they murmur now of him 'He will hardly come at all'.

'We will w[h]ile away the time with fiddle and dance, and song',
'The way', they say, 'is rough and the school too far to reach',
But wait – a stir at the door and in through the jostling throng
Comes the man skin-drenched from his wheel, who had said he would come
to teach.

He has come – like the bringer of fire, who in fighting days went out,
With news that the clans must rise, upholding a flaming brand;
Another and another grasped it and bore it about,
'Till the rally had gone with the fire o'er the width of the waiting land.

And the fire he has brought tonight through the winter rain and storm
Is the rallying hope that our race shall live and shall yet prevail.
See the eyes of the young men glisten, and the aged lean to listen
To the glorious glowing speech of the yet unconquered Gael.

So here at the end of the book I have gathered of hero boys,
That tell of great deeds done in battle mid flash of steel,
I set the last of my songs, the one I have made to praise,
The man whom I saw that night through rain and wind go past on his flying
wheel.[50]

Gaelic League cyclists ranged from the *timirí* and the rank and file enthusiasts who travelled to *feiseanna* on bicycles[51] to better-known members of the League, such as its president, Douglas Hyde,[52] and the poet and mystic, Susan Mitchell.[53] Eager students of Irish went on cycling holidays to Gaeltacht areas,[54] including, on at least one occasion, Patrick Pearse;[55] indeed, it became so common for Irish-language enthusiasts to cycle in Gaeltacht districts that, according to Arthur Clery, native speakers believed all 'Irish Irelanders' rode bicycles.[56] Although this was an exaggeration, it captured the essential truth about the importance of the bicycle to the Gaelic League.

In addition to those clubs, whose purpose was to cater for people with distinct sporting and recreational interests, a small number of clubs were also established or led by cycle agents, who thereby combined the pleasures of club life with promoting their business interests. These included Belfast's Osborne Cycling Club, named after its president, Thomas Edens Osborne, in 1890;[57] the Tipperary Cycling Club, whose captain in 1891 was D.J. Mc Carthy, an agent for the 'Energetic' Cycling Company;[58] Dublin's Leinster Cycling Club, whose captain in 1892 was Ben Wayte, who ran a cycle depot on Lemon Street;[59] and the Wanderers Cycling Club of Dublin, whose captain in 1893 was W.F. McCourt, the manager of the Pims' cycling department on South George's Street .[60] Others involved in the cycling trade and who played a prominent role in cycling clubs included

An advertisement for J.B. and A.R. Wayte's cycle repair workshop in Dublin, July 1891.

W.R. McTaggart, who was a vice-president of the Cork Cycle Club in 1894 (and a member since 1882) and president of the Church of Ireland Association Cycle Club;[61] E. Cole, a Limerick cycle agent who helped to found the Limerick Commercial Bicycle Club and Ben Turner, a Dundalk cycle dealer and captain of the Dundalk Cycle Club in 1895;[62] George Cooney, a Kells 'cycle factor' who established the Kells Round Tower Cycle Club in 1897;[63] Philip Duffield, who ran a cycle depot in Belfast's Donegall Pass and was a member of no less than seven cycling clubs in 1899: the Irish Road Club, Ulster Cycling Club, Belfast Cycling Club, Northern Cycling Club, Mountpottinger YMCA Cycling Club, Bloomfield Cycling Club and Ballynahinch Cycling Club[64] and Peter Murray of Dunshaughlin, a general shopkeeper and bicycle salesman who founded a cycling club, the Buffalo Bills, around 1900, who 'cycled the length and breadth of Meath'.[65]

The Buffalo Bills' fondness for cycling in the countryside was probably shared by all tricycle and bicycle clubs and also by most cyclists who were not club members. Club secretaries and other club members frequently sent accounts of their rides in the Irish countryside to editors of cycling journals and other publications,[66] as did cyclists who were not members of cycling clubs.[67] These sometimes included descriptions of thrilling incidents such as encounters with angry bulls or dogs,[68] headers,[69] or crashes against farmers' carts;[70] or they frequently waxed lyrical on the wonderful scenery and the soothing effects of a rural cycle trip.[71] When

A cyclist encounters a bull.

J.M. Synge wrote that he felt 'as happy as seven kings' after a long afternoon's
bicycle ride, he was undoubtedly voicing a widely held opinion about the thera-
peutic nature of cycling in the countryside.[72] A number of clubs were organised
whose main purpose was convivial rural spins: these included the Ohne Hast
and Fingal Cycling Clubs, discussed above, and the Middleton Cycling Club,
Nenagh's Ormond Cycling Club, and the Longford Cycling Club, established in
March 1894, the mid-1890s and April 1898, respectively.[73] For most other clubs,
runs to the countryside or to scenic coastal towns and villages were an essential
part of their collective activity. Good Friday was, surprisingly, the date chosen by
most clubs for their first run of the season.[74] Many clubs went on a large number
of runs during the cycling season (which was usually from April to September
– the inclement weather from October to March made roads impassable for tricycles and bicycles before the pneumatic tyre was developed, and unpleasant for
cyclists thereafter). The Civil Service club went on some thirty runs in 1889,[75]
while Belfast's Mossley went on twenty-one in the following year;[76] the Woodvale
Cycling Club of Belfast, which consisted of fifty-eight members, went on some
thirty-two runs in 1894, and another fourteen had to be cancelled due to bad
weather;[77] the Dal Riada Cycling Club, based in Coleraine and Ballymoney, went
on some twenty-four runs in 1898.[78] The enthusiasm of these clubs for group
trips in the countryside was typical of Irish cyclists generally. Popular destinations

The 'Crown and Shamrock' in Carnmoney, a popular hostelry with Antrim cyclists.

for Dublin clubs and other cyclists in the 1880s and 1890s included the Dublin and Wicklow mountains, especially Enniskerry and Glendalough;[79] Bray was another popular resort with Dubliners,[80] as were Strawberry Hall on the outskirts of the Phoenix Park,[81] Lucan (considered 'the Ripley of Ireland' in 1889)[82] and the small Meath village of Enfield.[83] The picturesque village of Crawfordsburn was a particular favourite of Belfast cyclists: as early as June 1886 it was referred to as 'Cyclonia' due to the large number of cycling visitors who wended their way there for Saturday tea.[84] Bangor and Ballycastle also attracted thousands of Belfast cyclists in the late 1890s.[85] Blarney, Passage West, Riverstown and Leemount were popular destinations with cyclists from Cork city in the 1890s, and cafés or 'cyclists' rests' were constructed in these places to serve them tea and refreshments.[86] By the late 1880s it was becoming common for cycling trippers to take photographs during club excursions, as 'Pacemaker' complained to *Sport* in April 1888:

> Amateur poets and photographers are now busy looking up their rhyming dictionaries and cameras. The cycling poet is generally a very delightful companion. He makes one long for a few pounds of strychnine or a keg of dynamite, judiciously applied; but still as a first-class exasperator he is not in it with the amateur cycling photographer. The fiend of the camera stops you just when you are spinning along the most delightful bit of road. He poses you on a rock or makes you bestride a wall, and then wastes half an hour focussing you. When he succeeds in providing a picture you feel that the laws of the land are very defective in not enabling you to punish with proper severity your unfeeling libeller.[87]

Some photographers, such as Luke Healy of Drogheda and two Dublin-based camera salesmen, J. Robinson of Grafton Street and Thomas Mayne of Lord Edward Street, directed advertisements at cyclists;[88] Mayne also sold 'paragon optical lanterns' to cyclists, enabling them to enlarge their negatives or make lan-

tern slides for showing at club entertainments.[89] By March 1892 almost every Dublin club contained several 'amateur photographers',[90] and the countless photographs of Dublin and other clubs in the 1890s attest to Irish cyclists' fondness for being photographed with their machines, either before, during or after runs in the countryside.[91]

Many cyclists undertook their trips as members of the Cyclists' Touring Club (CTC). This organisation, founded as the Bicycle Touring Club in Harrogate in August 1879, and changing its name to the Cyclists' Touring Club in 1883 due to touring cyclists' increasing fondness for tricycles, aimed to promote cycling touring. It appointed officials known as chief consuls and consuls throughout the United Kingdom (and, over time, on the European continent) who gave information to CTC members about roads, restaurants, accommodation and places of interest in their localities. The organisation also negotiated reduced rates for meals and accommodation with hoteliers and innkeepers throughout the United Kingdom, as well as recognising various workmen in each district as CTC-recommended cycle repairers.[92] As was the case with many other cycling clubs, the CTC had its own uniform, which was supposed to increase members' sense of belonging and exclusiveness.[93] Club uniforms were also intended to impress members of the public, but in at least one instance, in November 1888, the CTC's outfit did not have the desired impact – a startled old woman who encountered some CTC cyclists in their grey uniforms at Portadown, thought that they were escaped workhouse inmates![94] Louis Meldon of the Irish Champion Bicycle Club was one of the four vice-presidents elected at the Bicycle Touring Club's inaugural meeting; his bicycle touring credentials were

MAGAZINE HAND CAMERAS
Holding 24 Plates, 12s. 6d.!!

T. MAYNE'S,
10, Lord Edward Street, Dublin.

Right: The combined joys of cycling and photography: an advertisement for Thomas Mayne of Lord Edward Street, Dublin, in 1891.

Opposite: Crawfordsburn in 1890, a popular destination for Belfast cyclists.

firmly established when he and another Irishman, C.W. Fagan of the Temple Bicycle Club, who wrote numerous accounts of his Irish bicycling trips under the pen name of 'Sprig-o'-Shillelagh',[95] became in 1876 the second and third people to cycle over the Simpton Pass in the Alps.[96] In 1884 Northern, Southern, Eastern and Western divisions of the CTC were organised in Ireland, comprising of approximately 225 members who could avail of special rates in some 60 hotels and inns.[97] The Irish CTC membership slowly rose to 587 in September 1885, 646 in October 1888, 752 in October 1890 and 1,074 in October 1896.[98] There was a heavy concentration of CTC membership in Dublin, with over 600 CTC members residing there in July 1898.[99]

A network of hotels, inns and restaurants catered for the needs of the growing number of touring cyclists, whether these were members of the CTC on cycling holidays, cycling club members on weekend or day trips, or other cyclists on day trips to the countryside or coastal resorts. According to one source, in May 1893, in most Ulster hotels 'the wheelman finds that his needs and necessities are anticipated when he arrives';[100] one presumes these establishments offered more appetising fare than the 'dog biscuits' which A.W. Rumney consumed in one shop at Horn Head, Co. Donegal, on his five-hundred-mile trip on a geared Ordinary along the coast from Antrim to Sligo in June 1893.[101] In the rest of the country there was a marked improvement in accommodation and catering facilities for cyclists towards the end of the period in comparison to the situation that had existed in much of Ireland in the 1870s and 1880s. E.J. O'Reilly, who cycled throughout the eastern seaboard counties of Leinster in the 1870s and 1880s, recalled that:

Scenes from an Ohne
Hast lantern show,
April 1891.

Many Irish hotels were catering for cyclists by the late 1880s.

Bar the Imperial at Drogheda, and the hotels at Woodenbridge, Glendalough, and Roundwood, I have no particularly agreeable recollections of the houses of call at some distance from [Dublin] town. Some of them were too terrible for words, and if you asked for meat it was long odds that you couldn't have it.

The front cover of W. St John Joyce's *Rambles around Dublin* (1890).

There was only one item that never failed, and that was 'plain porther'. At one place they refused to put another and myself up one night, on the ground that the house was full. We had no idea that hotel accommodation at Ashbourne was so run on, but when we told a policeman he said, 'Divil a soul at all there's in it'. I believe they had not a bed to give us; but the place was called an 'hotel'.[102]

Two English tourists who cycled from Dublin to Waterford, and thence to Kilkenny, Tipperary, and back to Dublin again in 1885, recorded 'an amiable desire to bleed the *Sassenach*' along the route that they travelled; A.J. Wilson, who went on an Irish cycling tour three years later, complained of 'being fleeced right and left by every living soul at Killarney who could invent an excuse for levying blackmail upon us'.[103] G.W. Hurston and H.R. Stokes of the Melbourne Bicycle Club, who cycled round Ireland in August 1889 as part of their bicycle tour around the world, found that 'the old wizened landlord' of Dundalk's Imperial Hotel threatened to call in the police when they objected to the exorbitant price that he charged for their dinner.[104] Even some CTC-approved hotels had higher charges than other hotels in the same district.[105] Not surprisingly, some cyclists

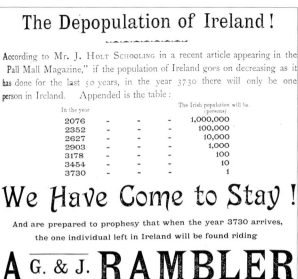

A topical advertisement for 'Rambler' bicycles, 1897.

preferred to combine cycling and camping on their holidays, rather than submit themselves to the frequently unpleasant and expensive alternative of an inn or hotel,[106] while others were the recipients of the peasantry's hospitality, receiving refreshment free of charge or for trifling sums.[107] According to Thomas Hiram Holding, who went on a cycle camping holiday in Sligo, Mayo and Galway in 1897, two bicyclists could live 'luxuriously' on 30*s* per week, and 'almost luxuriously' on 15*s*, whereas it would cost a non-bicyclist more than 70*s* to get by each week.[108]

The *Irish Cyclist*, recognising cyclists' enthusiasm for trips in the countryside, began a series of illustrated articles in its 18 May 1887 issue on recommended cycling routes in the vicinity of Dublin. The *Evening Telegraph's* Weston St John Joyce followed suit two years later, eventually publishing two books of his collected articles in 1890, *Rambles near Dublin* and *Rambles around Dublin*, which described sites of scenic and historic interest. That intrepid entrepreneur, W.J. Mecredy, produced his *Mecredy's Road Book of Ireland* in 1892, a publication which listed the distances between Irish towns and villages, described the (frequently poor) road conditions and provided useful maps for cyclists intent on seeing the countryside. A similar publication, R.T. Lang's *Irish Road Book*, was produced in 1899. The Belfast cycle agent, Thomas Edens Osborne, showed a similar entre-preneurial bent to R.J. Mecredy when, in 1897, he published a pamphlet aimed at tourists who wished to travel by bicycle and train in Ulster.[109] The Belfast and County Down Railway Company commissioned Robert Lloyd Praeger, in 1898, to write a guide for tourists travelling in Co. Down, which was partly aimed at cyclists; in the same year the Great Southern and Western Railway commissioned John O'Mahony to produce a similar guide, *The Sunny Side of Ireland*.[110] Stephen Gwynn got in on the act in 1899 with his *Highways and Byways in Donegal and Antrim*, a mixture of travel itinerary and Nationalist history lesson for the cyclist in northern Ulster (William Bulfin's later and better-known *Rambles in Eirinn* was wider in geographic scope and more acerbic in tone),[111] as did C.P. Redmond, editor of the *Waterford News* and leading member of the Waterford Bicycling Club, when he published *Beauty Spots in the South-East of Ireland and How to See them by Car and Cycle* in 1901.

Railway companies also encouraged cycling tours by offering reduced fares to cycling excursionists travelling to popular tourist destinations such as Killarney, which was described in one such promotion in August 1898 as 'the Irish Riviera',[112] or by selling cheap tickets to cyclists on weekends.[113] Others sold cheap single tickets to cyclists, who travelled by train to their chosen destination and then cycled home.[114] In July 1897 the Dublin, Wicklow and Wexford Railway Company and the Blessington Steam Tramway introduced a special package for cyclists, who could travel by rail from Dublin to any station in Wicklow, cycle across the latter county to Blessington, and return to Dublin by tram; the charge for bicycles was a mere one shilling.[115] The thousands of Irish and foreign cyclists who travelled through Ireland in the summer months of the 1890s were part of a general tourist boom in the country in this period.[116] Some of the foreign cyclists may have been attracted by the publicity efforts of the joint committee of the ICA and the Irish Tourist Association to promote cycling holidays in Ireland, which was formed in December 1895 on the suggestion of the lord lieutenant, Earl Cadogan, 'an ardent cyclist'.[117] The Irish Tourist Authority urged hoteliers to improve their facilities in order to attract greater tourist custom and, according to the *Irish Tourist* in May 1898, 'During the past few years a marked improvement has taken place in the cleanliness and general comfort of the hotels; greater atten-tion is given to the cooking; bills of fare are more varied, and in consequence, tourists, in general, and cyclists, in particular, grumble less of hotel discomforts'. Whether they cycled to enjoy Ireland's scenery, or combined cycling holidays with golfing or fishing,[118] or were 'returned Yanks', cycling in Ulster in order to find their ancestral homes,[119] cycling tourists were an important stratum of the Irish cycling world in the late nineteenth century.

Cyclists in the countryside braved a number of hazards, the worst of which was the frequently appalling condition of the roads. Cyclists' accounts usually

The poor state of many of Ireland's roads is illustrated in this *Irish Cyclist* cartoon of May 1888.

record a very favourable impression of the roads in Connemara[120] and Down,[121] and a mixed picture of road conditions in the rest of the country, although the general impression is that they were often poorly maintained and were dangerous for cyclists. Even Dublin and Belfast's streets were considered unfit for cyclists' needs,[122] so one can only imagine the conditions that cyclists met with elsewhere. Descriptions of abominable roads, even main roads between cities and large towns, were common.[123] The grand juries responsible for road maintenance tended to give maintenance contracts to those who tendered the lowest bids – the result being roads that suited farmers' carts (farmers were the main rate payers) and suited other heavy transport well enough, but that were hopelessly inadequate for tricycles and bicycles.[124] Conditions were bad enough for riders of solid-tyred or cushion-tyred machines, but were much worse for those with pneumatic-tyred cycles – particularly owners of machines with the earliest versions of the pneumatic tyre, as these could take at least one hour to mend when they were punctured, even if one were an expert on the complicated process involved in repairing the punctures.[125] According to the *Irish Cyclist*, in 1898 a cyclist in Ireland could, on average, expect one puncture every 1,500 miles; in

Dan Albone's 'Irish Ivel' safety bicycle, 1887.

counties Dublin and Antrim, however, the average was much worse, at one puncture in every 600 miles and 700 miles, respectively; one unfortunate Donegal cyclist notched up ninety-three punctures, an average of one for every thirteen miles that he cycled![126] More anecdotal evidence about the poor state of Irish roads came in 1899 from John Brown of Dunmurry, the inventor of the viagraph, a device for measuring road surfaces. Brown traced the variations in the surface of the road from Belfast to Lisburn with his machine, and calculated that negotiating the road's ruts and dips alone amounted to climbing a hill greater in height than Slieve Donard.[127] The abolition of the grand juries and their replacement with county councils did not lead to an immediate marked improvement in Irish roads, although some councils invested in steamrollers.[128] W. Fitzwalter Wray, an English cyclist who visited Ireland in May and June 1907, cycling from Dublin to Kerry via Wicklow, Carlow, Kilkenny, Tipperary and Cork, recorded a succession of deplorable roads which had much in common with descriptions throughout the late nineteenth century. After an abysmal journey from Bray onwards, which included a crash in which he hurt his hand, he reached Kilkenny:

> Here I told some members of the Royal Irish Constabulary of my physical
> sufferings by reason of their bad roads, but they only laughed. 'Ah, sure now,
> you've a good road right away to Clonmel, steamrolled, the best road you've

seen this year'….. So I set out from Kilkenny with a light heart, and found the road worse than ever before. My toes all went to sleep, numbed with vibration. I ached from head to foot. There was no footpath. The inch of soft grey dust that lay on the road failed to mitigate its turmoil. Downhill I must brake the machine to eight miles an hour, or be broken on the wheel. A thousand times I wished I had never brought the bicycle. Finally I resolved to take the train at the first station. After nine miles of it, and approaching Callan, it certainly improved, but I had to stop and bathe my wrists in a cold spring. My left hand had not yet recovered from the spill of Whit-Monday, and it was now painful. I came to a fork, and there was no finger-post. I have seen none anywhere, except round Dublin, and no mile-stones. A rustic directed me – 'a splendid steamrolled road right away to Clonmel'. There is an affection of the mind, it seems, which may be called steamroller on the brain. In half a mile it was so bad that I could stand it no longer, and I walked, pushing my bicycle on an Irish main road…..[129]

Conditions were no better in Cork: 'Cork was too filthy for words, most of its streets being bad macadam. For heartless and hateful road murder, commend me to the city of Cork'.[130] Wray continued on his doleful journey from Glengariff to Kenmare:

I have rarely cycled on a more villainously bad main road. Most of the eight miles I then covered lay in the twilight of dense woods, which kept it always wet: and the bad making of the road, and the donkeys and the coaches complete the wreck. Bang, bump, jump, crash, knock, rattle, and jolt you go, with now and then a skid right across the road for a change, and all this for a pace of eight miles an hour.[131]

When Wray eventually left 'the worst main road in the world' – the road from Kenmare to Killarney – his head 'ached badly with cerebro-spinal vibration'.[132]

It was taken for granted that Irish roads were generally in considerably poorer condition than those in England,[133] which explains why British cycle manufacturers produced sturdier versions of their machines for the Irish market in the 1870s and 1880s. A cyclist with considerable experience of cycling in England and Ireland in the 1870s felt that only three bicycles were suitable for Irish roads – these were the Singer 'Special Challenge', with forks specially adapted for the rough usage on Irish roads, the Coventry Machinists' Company's 'Irish Roadster' – a machine of 'extraordinary strength' – and the Bayliss and Thomas 'Duplex Excelsior'.[134] In 1887 Dan Albone's factory in Biggleswade began producing 'Irish Ivel' safety bicycles which were specially designed to withstand the 'rough usage' and the numerous breakages which affected other makes of machines on Irish roads;[135] in the same year the Swift company manufactured its 'Irish Swift' bicycle, which was '[c]onstructed specially strong for Irish roads'.[136]

Left: The Coventry Machinists' Company's 'Irish Swift' safety bicycle, 1890. Note the endorsement from Reverend E.A. Brandon of Ballacolla.

Opposite: In this cartoon the dog emerges victorious over the cyclist.

THE BROKEN STEED ;

Or, "Those who get people into mischief"——   ——"Must help people out of it."

The biter bit: one dog gets its comeuppance in this cartoon.

A TRIUMPH OF PERSEVERANCE.

In 1888 the Coventry Machinists' Company marketed bicycles and tricycles whose spring forks, which allegedly completely suppressed vibration, were stated to have been especially designed for cycling in Ireland, while all of the Pims' Quadrant Tricycle Company, Robinson and Price, and Marriott and Cooper machines were similarly advertised as having been especially constructed for travelling on Irish roads.[137] In 1890 extra-strong safety bicycles for the Irish market included the Singer Company's 'Irish Success', the Guest and Barrow 'Irish Girder' and the 'Ivy';[138] although these and other machines might have been more durable on Irish roads, because of their weight, they were regarded as 'heavy old crocks' by 'Ixion', *Sport*'s cycling correspondent.[139] It became rarer for cycle manufacturers to produce special models for the Irish market in the 1890s, as the almost universal practice of fitting pneumatic tyres to their machines rendered such special measures unnecessary; nevertheless, as late as 1897 the Dennis Company of Guildford made a 'Speed King' bicycle which was advertised as having been specially strengthened for riding on Irish roads.[140]

The danger of cycling on poorly maintained roads was heightened by the hazards posed by animals. Dog attacks were common[141] and were particularly dangerous to Ordinary riders, as evidenced by the fatal fall suffered by a cyclist named Matthews after he was attacked by a dog while riding through William Street in Waterford on 16 May 1885.[142] James Bennet of the Northern Bicycle Club wrote in 1881 that he always carried a whip when he went cycling and used it against dogs that attacked him.[143] John Townsend Trench shot threatening dogs with his revolver; after he killed a 'furious dog' in Kenmare in 1884 he successfully defended himself at petty sessions, proving that he had not endangered anyone's life by demonstrating that he was such a skilled marksman that he could shoot a cork out of a man's hand while riding his bicycle.[144] In 1897 a less drastic

IRATE CYCLIST—" Call off your dog, can't you ! '

MISS ALLTHAIR—" Come away, Sport, you silly dog ; these are not bones—these are the gentleman's legs."

There was little love lost between cyclists and dogs.

method of anti-canine defence than whips or revolvers was being used in Ireland in the form of an ammonia gun that cyclists sprayed into dogs' faces; the ammonia caused dogs to sneeze violently and rendered them temporarily harmless, allowing cyclists to make their escape. The Royal Society for the Prevention of Cruelty to Animals deplored the practice, arguing that 'A hearty kick would be just as effective'! [145] The dog was by no means 'man's best friend' as far as Irish cyclists were concerned, hence the almost gleeful account of the killing of a dog by a Kilmeague bicyclist that was printed in the *Leinster Leader* in June 1893. [146]

According to the pioneering motorist Charles Jarrott, 'the high roads in Ireland were used more or less as farmyards for the breeding of chickens and other birds and beasts', making driving there a frequently hair-raising experience. [147] For cyclists, encounters with pigs, [148] donkeys, [149] bulls, [150] cows, [151] goats, [152] horses, [153] geese, [154] and hens [155] were also often fraught with hazard, resulting in injury for many hapless wheelmen and wheelwomen. Even when animals were under some form of human control, cyclists' hearts sank when they met them. Asses driven by boys were the particular bugbear of one Limerick cyclist in 1880:

Cats on the road were another nuisance with which Irish cyclists had to contend.

The road from Askeaton to Foynes is, from a tricycle point of view, a good one, save when either a fresh supply of broken stones is laid down, or when there happens to be a fair, a butter-market, or other general gathering anywhere in the vicinity. The stones are bad enough, but the last-mentioned event is a magnet that draws many asses and carts, piloted by boys – a combination of misfortunes whereat the heart of the tricyclist goes down, and his hair stands up. I defy any man to predict, with the faintest approach of veracity, what will be the course of action, and what the path or orbit, of an ass propelled by a boy when the two are before you on the road. They defy calculation, upset all the theories of the scholiasts, and submit to no formula. Newton, no doubt, made a great discovery when he evolved a force that influences alike the rolling planets and the falling apple; Kepler earned commensurate fame when he formulated laws that pursue the most reckless and erratic of comets into space and predict its return with unerring precision; but it is deeply to be regretted that neither these [n]or any other of the master-minds of earth gave their attention to the discovery of a solution of the problem of an ass's orbit when propelled by a stick with a boy attached to the end thereof.

AN ASTONISHED COW.

An English tourist runs into an Irish cow.

...I doubt not but that a donkey *unaccompanied* would pursue some rational path that might fall within the domain of conic sections; but an ass *and a boy* form a combination and coalition of such diabolical perversity – such invincible and ineradicable tendency to all kinds of aggravation, that they defy all description and tend only towards the production of perspiration and terror.[156]

William Bulfin had an even more jaundiced opinion of the cattle drovers whom he encountered on Meath's roads:

They are lord and masters of the road for the moment, and they know it well. They will not open a way through their troop for you. They will not assist you in any way to get the cattle out of your way. In busy times they are prejudiced against cyclists, more or less, and they are more or less tired, and more or less drunk, and more or less defiant, and more or less blue-moulding for trouble. If you remonstrate with them they will say mordant things to you, and if you retaliate, they will use language most lurid and personal. If you become aggressive you will have to fight, and if you fight, you will have to smite them hip and thigh or be smitten into pulp. But it would be foolish and fatiguing and excessively risky to commit yourself to a belligerent policy regarding them; because as there are a great many troops of cattle on the march, you will have to fight drovers at every two or three hundred yards of the road from Kilmessan to Ballivor.[157]

Bulfin decided that discretion was the better part of valour:

> The better course is to use diplomacy. Praise the cattle, praise the weather if you
> can, ask them how prices ruled at the fair, and smile every time you have to get
> off your wheel to let them pass. You will have to get off for every troop, but no
> matter, it is better to smile than to fight three reckless characters armed with
> long ash saplings. I smiled and was diplomatic, and only fought once or twice in
> all the miles of purgatory I experienced. But I made a vow never to cycle again
> while the Meath men are on the trail; and I tried to console myself with the
> thought that if I had a few score of the dusky riders who are often my comrades
> in a certain stock country far away, [Argentina], I could clean out Meath in a
> week, graziers and drovers and cattle and all.[158]

The obstructions which cyclists encountered explain one cyclist's wistful longing for the day when James Bond-type gadgets for cyclists would be invented,
including a 'cow catcher' to be affixed to the front of bicycles to remove such
obstacles as asses, goats and pedestrians from cyclists' paths, and a valve-operated
pellet gun mounted on the lower part of bicycles 'to scare away those pugnacious
dogs which timid wheelmen dread so much'.[159]

It should be pointed out that cyclists were themselves at fault for some of the
dangers that were inherent in their pastime. Unlike the situation in Britain, where
cyclists were obliged to carry lamps, there was no such legal obligation for cyclists
in Ireland (except in a few urban districts such as Cork city, where a by-law in
1892 made lamps and bells compulsory),[160] and most chose not to,[161] with inevi-
tably fatal consequences for some cyclists and pedestrians. The folly of cycling
without lights was shown by the case of John Larkin, a prosperous carpenter
from Lisdoonvarna, who was killed while cycling without a light on the night
of 21 November 1878 at a dangerous bend on the Ennis to Lisdoonvarna road
– he was one of the first of many Irish riders to be killed in a cycling accident.[162]
Pedestrians were also endangered by cyclists riding machines without lamps at
night, as illustrated by the tragic case of an elderly man, James McMahon, who
was killed in Dundalk in May 1894 when he was struck by a lightless bicycle
being ridden by Bernard Mullen, a post office clerk.[163] The danger to pedestrians
was increased due to many Irish cyclists' refusal to fit bells on their machines (bells
on cycles were a legal requirement in Britain but not in Ireland); they preferred
to shout warnings at pedestrians instead.[164]

The perils inherent in cycling were heightened by the fact that cycle manufacturers did not begin routinely fitting brakes to machines until 1895, a practice
which began in the USA.[165] Serious injury or fatal crashes were inevitable for
some riders of brakeless machines. These included John Cullen, the manager
of O'Neill's creamery in Waterford, who was killed on a hired brakeless bicycle while speeding down Clonegam Hill at Curraghmore on Easter Monday,

1895.[166] Even some cautious cyclists who rode bicycles with brakes were killed in crashes resulting from faulty brakes snapping when they rode downhill – such unfortunates included Charles Boyle of Booterstown, who was killed in 1881 when riding his Ordinary down a steep hill at Killakee, Co. Dublin, and Sergeant McPhillips of the RIC, who received a fatal rupture in a 'header' over the handlebars of his Ordinary after the brakes on his machine failed when he was spurting down a hill at Dunfanaghy, Co. Donegal, in April 1888.[167] Most cycling accidents arose from riding brakeless bicycles, especially down hills;[168] according to the *Nenagh Guardian* in May 1896, a considerable proportion were caused by youths showing off by riding brakeless machines downhill with their legs crossed upon the handlebars.[169] Despite the obvious dangers of riding brakeless bicycles, Irish cyclists – particularly young men – continued to ride such machines in the late 1890s, scorning bicycles equipped with brakes as fit only for novice, nervous, or unskilled riders.[170] Riding a brakeless bicycle, according to E.J. O'Reilly, was considered 'a patent of cycling nobility'.[171]

Many cyclists tried to lessen the dangers by riding on footpaths instead of the roads. Not only was this practice common in cities such as Dublin and its suburbs,[172] but it was also common in rural areas, many of which had footpaths along the side of the roads. The footpaths were considerably safer than the roads and cyclists frequently preferred to cycle on the former than risk their necks by riding on the latter.[173] From the 1860s to the early 1890s, the RIC and DMP often turned a blind eye to cycling on footpaths, but this began to change following a case at the Exchequer Division of the Four Courts in February 1892, in which Justice Murphy upheld the decision of the Newtownards magistrates to fine a cyclist – a solicitor named McKee – 5s., as well as costs, for obstructing the footpath at Cunningburn, Co. Down, on which he was riding his bicycle. This was in spite of the fact that there were no pedestrians around at the time that McKee was arrested by an RIC sergeant for the alleged obstruction.[174] Thereafter, both the RIC and DMP conducted an episodic clampdown on cycling on footpaths, even when there were no pedestrians around and, therefore, no obvious obstruction occurring. The police efforts were often thwarted by magistrates who, as cyclists themselves, sympathised with offenders who felt they had little alternative but to ride on footpaths, and who either handed down trifling fines[175] or even refused to convict, despite the clarity of the law on the issue. The latter was the course adopted by the Tullamore magistrates in 1897, much to the frustration of Head Constable O'Neill; four of the five magistrates at Tullamore petty sessions were cyclists, and two of them admitted that they themselves broke the law. The chairman, Colonel M. W. Biddulph, refused to convict offenders who rode on footpaths outside of a one-mile radius from the town.[176] The fact that cycling on footpaths was widespread is suggested by the claim of a Derry barrister in July 1897 that all cyclists, including the police themselves, indulged in the practice, and he condemned the hypocrisy involved in such prosecutions.[177] In November 1897

A contemporary comment on the foolhardiness of Irish cyclists.

Inspector General Andrew Reed surprised Irish cyclists by ordering the RIC to prosecute footpath cyclists only in cases where there was a clear case of obstruction,[178] a development which was welcomed by the force's rank and file, who disliked 'the objectionable and unpopular duty of prosecuting peaceable citizens' who rode on footpaths.[179] The *Weekly Irish Times* speculated that Reed's decision was partly influenced by the unpopularity of such prosecutions with the public,

THE WHEELER AND THE PEELER

I passed a peeler on the path
  Who walked the way that I was going
It stirred his high and righteous wrath
To pass that peeler on the path.
Swear-words, of which the peeler hath
  Command, from him came swiftly flowing
When I passed that peeler on the path
  Who walked the way that I was going

Left: 'The Wheeler and the Peeler': a 'scorcher' on a footpath speeds past a policeman.

Opposite: 'The Scorcher Snatcher': a Jack B. Yeats cartoon.

and also by embarrassing cases such as the conviction of a constable in Ulster for riding on a footpath and the jailing of a Belfast-based major, S.K. Cowan, who refused to pay the fine of 10s and costs inflicted on him by the Lurgan magistrates for a similar offence, on the grounds that the roads had been in an unrideable condition and that he had had no alternative but to cycle on the footpath.[180] Whatever Reed's reasons may have been, his volte-face was short-lived: in March 1898 he instructed the RIC to resume prosecuting in all cases of cycling on the footpath, regardless of whether there was an actual obstruction or not.[181]

The police also prosecuted 'scorchers', cyclists who rode at excessive speed; their attempts to catch speeding cyclists were the subject of a Jack B. Yeats cartoon, 'The Scorcher Snatcher', in the *Irish Cyclist* of 3 April 1895. The urge to ride speedily and recklessly was irresistible to many cyclists, as recognised by the *Midland Reporter* in June 1898. In an article which discussed a proposal to

THE SCORCHER SNATCHER.

(1) Flip-flaps is here depicted showing his patent *scorcher-grabber* to the police authorities. (2) A. is the first peeler with the grabber fitted (3) This is the moment when the peeler is grabbing the *scorcher*. (4) But the scorcher didn't stop. (5) He dashed on through towns and villages. (6) But when he started to race down a hill like this. (7) The peeler's heart failed him, and he struck off the grabber.

erect a notice board at the top of steep hills, warning cyclists of the dangerous nature of riding down these slopes, the newspaper commented that for most cyclists 'such a notice would be a direct incentive to raise the legs in the air, lose the pedals and the presence of mind at the same time, and dash full speed down the declivity at a "scorching" rate'. It recommended instead that notices should be posted giving cyclists information on the locations of the nearest ambulance, police barracks (where a stretcher might be obtained), chemist's shop (for procuring splints, bandages, sticking plaster, lint and chloroform for operations); the addresses of local surgeons, whose services would be called on to perform operations on cyclists who were foolhardy enough to cycle down dangerous hills; and the location of the nearest mortuary, if the descent should prove fatal. This, the newspaper felt, would have a more sobering effect than posting a notice that merely stated 'Dangerous for cyclists'.[182] The 'scorcher' cyclist was satirised in a poem in the *Irish Cyclist* of 20 September 1893:

An advertisement for Dunlop tyres in 1896 attempts to cash in on cyclists' desire for speedy machines.

A Dublin magistrate urges a cabby to run over a cyclist.

The Scorcher

'Hi! I say –
Clear the way!'
Hark the furious shrieking!
Flying fowls –
Canine growls –
Porkers scudding, squeaking.

Language loose;
Loud abuse;
Village idlers yelling –
Here and there –
Everywhere –
Loud commotion swelling.

Baby throats,
Highest notes,
In a chorus squalling;
Grown-up boys
Make a noise
Hideously appalling.

What's amiss?
Why is this
Horrible excitement?
Are there laws?
For the cause
Well deserves indictment.

There he goes!
Sunlight shows
Just a flashing pedal –
Someone groans,
'Scorcher Jones
Going for a medal!'

'Cads on castors' – cyclists who placed pedestrians in danger by riding recklessly
– generated a certain amount of understandable hostility towards cyclists,[183] especially
when elderly pedestrians were killed as a result of cyclists' heedless riding.[184] This hostility manifested itself in several ways: in the award of £120 damages against Charles
Strangman, a Waterford cyclist, who seriously injured a priest when he rode into him

on a footpath on the Newtown road in August 1876;[185] the decision to bar cyclists from the Kingstown piers and the seafront promenade at Bray, due to the dangers posed by 'scorching' cyclists;[186] and the speed restrictions imposed by the Cork and Belfast municipal authorities on cycling within their respective cities.[187] 'Scorchers' who were killed as a result of their careless cycling, such as the Dubliner who died as a result of riding into the shaft of a stationary cart on D'Olier Street in 1894, which he did not see as he was 'scorching' with his head down over the handlebars of his bicycle,[188] and Patrick Burke, a GPO employee who was killed after colliding with a Lipton's van on Harcourt Street in August 1897, received scant sympathy from coroners; indeed, in the latter case the coroner commented instead on the scandalous speeds of twenty to thirty miles per hour at which some cyclists travelled through Dublin's streets.[189] No official was more outspoken in his hostility towards cyclists than the Recorder for Dublin city, Frederick Falkiner. Falkiner explained in 1888 that he found against cyclists in court cases whenever he could as he considered them to be dangerous nuisances who frightened horses on the roads;[190] he described cyclists as snakes who sneaked up silently behind their unsuspecting victims, and likened their approach to the rapid and deadly attack of a flash of lightning or a typhoid bacillus.[191] Dublin cyclists were astonished in May 1898 when the Recorder found in favour of two cyclists who claimed damages (one case involved a bicyclist who was knocked down by a horse and trap and the other involved a bicyclist whose machine was damaged in a crash caused by the unsafe condition of tram lines),[192] as it was a widespread perception that Falkiner believed that cyclists 'went forth on the highways with no other object in view than to slay innocent children and harmless ladies'.[193] The perception that cyclists did not receive justice in Dublin's courts was summed up by a cartoon in the 18 September 1894 issue of the *Irish Wheelman*, in which an excited magistrate urges a car driver to run over a bicyclist and promises to let him off with a trifling fine for the offence. Such an offer would probably have appeared enticing to some drivers, as there is plenty of evidence from as far afield as Dublin, Cork, Tralee and elsewhere that jarvies resented the spread of cycling because it lost them fares;[194] their hostility manifested itself in various ways, such as obstructing roads with their cars or strewing nails and broken glass on roads, to the more common practice of forcing cyclists off the roads by deliberately driving their cars dangerously close to them.[195]

Despite the numerous obstacles that they encountered, Irish cyclists indulged their love of speed either by 'scorching' on their own or engaging in organised speeding contests, including attempts to achieve the quickest times for cycling between various towns, such as those between Belfast and Dublin,[196] Limerick and Dublin,[197] or Dublin and Cork,[198] or cycling from Mizen Head to Fair Head,[199] a rough Irish equivalent of the John o' Groats to Land's End ride in Britain. The Irish Road Club (IRC) was formed in April 1890 to promote fast, long-distance cycling, with membership open to any amateur rider who cycled at least one hundred miles in twenty-four hours,[200] a development which had already been anticipated by the practice of such outfits as the Leinster Cycling Club and the Newry Cycling

Michael Walsh on the velocipede which he rode in a race in Co. Wexford in 1870.

Club of awarding medals to members who rode certain long distances in twenty-four hours.[201] A Northern branch of the IRC was formed in May 1892, attaining a membership of fifty-five by March 1893; by February 1894 there were over 200 members in the IRC throughout Ireland.[202] In 1893 the IRC awarded a gold medal to cyclists who rode at least 175 miles in twelve hours, and a silver medal to those who rode at least 140 miles and a bronze medal to those covering at least 112 miles in the same time; for its twenty-four-hour time trials, gold medals were awarded to riders who covered at least 280 miles, while silver medals were given to those who rode at least 240 miles and bronze medals were awarded to riders who cycled at least 180 miles.[203] The IRC also held road races from Dublin to Waterford, Cork, Athlone and Dundalk,[204] but the favourite starting point for its races and speed trials in the 1890s was Enfield, Co. Meath, as most of the nearby roads were relatively level and conducive to rapid cycling.[205] For a number of years Barrington's Hotel in Enfield was regarded as virtually the IRC's headquarters, such was the frequency with which this elite cycling outfit assembled there for races, meetings and club dinners.[206]

The IRC's competitions were just one example of the enthusiasm of Irish cyclists for bicycle and tricycle races. Such enthusiasm manifested itself at an early stage. The three-quarters of a mile velocipede race between four military officers for a stake of £3, which formed part of the sports organised by officers of the 72nd Highlanders in Limerick on 14 August 1869, was one of the earliest recorded cycling races in Ireland.[207] Some of the earliest velocipede races in Dublin were held on 4 June 1870 in the grounds of the Exhibition Palace at Earlsfort Terrace. A Mr P. Kavanagh, an Arklow coachbuilder who rode a velocipede which he had made himself, initially thought that he had won the third race, but the organising committee awarded first place to William Black, of 145 Capel Street (who, in 1875, became manager of a bicycle depot, the Dublin Bicycle Factory, at the same address). Black, the second-placed rider, successfully appealed against the initial race result, on the grounds that Kavanagh had fouled him twice by riding into his back wheel, and that following the first of these collisions Kavanagh had been helped to remount his machine, which was against the rules. This was to be the first of many Irish races whose outcome was disputed by at least one of the contestants. An enraged Kavanagh responded by challenging the contestants to a re-run of the race, for a prize of £1.[208] In the return contest at Enniscorthy, Kavanagh, whose iron-tyred boneshaker weighed 75lbs, was easily defeated by the Dublin bicycle maker, Neal of Clarendon Street and his foreman, Michael Walsh, both of whom astonished the coachmaker by turning up on two of the latest, rubber-tyred velocipedes[209] – this was not the last time that the scales were to be tipped in favour of racers who had the advantage of the latest advances in cycling technology.

The first bicycle races in Dungarvan were held in September 1870, over a four-mile course along the roads to Barnabue. Thousands of spectators turned up to watch the novel spectacle, and the race day was treated as a public holiday; the RIC offered their services in keeping the roads free of traffic, which was partly accomplished by Sub-Inspector Edmond McDermott and several magistrates (including Resident Magistrate Henry Edward Redmond) riding before and behind the cyclists on their horses. Some of the magistrates almost ran down the competitors in their zeal, and the sub-inspector twice nearly ran over R.E. Brenan of the Dungarvan Ramblers Club. County Inspector John Loch wagered £10 that Brenan could defeat a local favourite, a land agent named Shaw; the policeman won his bet, but it was a close affair, as the powerfully built Shaw put his machine across his back after he had been passed by Brenan and took a short-cut across some fields to establish a lead, but Brenan still managed to overtake him. Although the races were tremendously exciting for the spectators, they were not particularly fast affairs, as some soldiers of the 67th Regiment who took their tunics off were able to keep pace with the racers for most of the route.[210]

As the evidence from Dungarvan suggests, cycling races were often rough-and-ready affairs, particularly before the establishment of the ICA. In Ulster in the 1870s and 1880s, for example, cycling races often constituted a small part of general sports meetings organised by cricket and athletic clubs.[211] Not sur-

A fanciful view of a bicycle race in rural Ireland in 1885.

prisingly, the courses often fell far short of the standards desired by cyclists. For instance, a race which was organised in 1873 to raise funds for the Whiteabbey Amateur Band was held in a meadow on Cave Hill – the course had a steep slope on one side, the grass in the meadow was only partially cut, the turf was slippery, and most of the contestants, who were riding boneshakers, had to dismount when they reached the long grass; the race was easily won by Sam McCombe of Carrickfergus, the rider of the only rubber-tyred 'Ariel' bicycle in the contest.[212] In October 1881 a Belfast cyclist watched a bicycle race in Coleraine 'over the most despicable ground' for racing that he had ever seen, which consisted simply of a clay field whose ridges had been filled with cinders in an attempt to make it even.[213] However, primitive racing conditions were not an Ulster monopoly. A member of the Irish Champion Bicycle Club wrote of a bicycle race at Clonmel on 6 July 1876, that 'the "Velocipede" race was thoroughly a country event. The course was on the side of a hill, and had never been rolled, the grandstand was made of unbarked trees, and our whole time was occupied in preventing our bicycles from being broken up'.[214] A Dubliner was appalled at the shambles which he witnessed at the Lismore College sports on Whit Monday, 1878. The sports were held on the grounds of the college, and, according to the visitor:

> ...a place more unsuited for such a sport could not have been selected. It illustrates what we have often observed at provincial sports, when the entire management is entrusted to local gentlemen only – persons who possess no

knowledge of the sports they profess to manage. They imagine that when they secure a brass band, a few prizes, and a badly-laid out course, they have done their duty. Far from it.

On this occasion there was confusion over where the seven-mile bicycle race was supposed to finish, so that there was no official and no finishing tape or flag at the supposed terminal point of the race; instead, there was 'nothing but an excited crowd, who could not tell the exact spot to be considered the winning-post'.[215] Even if an official had been present at a clearly demarcated finishing line there is no guarantee that the race would have had a clear result as, according to R.J. Mecredy in 1891, cycling races outside of Dublin were frequently in the hands of incompetent judges. According to Mecredy, judges at these races were often 'some local big wigs' who were as carried away with excitement by the proceedings as the rest of the specta- tors were; consequently, as the leading competitors swept round the final bend, they often watched the approach of the race leaders instead of fixing their eyes on the finishing line. If the finish was a close one, this caused difficulties for the judges:

> As they pass the tape a look of doubt generally crosses their faces, and they settle the difficulty by giving it a dead heat, or each judge gives his opinion (and it is nothing more than an opinion), and the majority carries the day and decides – often wrongly – as to who shall get first prize. In Belfast each judge writes on a slip of paper the name of the man whom he thinks has won, and almost invariably, if a finish is close, opinions are divided.

In Mecredy's opinion, the competitor who was adjudged to have finished second in such close contests 'cannot always feel that the winner is a man and a brother; but he is not naturally permitted to give physical expression to his feelings'. He felt that there was 'more latitude to natural human feelings' at races held at GAA meetings, instancing the case of a race meeting held near Carlingford Lough 'some good while ago'. In a closely contested finish between two Ordinary riders, the second rider, realising that he was not going to overtake the leader, deliberately crashed into his rival's machine, causing both riders to have 'a first-clash smash' and allowing another rider to win the race. Rather than condemning the foul, the crowd cheered for what they saw as a brave deed![216]

Provincial cycling races may not always have met the standards of Mecredy and other critics, but they were still highly popular with locals, especially when they were a novelty.[217] These races brought colour and excitement to the countryside, as a correspondent explained to the *Irish News* in July 1897: 'We don't see much sport in the country, and indeed it is a welcome sight to see a turnout of cyclists along our country roads on the occasion of a road race'.[218] The enthusiasm which bicycle races often evoked amongst spectators in villages and small towns was vividly described by the *Irish Cyclist* in May 1893:

The cycling track at the Royal Dublin Society's grounds, 1886.

The interest excited by the hundred-mile race in the Co. Down on Whit Monday was extraordinary. At all the towns along the route the people turned out in hundreds, cheering the competitors vigorously, and questioning everyone as to whether there were any more coming. At Warrenpoint the riders passed through a living avenue, and how they escaped without injury to themselves is a mystery. One of them knocked down a small boy, but happily without hurting him. At Rostrevor it was the same, while at Annalong the inhabitants were lavish in their attentions to the competitors. The sporting fishermen of this village handed drinks of water to everyone who passed, and the rider who refused the proffered lubricant generally got the contents of the tin over his head. Some of them seemed rather to enjoy this attention. But Banbridge eclipsed, both in numbers and enthusiasm, any town on the route. The course lay through the main street of the town, and the gradient of this street is so steep that it has been found necessary to make a cutting through the centre to enable horses to bring their loads to the top. Half way down this cutting is spanned by a viaduct, and on this, as well as on both sides of the cutting, the people were in lines of three deep… The crowds cheered themselves hoarse, and everyone got a royal reception, from the leader to the whipper-in.[219]

Similar enthusiasm was evident during the IRC's fifty-mile road race from Enfield in April 1894, a contest which was watched 'with keen interest by the inhabitants

I. C. A. TOURNAMENT, 1887.

of the district, who lined the ditches at every village and cross-roads' on the route. A journalist who was present provided rare evidence about the hangers-on at such events, the poseurs or 'masher' riders who did not themselves compete in races but who wanted to bask in the reflected glory accorded to racing cyclists at the time. He wrote :

> If the stewards of the Road Club intend to abolish a source of very great annoy-ance – a veritable nuisance – in connection with their road race competitions they should get rid of the gang of masher wheelers who attend at the finish of a race to display their forms and costumes and obstruct the competitors. This form of 'road nuisance' was very noticeable on Saturday evening, when at least one competitor, [J.] George, had to pull up towards the final rather than rush into a number of machines that were in his way. Perhaps if a strong rider went slap-bang with his machine amongst those ornamental dudes that surround the winning post on an occasion or two, it would be a good way of abating the nuisance.[220]

"The Rover has set the fashion to the world."
—*The Cyclist.*

ROVERS
AND
CHAMPIONSHIPS

Of the many CHAMPIONSHIPS won on ROVERS during 1895, the following are a few:

Ireland, 10 Miles.	North-Western District, 1	Humber C C. (Coventry).
„ 25 Miles.	Mile.	Isle of Wight.
„ Ulster, 25 Miles.	Club Championship of Eng-	Italian B.C.
N.C.U. (Sussex Centre) 25 Mls.	land (Juniors).	London Central B.C.
N.C.U. (West of England)	Catford C.C., 1 Mile and 50	Mid-Surrey B C.
Centre) 10 Miles.	Miles.	Newcastle C.C.
N.C.U. (South Durham Centre)	Argus B.C., 5 Miles.	Newhaven B.C.
25 Miles.	Carlisle.	Salford Harriers.
Essex, 1 Mile.	Cork C.C.	Tottenham C.C.
Essex, 10 Miles.	Castle Douglas.	Wellingboro' C.C.
Scotland (North) 1 Mile.	Dagonet C C.	

Mr. HARRY LARGE, 10 and 25 Miles Irish Champion.

J. K. STARLEY & CO., Ltd., METEOR WORKS, WEST ORCHARD, COVENTRY.

DEPOTS—LONDON: 5, Holborn Viaduct, E.C.   157, New Bond St, W.   55, Farringdon St. (Wholesale Department and Warehouse).   PARIS: 47, Avenue Parmentier.

Agents in Ireland:— [agent listing in small print]

Right: An advertisement from March 1896 lauding the success of 'Rover' bicycles in Ireland and Britain.

Opposite: Competitors in the ICA's 1887 championships.

Evidence from Drogheda shows the lengths to which some 'ornamental dudes' were prepared to go in order to cut a dashing figure. In July 1896 a 'professional gentleman' observed a young man from the country behaving strangely outside his premises. At first the Drogheda witness thought that the young man, a cyclist, had injured himself and was tending to his injury, but when he approached him the startled cyclist sped off on his bicycle. It turned out that 'The poor fellow was manufacturing a pair of false calves, with which, when mounted, to delight all beholders and bewitch the female mind'. He was constructing these false calves by putting strips of bacon down his stockings! In his embarrassed haste to get away, the young man left one strip of bacon behind on the road.[221]

Founded in 1882, the ICA – one of whose main functions was the convening of annual championship cycling races – was partly responsible for the image of racers as the elite of the Irish cycling world. The ICA spent some £1,500 on constructing a gravel racing track at the Royal Dublin Society's grounds in Ballsbridge, holding its first race meeting there on Easter Saturday and Easter Monday in 1885.[222] Thereafter, most Irish championship races were held there or in the Phoenix Park, despite such unsavoury aspects as the foul language frequently used by spectators and the open business conducted by bookmakers at these venues.[223]

BE WISE IN TIME.

Don't purchase your Bicycle for coming season, until you have seen

"THE PIERCE"
TEN GUINEA CYCLE,

Already the Sensation of 1900.

Built throughout of our own Component Parts, produced from the finest raw material procurable, *not of cheap collected rubbish.*

THE PIERCE Model A	-	Roadster	-	£15 15 0
THE PIERCE Model B	-	Perfection	-	18 5 0
THE PIERCE Model C	-	Light Roadster	-	15 5 0
THE PIERCE Model D	-	Perfection	-	16 5 0
THE PIERCE Model E	-	Ladies' Safety	-	16 16 0
THE PIERCE Model F	-	,, ,, Perfection		18 5 0

Specimens of each just sent for Competition to World's Exhibition, Paris.
SOLE AGENCIES NOW ARRANGING.

PIERCE'S, Cycle Manufacturers, WEXFORD & PARIS.

An advertisement for Pierce's of Wexford, 1900.

Other purpose-built race tracks followed, the best of which were at Tralee, Waterford, Wexford, Kilkenny and Ballymena. The Tralee track, 'the admiration of all racing men in the bicycle world', was constructed by a railway engineer at the town's cricket grounds in 1888.[224] The Waterford track at the People's Park, which cost £400 to construct in the early 1890s, was paid for by W.G.D. Goff, JP, vice-president of the Waterford Bicycle Club – it could hold crowds of an estimated 7,000 to 8,000 people.[225] Some £1,500 was spent by the Wexford Sports Company on a race track and sports grounds in 1893. Kilkenny's cycling track, which was constructed in 1897, could accommodate some 1,500 seated spectators.[226] Victorian Ireland's only cement racing track, which was probably the finest bicycle track in the country, was opened at Ballymena on 22 June 1897.[227] These permanent tracks, and a host of other grass and turf tracks, illustrated the Irish public's keen interest in cycling races. It is no coincidence that Irish cycle dealers frequently stressed in their advertisements how quickly their machines travelled, often by claiming or suggesting that particular racing triumphs were due to rac-ers riding the brand of machine or tyre that they sold.[228] Some racers probably colluded in this, as it is likely that many leading Irish racers were 'makers' ama-teurs' – allegedly amateur riders who received cheap or free machines from cycle manufacturers or who had their hotel or other expenses paid by them, in return for riding their bicycles in races.[229] The link between racing success and cycling product was made explicit by the Birmingham firm of William Bown Limited in an interesting way in October 1897, when they displayed in the window of their Bachelor's Walk, Dublin, depot the 'Æolus' bicycle on which W.L. Martin of the Irish Road Club set a new twelve hours' distance record, attracting 'a great deal of attention' from passers-by for doing this.[230] This was probably a more effec-tive advertising ploy than that adopted by another Bachelor's Walk business in March 1891, which consisted of posing a stuffed monkey, which had 'a terrified look' on its face, 'in the most picturesque attitudes on the various machines on view', including an Ordinary bicycle and some perambulators.[231] The conceptual link between rapid and easy movement and the tricycles and bicycles for sale in cycle shops was probably also enhanced by the fact that cycle dealers were often well-known ex-racers who entered into the cycle business on their retirement from the track[232] or, indeed, in some cases were still pursuing racing careers – for instance, the *Irish Cyclist* in June 1895 attributed a good deal of the business suc-cess of F.O. Maxwell and Cecil K. Harding of Derry to the fact that they had won almost one hundred prizes in races and were still 'racing men of more than ordi-nary ability'.[233] The most illustrious ex-racer to set up in business for himself was undoubtedly Harry Reynolds of Balbriggan, who became Ireland's first world champion cyclist when he won the one-mile amateur world championship in Copenhagen on 15 August 1896. He endeared himself to Irish Nationalists by refusing to acknowledge the Union flag or 'God Save the Queen' at the medal-awarding ceremony; on his insistence, the Danish officials lowered the Union flag and replaced it with a green flag, and 'an Irish tune' was played instead of 'God Save the Queen'. After a brief stint as a professional racer in Australia and New Zealand he returned to Ireland, opening a cycle shop at 4 Crampton Quay, Dublin, in 1900.[234] Reynolds's racing successes, and the fact that an estimated 30,000 bicycles were being purchased annually in Ireland in the late nineteenth and early twentieth centuries,[235] are just two indications of the energetic Irish cycling scene in existence in the late Victorian era. The days in which Irish peo-ple were terrified by the sight of passing bicycles and tricycles were gone forever.

References

Chapter 1 (pp 9-12)

1. *Irish Cyclist*, 29 December 1886. The cyclist received the nickname of 'Dick the Devil' as a result of this incident.
2. *Wheel World*, December 1883.
3. *Irish Cyclist*, 24 June 1891.
4. Ibid, 25 May 1887.
5. For a discussion of women's cycling in nineteenth-century Ireland see Brian Griffin, 'Cycling and Gender in Victorian Ireland', in *Éire-Ireland*, vol. xli, numbers 1 & 2 (Spring/Summer 2006), pp 213-241.
6. *Irish Cyclist*, 27 September 1893. The phrase occurs in an article in which the author laments that the old 'freemasonry of the wheel is out of place in these levelling days'.
7. Ibid.
8. *Weekly Irish Times*, 21 November 1896.
9. *Irish Cyclist,* 22 July 1896.
10. *Irish Tourist*, July 1898.
11. *Irish Wheelman*, 9 November 1897; *Irish Cyclist*, 16 September 1898.
12. *Irish Cyclist*, 7 May 1902.

Chapter 2 (pp 13-32)

1. Details from James McGurn, *On Your Bicycle: An Illustrated History of Cycling* (London: John Murray, 1897), pp 14-24; Wiebe E. Bijker, *Of Bicycles, Bakelites and Bulbs: Toward a Theory of Sociotechnical Change* (Cambridge, Mass.: MIT Press, 1995), pp 21-25; David V. Herlihy, *Bicycle: The History* (New Haven and London: Yale University Press, 2004), pp 19-52.
2. Herlihy, *Bicycle*, p. 51.
3. *Irish Cyclist*, 10 February 1886, 5 March 1890.
4. McGurn, *On Your Bicycle*, pp 30-31; Derek Roberts, *Cycling History: Myths and Queries* (n.p.: John Pinkerton, 1991), pp 19-20.
5. McGurn, *On Your Bicycle*, p. 31; Roberts, *Cycling History*, pp 26-27.
6. McGurn, *On Your Bicycle*, p. 30.
7. Ibid, p. 27.

8. David Harrel's manuscript memoirs, pp 5-6 (Trinity College Dublin, Ms 3918a); *Irish Cyclist,* 8 June 1887; *Irish Wheelman*, 25 September 1894.

9. 'Velox', *Velocipedes, Bicycles and Tricycles: How to Make, and How to Use Them* (London: George Routledge, 1869), pp 70-71.

10. McGurn, *On Your Bicycle*, pp 24-27.

11. *Irish Cyclist*, 27 January 1892. Italics in original.

12. Ibid, 5 March 1890.

13. Details from Frederick Alderson, *Bicycling: A History* (Newton Abbot: David and Charles, 1972), pp 23-24; McGurn, *On Your Bicycle*, pp 34-35, 45-46.

14. Andrew Ritchie, 'The Origins of Bicycle Racing in England: Technology, Entertainment, Sponsorship and Advertising in the Early History of the Sport', *Journal of Sports History*, vol. 26 (Autumn, 1999), pp 489-550.

15. Details from Alderson, *Bicycling*, pp 38-41; Herlihy, *Bicycle*, pp 160-164.

16. Roberts, *Cycling History*, p.1.

17. R.J. Mecredy and Gerald Stoney, *The Art and Pastime of Cycling* (Dublin: Mecredy and Kyle, 1890), p.25; Herlihy, *Bicycle*, p.169.

18. Farrell and Turner's patent, 1869/1281 (British Library Patent Library); *Irish Times*, 17 June 1870; *Thom's Irish Almanac and Official Directory of the United Kingdom of Great Britain and Ireland: for the Year 1870* (Dublin: Alexander Thom, 1870), p.1501.

19. Bijker, *Bicycles, Bakelites, and Bulbs*, p.54.

20. Blood's patent, 1876/4250 (British Library Patent Library). Blood was not the first to think of a tricycle that could be ridden by invalids. In 1869 Reverend R.H. Charsley invented his 'Velociman', which was especially designed for cripples, His machine was still being ridden by disabled cyclists in 1900: see Arthur Judson Palmer, *Riding High: The Story of the Bicycle* (New York: Dutton, 1956), p.40.

21. *Irish Cyclist*, 6 November 1889.

22. *Wheel World*, December 1883; *Irish Cyclist*, 19 March 1890. The Careys' mechanic, 'the best mechanic in the metropolis', who later became the foreman of the repair department of the Pneumatic Tyre and Booth's Cycle Agency, built the first 'Dublin' tricycle: *Irish Cyclist*, 13 September 1892.

23. Details from *Irish Cyclist*, 19 March 1890; McGurn, *On Your Bicycle*, pp 81-82; Bijker, *Bicycles, Bakelites, and Bulbs*, pp 54-57; Herlihy, *Bicycle*, pp 209-214.

24. *Irish Cyclist*, 11 November 1885, 6 November 1889.

25. Ibid, 10 February 1886.

26. Alderson, *Bicycling*, p.23.

27. Samuel Dawson, *Incidents in the Course of a Long Cycling Career* (Lancaster: Beeley Brothers, 1906), pp 5, 54.

28. *Irish Cyclist*, 26 March 1890.

29. Details from ibid, 5 March 1890, 25 September 1895. In an interview in 1888 Trench stated, 'I am quite confident that the bicycle I speak of was the first that was brought to, and ridden in, Ireland, as Michaux had only made a few of them at the time; and, when I rode it through the streets of Paris, people used to stop and stare at me, as the thing, even in Paris, was quite unknown': ibid, 2 May 1888.

30. *Irish Athletic and Cycling News*, 9 April 1889.

31. *Irish Cyclist*, 9 May 1894.

32. Ibid, 18 April 1894.

33. *Irish Wheelman*, 25 September 1894.

34. *Irish Times*, 6 June 1870.

35. *Irish Cyclist*, 21 February 1894.

36. Ibid, 12 March 1890, 16 April 1890.

37. Ibid, 19 March 1890. For a discussion of the Hutton coachbuilding business see Jim Cooke, *Ireland's Premier Coachbuilder: John Hutton and Sons, Summerhill, Dublin* (Dublin: Jim Cooke, 1992).

38. *Thom's Irish Almanac and Official Directory of the United Kingdom of Great Britain and Ireland: for the Year 1867* (Dublin: Alexander Thom, 1867), p.1422; *Irish Cyclist*, 16 April 1890.

39. *Thom's Irish Almanac and Official Directory of the United Kingdom of Great Britain and Ireland: for the Year 1872* (Dublin: Alexander Thom, 1872), p.1523; *Irish Cyclist*, 7 May 1890; *Irish Wheelman*, 25 September 1894.

40. *Irish Cyclist*, 12 March 1890; *Irish Wheelman*, 29 August 1899. For a discussion of the Pierce agricultural implement manufacturing firm, including a very brief account of its production of bicycles from the late 1890s to the 1930s, see Anthony O'Sullivan, 'Pierces of Wexford', *Journal of the Wexford Historical Society*, no. 16 (1996-1997), pp 126-143.

41. *The Leader*, 23 March 1901.

42. *Irish Cyclist*, 12 March 1890.

43. Ibid, 18 March 1896.

44. Ibid, 7 February 1894; C.P. Redmond, *Beauty Spots in the South-East of Ireland and How to See them by Car and Cycle* (London and Dublin: Henry Gaze, 1901), p.32.

45. *Irish Cyclist*, 7 February 1894.

46. *The Belfast and Province of Ulster Directory for 1865-66* (Belfast: *Belfast Newsletter*, 1865), p.111; *Irish Cyclist*, 16 April 1890.

47. *Irish Cyclist*, 16 April 1890.

48. Ibid, 7 February 1894.

49. *Sport*, 17 December 1892.

50. *Irish Cyclist*, 16 April 1890.

51. Ibid, 24 June 1896.

52. Roberts, *Cycling History*, p.34.

53. *Irish Cyclist*, 7 February 1894, 14 February 1894.

54. Ibid, 14 February 1894.

55. *Wheel World*, June 1883. Cromie caused bitter disappointment to the expectant audience by refusing to ride his new bicycle straightaway. He preferred to save himself potential embarrassment by practising riding the machine in secret for a few days, before venturing forth on it in public.

56. Edward O'Toole, *Whist for Your Life, That's Treason: Recollections of a Long Life* (Dublin: Ashfield Press, 2003), p.90.

57. *Irish Cyclist*, 14 February 1894. For other accounts of horsemen challenging cyclists to race in Tipperary and Mayo (contests which the cyclists won), see *Bicycling News*, 1 September 1876, 8 December 1876.

58. *Bicycling News*, 8 September 1876.

59. Ibid, 3 November 1876, 24 November 1876, 16 February 1877.

60. Ibid, 23 March 1877.

61. Ibid, 21 December 1877, 28 December 1877.

62. Account by 'Medicus' in ibid, 14 December 1877.

63. *Limerick Chronicle*, 19 October 1880. My thanks to Tom Hayes for this reference.

64. *Bicycling News*, 11 February 1881.

65. *Morning Mail*, 24 October 1881.

66. Account by 'A.T.F.' in *Wheel World*, September 1883.

67. *Wheel World*, December 1883.

68. *Irish Cyclist*, 17 February 1892.

69. Ibid, 5 May 1886.

70 *Wheel World*, October 1886.

71. *Irish Cyclist*, 16 September 1885.

72. A.J. Wilson, *Two Trips to the Emerald Isle* (London: Iliffe, 1888), p.27. For a biography of Wilson, including a brief account of his cycling in Ireland, see Arthur F. Dimmock, *Arthur James Wilson 1858-1945* (Feltham: British Deaf History Society, 1996).

73. *Sligo Champion*, 1 September 1894.

74. O'Toole, *Whist*, p.92.

75. Tim Pat Coogan, *De Valera: Long Fellow, Long Shadow* (London: Arrow Books, 1995), p.16.

76. Account by 'H.M.W.' in *Bicycling News*, 25 January 1878.

77. *Wheel World*, December 1883.

78. *Irish Cyclist*, 7 January 1891.

79. Stephen Gwynn, *Highways and Byways in Donegal and Antrim* (London: Macmillan, 1899), p.106.

80. *Irish Cyclist*, 13 February 1895.

Chapter 3 (pp 33-101)

1. *Irish Cyclist*, 8 June 1887.
2. *Thom's Irish Almanac and Official Directory of the United Kingdom of Great Britain and Ireland: for the Year 1869* (Dublin: Alexander Thom, 1869), p.1400; *Irish Cyclist*, 26 March 1890.
3. *Irish Wheelman*, 25 September 1894.
4. *Irish Cyclist*, 7 May 1890.
5. *Icycles*, December 1880; *Irish Cyclist*, 21 May 1890, 2 July 1890. William Bindon Blood was the club president; William Persse Blood was its secretary, and Louis Meldon, – a solicitor, and brother of Dr Austin Meldon – was its captain.
6. *Irish Cyclist*, 11 June 1890. For accounts of the Dublin University Bicycle Club and of cycling at Trinity College Dublin in the nineteenth century see Kenneth Bailey, *A History of Trinity College Dublin 1892-1945* (Dublin: The University Press, 1947), pp 130-133, 164; Trevor West, 'Football, Athletics and Cycling: The Role of Trinity College, Dublin in the Evolution of Irish Sport' in Sarah Alyn Stacey (ed), *Essays on Heroism in Sport in Ireland and France* (Lewiston, Queenston and Lampeter: Edwin Mellen Press, 2003), pp 141-142.
7. *Bicycling News*, 20 September 1878.
8. *Morning Mail*, 14 September 1881.
9. *Icycles*, December 1880; *Irish Cyclist*, 12 March 1890.
10. *Irish Cyclist*, 7 February 1894, 14 February 1894.
11. Ibid, 14 February 1894.
12. *Wheel World*, June 1882; *Irish Cyclist*, 30 April 1890.
13. *Limerick Chronicle*, 29 December 1874, 4 March 1879. My thanks to Tom Hayes for bringing these references to my attention.
14. *Bicycling News*, 3 August 1877. Its president was the Honourable T. Stopford, and its vice-presidents were a Captain Thomas and a Dr Carey.
15. *Icycles*, December 1880; George Henry Bassett, *Louth County Guide and Directory, including the Town and County of the Town of Drogheda* (Dublin: Sealy, Bryers and Walker, 1886), pp 35, 287.
16. *Wheel World*, June 1881; *Irish Cyclist*, 17 March 1886. According to the *Irish Cyclist* of 25 November 1885 the first cyclist in Tralee had taken up the pastime around twenty years previously, when he would impress 'the young lads' of the town with exhibitions on his bicycle.
17. *Irish Sportsman and Farmer*, 7 June 1879, 28 June 1879; *Bicycling Times*, 26 June 1879; *Bicycling*, July 1879; *Morning Mail*, 14 September 1881.
18. *Icycles*, December 1880; undated newspaper extract from mid 1890s in scrapbook of cycling newspaper cuttings (National Library of Ireland [hereafter NLI], Ms 32624).
19. *Limerick Chronicle*, 4 March 1879.
20. *Cyclists' Touring Club Monthly Gazette*, August 1884; *Irish Cyclist*, 3 March 1886.
21. *Irish Cyclist*, 20 May 1885.
22. *Limerick Chronicle*, 4 March 1879; *The Cyclist*, 1 April 1885; *Irish Cyclist*, 14 April 1886.
23. *Wheel World*, February 1884, April 1884.
24. Mecredy and Stoney, *Art and Pastime*, pp 193-194. The Irish Bicycling Association was formed by representatives of the Dublin University Bicycle Club, Phoenix Bicycle Club, Leinster Bicycle Club and Metropolitan Bicycle Club. See *Wheel World*, August 1882.
25. R.J. Mecredy, *Xmas Number of the Irish Cyclist and Athlete* (Dublin: A. and E. Cahill, 1886), p.19.
26. Lombe Atthill, *Recollections of an Irish Doctor* (London: Religious Tract Society, 1911), pp 97-98.
27. *Icycles*, December 1880; *Irish Cyclist*, 22 April 1891.
28. *Limerick Chronicle*, 20 April 1880. My thanks to Tom Hayes for this reference.
29. *Icycles*, December 1880.
30. *Morning Mail*, 6 September 1881, 14 September 1881; *Wheel World*, July 1881.
31. *Wheel World*, September 1881.
32. Ibid, October 1881.
33. Ibid, June 1882; Tom Hunt, 'The Development of Sport in County Westmeath 1850-1905' (unpublished Ph.D. thesis, De Montfort University, 2005), p.156. For a discussion of cycling in Meath in the late nineteenth century see Brian Griffin, 'The Early History of Cycling in Meath and Drogheda', *Ríocht na Midhe*, vol. xv (2004), pp 123-151.

34.. *Irish Cyclist*, 21 April 1886. This club ceased to exist in 1886, and all of its members joined the Limerick Amateur Athletic and Bicycle Club.
35. *Wheel World*, March 1882, April 1882.
36. *Irish Cyclist*, 19 November 1890.
37. *Wheel World*, July 1883; *Irish Cyclist*, 21 November 1888.
38. *Wheel World*, July 1883, August 1883.
39. Ibid, August 1884; *Irish Cyclist*, 1 July 1885, 21 April 1886.
40. *The Cyclist*, 1 April 1885; *Irish Cyclist*, 20 May 1885, 10 November 1886; George Henry Bassett, *County Down Guide and Directory, including the Borough of Newry* (Dublin: Sealy, Bryers and Walker, 1886), pp 287, 335.
41. *Wheel World*, March 1885.
42. *Irish Cyclist*, 20 May 1885.
43. Ibid, 1 July 1885.
44. Ibid, 27 October 1886; George Henry Bassett, *The Book of Antrim. A Manual for Manufacturers, Merchants, Traders, Professional Men, Land-Owners, Farmers, Tourists, Anglers and Sportsmen Generally* (Dublin: Sealy, Bryers and Walker, 1888), pp 55, 283.
45. *Irish Cyclist*, 5 May 1886.
46. *Ulster Cycling News*, 8 February 1893.
47. *Irish Cyclist*, 7 April 1886.
48. Ibid, 23 June 1886; George Henry Bassett, *The Book of County Tipperary. A Manual and Directory for Manufacturers, Merchants, Traders, Professional Men, Land-Owners, Farmers, Tourists, Anglers and Sportsmen Generally* (Dublin: Sealy, Bryers and Walker, 1889), p.319.
49. *Irish Cyclist*, 21 April 1886.
50. Ibid, 28 April 1886.
51. *The Cyclist*, 10 November 1886.
52. Ibid, 8 December 1886.
53. Mecredy (ed.), *Xmas Number 1886*, p.19.
54. *The Cyclist*, 20 April 1887.
55. *Irish Cyclist*, 26 November 1890.
56. For some examples see *The Country*, 8 July 1875; *Bicycling News*, 27 October 1876, 3 November 1876, 25 October 1878, 30 January 1880, 2 September 1881; *The Cyclist*, 7 May 1884; *Irish Cyclist*, 29 September 1886.
57. *Irish Cyclist*, 17 November 1886.
58. Ibid, 7 January 1891.
59. *Bicycling News*, 25 October 1878; *Wheel World*, September 1883.
60. *Wheel World*, September 1885.
61. *Cyclists' Touring Club Monthly Gazette*, July 1884.
62. *Irish Cyclist*, 10 November 1886; *Social Review*, 30 July 1898. The Coleraine cyclist later became a solicitor, with a practice near Stephen's Green in Dublin.
63. *The Cyclist*, 11 May 1887.
64. *The Jarvey*, 2 February 1889.
65. *Irish Cyclist*, 28 April 1886.
66. Ibid, 9 February 1887.
67. O'Toole, *Whist*, p.90.
68. *Irish Cyclist*, 12 May 1886.
69. Details about the development of the pneumatic tyre from Eric Tompkins, *The History of the Pneumatic Tyre* (Lavenham: Eastland Press, 1981), pp 7-10; Jim Cooke, 'John Boyd Dunlop 1840-1921, Inventor', *Dublin Historical Record*, vol. xliv (Spring 1996), pp 16-31; idem, *John Boyd Dunlop* (Garristown: Dreoilín, 2000), pp 6-11.
70. W.F. Grew, *The Cycle Industry: Its Origin, History and Latest Development* (London: Sir Isaac Pitman, 1921), p.53; Arthur du Cros, *Wheels of Fortune: A Salute to Pioneers* (London: Chapman and Hall, 1938), p.56.
71. *Irish Cyclist*, 9 October 1889, 13 January 1892. Evidence from the South of the country shows that some eleven of the thirty-one riders on a club run in Waterford in March 1890 rode 'Rapid' safeties: ibid, 23 March 1890.
72. *Irish Athletic and Cycling News*, 17 September 1889.
73. *Irish Cyclist*, 9 April 1890, 2 July 1890, 6 August 1890, 3 September 1890.

74. Ibid, 30 July 1890.
75. Ibid, 11 February 1891.
76. Ibid, 26 April 1891.
77. *Ulster Cycling News*, 15 April 1893.
78. *Leinster Leader*, 15 April 1893.
79. *Irish Cyclist*, 14 March 1894.
80. *Sport*, 12 May 1894.
81. *Irish Weekly Independent*, 12 January 1895.
82. *Irish Cyclist*, 26 June 1886.
83. *Irish Athletic and Cycling News*, 18 August 1889.
84. *Irish Cyclist*, 21 November 1888.
85. Ibid, 29 February 1888.
86. *Ulster Football and Cycling News*, 14 June 1889.
87. *Irish Cyclist*, 16 April 1890.
88. *Irish Times* extract quoted in *Sport*, 6 June 1891.
89. *Irish Cyclist*, 24 June 1891.
90. Letter from 'T.W.' in *Limerick Chronicle*, 21 July 1870.
91. *Limerick Chronicle*, 30 September 1880. My thanks to Tom Hayes for this and the preceding reference.
92. Cycling diary of a member of the Bonaparte-Wyse family, possibly A.N. Bonaparte-Wyse, in Co. Waterford, 1886 (NLI, Ms 34233).
93. *Irish Cyclist*, 12 January 1887, 26 March 1890; *Irish Wheelman*, 28 August 1894.
94. *Irish Cyclist*, 16 January 1895, 15 January 1896.
95. *Irish Weekly Independent*, 11 December 1895.
96. *Irish Cyclist*, 29 January 1896; *Irish Wheelman*, 26 February 1901.
97. *Wheel World*, February 1884.
98. *Irish Cyclist*, 24 March 1886.
99. *Sport*, 30 January 1892.
100. *Ulster Cycling News*, 22 February 1893.
101. *Irish Wheelman*, 5 January 1897, 19 October 1897.
102. *Irish Athletic and Cycling Record*, 5 May 1899.
103. *Irish Cyclist*, 17 December 1890.
104. Ibid, 3 October 1888, 24 February 1892.
105. Harry Hewitt Griffin, *Bicycles and Tricycles for the Year 1879-80* (London: *The Bazaar*, 1880), pp 50, 104.
106. *Belfast and Province of Ulster Directory for 1884* (Belfast: *Belfast Newsletter*, 1884), pp x, 260.
107. *Irish Cyclist*, 31 March 1886.
108. *Sport*, 28 April 1888.
109. *Irish Cyclist*, 10 July 1889.
110. *Sport*, 11 June 1892.
111. *Weekly Irish Times*, 8 May 1897, 7 August 1897.
112. Penny Bonsall, *The Irish RMs: The Resident Magistrates in the British Administration of Ireland* (Dublin: Four Courts Press, 1997), p.158; James Pethica (ed.), *Lady Gregory's Diaries 1892-1902* (Gerrards Cross: Colin Smythe, 1996), p.142.
113. *Irish Cyclist*, 25 April 1894.
114. Tony Farmar, *Ordinary Lives: Three Generations of Irish Middle Class Experience 1907, 1932, 1963* (Dublin: Gill and Macmillan, 1991), p.32.
115. *Irish Cyclist*, 17 December 1890.
116. Hunt, 'Sport in Westmeath', p.157.
117. *Irish Cyclist*, 21 April 1886.
118. *The Cyclist*, 4 May 1887.
119. Masthead of *Irish Cyclist*, 11 December 1889.
120. *Irish Cyclist*, 28 February 1894.
121. *Irish Athletic and Cycling Record*, 31 March 1899.
122. *Bicycling News*, 15 June 1877; *Wheel World*, February 1884.
123. *Irish Cyclist*, 10 November 1886, 15 December 1886. In 1897 Lord Athlumney was on the board of directors of the Ormonde Cycle Company: *Irish Times*, 22 February 1897.
124. *Irish Cyclist*, 22 April 1891, 31 March 1897.

125. Ibid, 18 May 1887, 29 June 1887.
126. *Sport*, 21 March 1891, 26 March 1892; *Irish Cyclist*, 25 March 1891.
127. *Irish Cyclist*, 8 April 1891, 5 June 1895.
128. *Sport*, 13 February 1892.
129. Ibid, 10 June 1893.
130. *Freeman's Journal*, 22 March 1890.
131. *Irish Cyclist*, 16 January 1895; *Weekly Irish Times*, 20 July 1895.
132. *Weekly Irish Times*, 20 July 1895.
133. *Irish Wheelman*, 19 January 1897.
134. *Irish Cyclist*, 5 May 1897.
135. *Ulster Cycling News*, 1 March 1893.
136. *Derry Journal*, 21 August 1896.
137. David Rubinstein, 'Cycling in the 1890s', *Victorian Studies*, vol. 21 (Autumn, 1977), p.49.
138. *Irish Wheelman*, 25 June 1895.
139. *Social Review*, 2 November 1895; *Irish Society*, 2 January 1897.
140. *Irish Cyclist*, 11 March 1896.
141. *Irish Wheelman*, 12 January 1897.
142. *Weekly Irish Times*, 23 January 1897.
143. *Social Review*, 2 May 1896, 9 May 1896; *Irish Cyclist*, 6 May 1896.
144. *The Wheelwoman*, 14 November 1896.
145. *Irish Cyclist*, 24 June 1896.
146. *Nenagh Guardian*, 24 June 1896.
147. Ibid, 27 May 1896.
148. *The Wheelwoman*, 24 October 1896.
149. *Irish Wheelman*, 15 June 1897.
150. *Irish Cyclist*, 20 May 1896; *Nenagh Guardian*, 3 June 1896, 6 June 1896.
151. *Irish Cyclist*, 4 November 1896.
152. Ibid, 12 May 1897.
153. Ibid, 26 May 1897.
154. Ibid, 5 October 1897.
155. *Irish Wheelman*, 7 April 1896; *Irish Cyclist*, 28 October 1896; Mary Colum, *Life and the Dream* (London: Macmillan, 1847), p.80; William Magan, *Umma-More: The Story of an Irish Family* (Salisbury: Element Books, 1983), p.348. A group of Kilkenny cyclists followed an otter hunt in July 1890: see *Irish Cyclist*, 23 July 1890. For fictional references to hunt followers on bicycles see Edith Somerville and Violet Martin ('Martin Ross'), *Some Experiences and Further Experiences of an Irish R.M.* (London: J.M. Dent, 1991), pp 75, 118.
156. *Bicycling News*, 15 September 1876.
157. *Irish Cyclist*, 12 May 1886.
158. Ibid, 16 May 1894, 30 April 1898; Bicycle Polo Association of Great Britain, *Bicycle Polo* (London: Bicycle Association of Great Britain, n.d.), p.5.
159. *Irish Cyclist*, 18 April 1894; Hunt, 'Sport in Westmeath', p.160.
160. *Irish Cyclist*, 16 May 1894.
161. *Irish Athletic and Cycling Record*, 5 August 1898; *Irish Wheelman*, 17 April 1900.
162. *Irish Cyclist*, 14 September 1898.
163. Ibid, 21 September 1898; *Irish Athletic and Cycling Record*, 7 July 1899; *Irish Wheelman*, 25 July 1899, 5 September 1899. The first international bicycle polo match was held at Crystal Palace, London, on 28 September 1901, between Ireland and England, with the Irish team winning by a score of 10 to 5: Polo Association of Great Britain, *Bicycle Polo*, p.7.
164. *Social Review*, 23 July 1898.
165. *Weekly Irish Times*, 1 May 1897; Windham Thomas Wyndham Quin (4th Earl of Dunraven), *Past Times and Pastimes* (London: Hodder and Stoughton, 1922), p.6.
166. *Irish Cyclist*, 18 August 1897. In the following year the *Midland Tribune* complained that the close police supervision of cyclists in the Birr district was a direct consequence of 'aristocratic cads and their female relatives' who cycled on the footpaths instead of the public roads: see issue of 12 March 1898.
167. *Freeman's Journal*, 25 March 1890; *Irish Cyclist*, 17 September 1890.
168. *Irish Cyclist*, 26 March 1890.
169. Ibid, 6 August 1890.

170. *Sport*, 1 April 1893, 9 September 1893.

171. Ibid, 3 February 1894.

172. Ibid, 17 June 1893; *Irish Cyclist*, 29 June 1898.

173. *Irish Cyclist*, 26 April 1893.

174. *Sligo Champion*, 31 March 1894.

175. *Irish Weekly Independent*, 19 January 1895.

176. *Irish Cyclist*, 29 April 1896; *Kerry Sentinel*, 8 July 1896.

177. *Kerry News*, 11 January 1896; *Irish Cyclist*, 29 April 1896.

178. *Hansard's Parliamentary Debates*, 4th series, vol. lxi, 7 July 1898, col. 182; *Irish Athletic and Cycling Record*, 23 September 1898.

179. *Wheel World*, May 1886.

180. *Irish Athletic and Cycling News*, 1 January 1889.

181. *Irish Cyclist*, 8 July 1896.

182. *Hansard's Parliamentary Debates*, 4th series, vol. lxi, 7 July 1898, cols 178-179; *Irish Cyclist*, 5 June 1900.

183. *Ulster Cycling News*, 1 March 1893; *Irish Cyclist*, 22 June 1898.

184. *The Cycle*, 23 January 1897.

185. Ibid.

186. *Irish Figaro*, 21 August 1897.

187. *Hansard's Parliamentary Debates*, 4th series, vol. lxi, 7 July 1898, col. 186.

188. *Irish Cyclist*, 22 June 1898.

189. *Irish Wheelman*, 11 July 1899.

190. *Daily Graphic*, 15 October 1896; *Irish Cyclist*, 30 December 1896.

191. *Weekly Irish Times*, 24 April 1897.

192. Matthias McDonnell Bodkin, *Recollections of an Irish Judge: Press, Bar and Parliament* (London: Hurst and Blackett, 1914), p.212. My thanks to James McConnel for this reference. Bodkin records in his memoirs (p.258) that he invented a combined cycling lamp bracket and carrier, the patent to which he subsequently sold to Messrs Brown and Son of London.

193. *Sligo Champion*, 20 May 1893, 21 April 1894; *Irish Wheelman*, 4 May 1897.

194. *Irish Cyclist*, 3 March 1897.

195. *Irish Athletic and Cycling Record*, 17 February 1899.

196. *Irish Cyclist*, 9 March 1887, 8 January 1890.

197. *Sport*, 25 February 1893; *Sligo Champion*, 20 May 1893.

198. *Irish Wheelman*, 4 May 1897.

199. *Irish Athletic and Cycling Record*, 17 March 1899.

200. *Irish Cyclist*, 9 June 1886. Irish doctors' approval of the health benefits offered by cycling, were given prominent publicity: for examples, see *Bicycling News*, 2 August 1878; Mecredy and Stoney, *Art and Pastime*, pp 160-161.

201. *Irish Cyclist*, 22 April 1891.

202. *Meath Herald*, 3 April 1897.

203. *Irish Athletic and Cycling Record*, 31 March 1899.

204. *Irish Figaro*, 10 April 1897.

205. *Kerry Sentinel*, 25 January 1896; *Rathmines News*, 29 August 1896; *Weekly Irish Times*, 29 August 1896; Annie P. Smithson, *Myself – and Others: An Autobiography* (Dublin: Talbot Press, 1944), pp 175, 186.

206. *Social Review*, 8 January 1898; Smithson, *Myself*, pp 170, 174-175, 186.

207. *Irish Cyclist*, 19 March 1890.

208. *Limerick Chronicle*, 11 November 1880. My thanks to Tom Hayes for this reference.

209. *Irish Cyclist*, 7 March 1888. I would like to thank Raymond Refaussé, archivist of the Church of Ireland's Representative Church Body Library, for biographical information on Reverend Whelan.

210. *Irish Cyclist*, 11 November 1885. For an interesting fictional parallel involving a curate, Reverend Corkran, 'a callow youth from Trinity College, Dublin', and Miss Francie Fitzpatrick, who crashes while riding his tricycle, see Edith Somerville and Violet Martin ('Martin Ross'), *The Real Charlotte* (London: Zodiac Press, 1972; first published 1894), p.106.

211. *Irish Cyclist*, 22 April 1891.

212. Ibid, 16 June 1886.

213. Ibid, 31 December 1890.

214. Ibid, 12 September 1888, 17 September 1890.

215. Ibid, 12 September 1888.
216. Ibid, 15 August 1888.
217. *Freeman's Journal*, 6 June 1890.
218. *Irish Cyclist*, 25 March 1891.
219. *Leinster Leader*, 18 August 1894; *Irish Cyclist*, 9 January 1895. The latter source claimed that a Dublin firm of cycling agents had received an order for over 200 safety bicycles for the students of Maynooth College, for their use during their summer holidays.
220. Catherine Candy, *Priestly Fictions: Popular Irish Novelists of the Early 20th Century* (Dublin: Wolfhound Press, 1995), p.80.
221. *Weekly Irish Times*, 16 May 1896.
222. John B. Cunningham and Joe O'Loughlin, 'O'Loughlin's Cycle Shop, Belleek, Co. Fermanagh and the Coming of the Bicycle', *Ulster Folklife*, vol. 44 (1998), p.94; James Owen Hannay ('George Birmingham'), *Pleasant Places* (London: William Heinemann, 1934), pp 108-110. See also *Irish Cyclist*, 11 January 1893, for a discussion of the case of Reverend Murphy, rector of St George's Church on High Street, Belfast, whose occasional bicycle rides on Sundays were regarded by clergy of a more conservative bent as Sabbath-breaking.
223. Ignatius Murphy, *The Diocese of Killaloe 1850-1904* (Dublin: Four Courts Press, 1995), pp 427-428. In 1900 another member of the Catholic hierarchy, Bishop Clancy of Elphin, purchased a 'McTaggart Royal' bicycle: *Irish Wheelman*, 8 May 1900.
224. Thomas J. Morrissey, *William J. Walsh: Archbishop of Dublin, 1841-1921* (Dublin: Four Courts Press, 2000), p.173.
225. *Irish Cyclist*, 6 February 1895.
226. Ibid, 8 May 1895.
227. *The Cycle*, 23 January 1897.
228. *Irish Figaro*, 24 July 1897.
229. *Irish Catholic*, 9 January 1897, 21 August 1897.
230. *Irish Cyclist*, 4 March 1891, 11 March 1891.
231. *Leinster Leader*, 19 August 1893.
232. Otway, *Pleasant Places*, pp 109-110.
233. *Irish Cyclist*, 15 February 1893.
234. *Irish Athletic and Cycling Record*, 14 January 1897.
235. *Royal Commission on Liquor Licensing Laws. Minutes of Evidence taken before the Royal Commission on Liquor Licensing Laws, with Appendices and Index. Vol. VI [Ireland]* H.C. 1898 [c.8980] xxxviii 527, p.247.
236. Sean O'Casey, *Autobiography Book 3: Drums under the Windows* (London: Pan Books, 1972; first published 1945), p.145.
237. *Irish Wheelman*, 18 July 1899.
238. *Irish Cyclist*, 3 June 1891.
239. Ibid, 24 June 1891.
240. Ibid, 18 January 1893.
241. *Tuam Herald*, 24 July 1897.
242. Hunt, 'Sport in Westmeath', p.162.
243. *Irish Cyclist*, 27 March 1895.
244. *Irish Wheelman*, 12 April 1896; *Irish Cyclist*, 10 June 1896. My thanks to Raymond Refaussé for biographical information on Reverend Charlton.
245. *Irish Cyclist*, 16 June 1897.
246. Dal Riada Cycling Club rules and regulations (Public Record Office of Northern Ireland [hereafter PRONI], D2800/13); *Irish Athletic and Cycling Record*, 6 May 1898.
247. *Irish Wheelman*, 15 May 1900, 26 June 1900.
248. Stephen Ball (ed.), *A Policeman's Ireland: Recollections of Samuel Waters, RIC* (Cork: Cork University Press, 1999), p.68.
249. *Bicycling News*, 3 November 1876.
250. *Wheel World*, November 1883. There were eleven competitors in the 2-mile race.
251. *Irish Cyclist*, 8 September 1886.
252. *Limerick Chronicle*, 8 January 1984. This source states that Constable Lowry was the first person to ride a safety bicycle, fitted with solid tyres, from Dublin to Limerick. My thanks to Constable Lowry's grandson, Dr Donal Lowry of Oxford Brookes University, for this reference.

253. *Irish Weekly Independent*, 23 February 1895; *Weekly Irish Times*, 4 April 1896.

254. *Sport*, 6 February 1891.

255. RIC circulars, 23 April 1892, 1 November 1892 (NLI, Royal Irish Constabulary circulars, August 1882-July 1900, IR 3522 r 3).

256. *Irish Wheelman*, 14 August 1894.

257. *Irish Cyclist*, 9 September 1891, 4 October 1893; *Sport*, 18 February 1893.

258. *Sport*, 24 December 1892; *Irish Cyclist*, 8 February 1893, 3 January 1894.

259. *Sport*, 11 March 1893; *Weekly Irish Times*, 9 March 1895.

260. *Weekly Irish Times*, 25 April 1896.

261. Ibid, 29 June 1895.

262. The following are some examples. In March 1892 the Lisnaskea RIC, 12 of whose twenty-six members were cyclists, formed their own cycling club; by May of the same year a cycling club for the Co. Fermanagh RIC was in existence. In Athlone a cycling club for the RIC was formed early in 1893 with a membership of forty. See *Irish Cyclist*, 2 March 1892, 4 May 1892; Hunt, 'Sport in Westmeath', p.161.

263. *Irish Cyclist*, 27 March 1895.

264. Ibid, 6 February 1895.

265. Thomas Fennell, *The Royal Irish Constabulary – a History and Personal Memoir* (ed. Rosemary Fennell) (Dublin: University College Dublin Press, 2003), p.19.

266. *Weekly Irish Times*, 19 October 1895.

267. Ibid, 6 April 1895, 18 May 1895.

268. *Constabulary Gazette*, 12 March 1898.

269. *Waterford News*, 22 March 1901.

270. *Constabulary Gazette*, 23 May 1903; Marian Raiswell (ed.), 'Private Notes of George McKee, Royal Irish Constabulary, Castlebar, 1880-1915', *Cathair na Mart*, vol. 18 (1998), p.117.

271. *Sport*, 23 June 1894; *Weekly Irish Times*, 18 April 1896. Captain A.H. Burdett, High Sheriff of King's County, was on the Banagher club's committee, as were two justices of the peace, as well as J.G. Taaffe and W.H. Lawrence of the Bank of Ireland: *Irish Wheelman*, 14 April 1896.

272. *Weekly Irish Times*, 22 August 1896.

273. Ibid, 4 September 1897.

274. *Irish Cyclist*, 30 June 1897.

275. *Irish Athletic and Cycling Record*, 17 February 1899.

276. *Royal Irish Constabulary. Evidence taken before the Committee of Enquiry, 1901. With Appendix* H.C. 1902 Cd. 1094 xlii 313, pp 92, 102.

277. *Irish News*, 13 September 1897. The policemen cornered the dog in a house near Newry and shot it. For the central role of the police in suppressing rabies in Ireland see Brian Griffin, '"Mad Dogs and Irishmen": Dogs and Rabies in the Eighteenth and Nineteenth Centuries', *Ulster Folklife*, vol. 40 (1994), pp 1-15.

278. For some examples see *Irish Cyclist*, 1 July 1885, 29 October 1890, 9 March 1892, 19 July 1893, 14 March 1894; *Sport*, 22 July 1893; *Irish Wheelman*, 18 September 1894, 11 June 1901; *Weekly Irish Times*, 2 February 1895, 9 March 1895, 14 September 1895, 17 April 1897, 29 May 1897.

279. *Weekly Irish Times*, 18 April 1896.

280. *Irish Cyclist*, 18 December 1889.

281. *Irish Figaro*, 30 January 1897. The counties with no mounted police were Dublin, Wicklow, Carlow, Kildare, Meath, Westmeath, Longford, King's County, Queen's County, Leitrim, Derry, Antrim, Down, Armagh, Tyrone, Cavan, Monaghan and Fermanagh; the constabulary districts of West Galway and North Tipperary also had their mounted sections disbanded.

282. *Constabulary Gazette*, 27 November 1897.

283. *Sport*, 9 January 1892.

284. *Irish Cyclist*, 13 May 1891. The Seddon Pneumatic Tyre Company also had machines specially built to their own design, for use by the RIC: see *Sport*, 23 December 1893.

285. *Irish Cyclist*, 2 March 1892.

286. Ibid, 1 February 1893.

287. Ibid, 19 July 1893.

288. Advertisement in District Inspector George Amyralde de Montmorency Edwin Dagg, *"Devia Hibernia". The Road and Route Guide for Ireland of the Royal Irish Constabulary* (Dublin: Hodges and Figgis, 1893), unnumbered page.

289. For a discussion of Dagg's guide see Angela Bourke, *The Burning of Bridget Cleary: A True Story* (London: Pimlico, 1999), pp 8-9.

290. Dagg, *"Devia Hibernia"*, unnumbered page.

291. *Constabulary Gazette*, 24 January 1903, 14 February 1903.

292. *Sport*, 4 March 1893. By September 1893 there were some 80 members in the DMP's cycling club, which was stated to be 'developing rapidly': *Irish Cyclist*, 20 September 1893.

293. *Weekly Irish Times*, 13 March 1897.

294. Christopher Lynch-Robinson, *The Last of the Irish R.M.s* (London: Cassell, 1951), pp 31-34.

295. *Constabulary Gazette*, 10 January 1903.

296. Ibid, 28 February 1903; Maurice Gorham, *Ireland from Old Photographs* (London: B.T. Batsford, 1971), illustration no. 55. This policeman's surname is often spelt as 'Woulfe' in contemporary sources, but as the DMP general register spells his surname as 'Wolfe', this is the spelling adopted by the author.

297. *Constabulary Gazette,* 21 February 1903.

298. Séamus Ó Riain, *Maurice Davin (1842-1927): First President of the GAA* (Dublin: Geography Publications, 1994), p.21.

299. *Bicycling Times*, 31 May 1877.

300. *Irish Cyclist*, 16 February 1887.

301. Michael J.F. McCarthy, *Five Years in Ireland 1895-1900* (Dublin: Hodges and Figgis, 1901), p.356.

302. *Irish Cyclist*, 7 May 1890, 30 March 1892, 29 April 1896; *Irish Wheelman*, 29 May 1900.

303. *Ulster Cycling News*, 22 March 1893.

304. *Irish Cyclist*, 16 June 1886.

305. See *Irish Cyclist*, 23 June 1886, for a description of the 1886 races, which were attended by over 5,000 spectators.

306. For a biography of Mecredy see Bob Montgomery, *R J Mecredy: The Father of Irish Motoring* (Garristown: Dreoilín, 2003).

307. See *Irish Cyclist*, 1 October 1890, for a lengthy interview with Count Stadnicki.

308. *Irish Cyclist*, 2 March 1892.

309. Ulick O'Connor, *Oliver St John Gogarty: A Poet and His Times* (London: Jonathan Cape, 1964), pp 24-25, 39-40. For Gogarty's accounts of his racing career see Oliver St John Gogarty, *Tumbling in the Hay* (London: Sphere Books, 1982; first published 1939), pp 17-20, 106-122; *It Isn't This Time of Year At All!* (London: Sphere Books, 1983; first published 1954), pp 39-46.

310. Ann Saddlemyer (ed), *Letters to Molly: John Millington Synge to Maire O'Neill* (Cambridge, Mass.: Belknap Press, 1971), pp 50, 131, 136, 165, 169, 173, 191, 230; Andrew Carpenter (ed), *My Uncle John: Edward Stephens's Life of J.M. Synge* (London: Oxford University Press, 1974), pp 43, 45, 69, 75, 123, 146, 154-155.

311. Carpenter, *My Uncle John*, p.75.

312. Ibid, pp 42, 51. On one occasion Synge carried a bullfinch on his bicycle to amuse his nephews: Maurice Bourgeois, *John Millington Synge and the Irish Theatre* (London: Constable, 1913), p.8.

313. *Irish Cyclist*, 4 March 1891; John A. Murphy, *The College: A History of Queen's/University College Cork 1845-1995* (Cork: Cork University Press, 1995), p.158.

314. Letter from 'Cyclostyle' in *Q.C.B.*, vol. II, no. 7 (May 1901). My thanks to Neal Garnham for this reference.

315. O'Toole, *Whist*, pp 90-92; *The Fifty-Eighth Report of the Commissioners of National Education in Ireland (for the Year 1891)* H.C. 1892 [c.6788-1] xxx 63, p.286; *Irish Cyclist*, 11 April 1894; *Kerry Sentinel*, 25 January 1896.

316. *Irish Teachers' Journal*, 22 February 1890, 8 March 1890.

317. Ibid, 20 September 1890.

318. O'Toole, *Whist*, pp 96-102; *Irish Cyclist*, 27 May 1896.

319. *Kerry News*, 11 January 1898.

320. Sean Murphy (ed.), *Pedal Power by Shannonside: The Story of Limerick Cycling 1876-1991* (Limerick: Limerick Treaty 300 Cycling History Committee, 1991), p.23. My thanks to Tom Hayes for bringing this source to my attention.

321. Details from *Irish Teachers' Journal*, 28 March 1896, and Patrick Loughrey, 'Commerce, Cycling or the Classroom?', *Ulster Local Studies*, vol. 8, no. 3 (Winter 1983), pp 25-29.

322. For the examples of King's County, Queen's County and Meath, respectively, see *Irish Athletic and Cycling Record*, 5 April 1893; *Leinster Leader*, 8 April 1893; *Irish Wheelman*, 16 March 1897.

323. Emily Lucy de Burgh Daly (ed.), *Chronicles and Poems of Percy French* (Dublin: Talbot Press, 1922), pp 50, 56, 100-101.

324. *Irish Cyclist*, 4 January 1893.

325. P.N. Wyse Jackson, 'On Rocks and Bicycles: A Bio-bibliography of Grenville Arthur James Cole (1859-1924) Fifth Director of the Geological Survey of Ireland', *Bulletin of the Geological Survey of Ireland*, vol. 4 (1989), pp 151-163; Paul Mohr, *Wind, Rain and Rocks: The Discovery of West Connacht Geology, 1800-1950* (Indreabhán: Clódóirí Lurgan, n.d.), pp 40-41. According to Robert Lloyd Praeger, who was best man at their wedding, Cole and his wife were 'earnest addicts of the wheel'. In 1902 they published an account of a cycling tour which they undertook in France, Germany, Poland, and the Balkans. See Blanche Cole and Grenville Arthur James Cole, *As We Ride* (Dublin: Royal City of Dublin Hospital, 1902), and Robert Lloyd Praeger, *Some Irish Naturalists: A Biographical Note-Book* (Dundalk: W. Tempest and Dundalgan Press, 1949), p.28.

326. Stephen Gwynn, *Today and Tomorrow in Ireland: Essays on Irish Subjects* (Dublin: Hodges and Figgis, 1903), pp 183-184.

327. R.A. Anderson, *With Plunkett in Ireland: The Co-Op Organiser's Story* (London: Macmillan, 1935), p.32.

328. George Moore, *Hail and Farewell: Ave, Salve, Vale* (Gerrards Cross: Colin Smythe, 1975; first published 1911), p.279; John Eglinton, *A Memoir of AE: George William Russell* (London: Macmillan, 1937), p.50; Henry Summerfield, *That Myriad-Minded Man: A Biography of George William Russell 'A.E.' 1867-1935* (Gerrards Cross: Colin Smythe, 1975), p.100.

329. *Wheel World*, August 1884.

330. *Irish Cyclist*, 3 June 1885.

331. *Irish Athletic and Cycling News*, 18 August 1889.

332. *Sport*, 14 February 1891.

333. *Irish Weekly Independent*, 26 January 1895.

334. *Irish Cyclist*, 21 April 1886. It is of interest that William George Russell, a very keen cyclist, started work as a clerk in the Pims' establishment in 1890.

335. Ibid, 20 June 1888.

336. Ibid, 13 August 1890; *Thom's Irish Almanac and Official Directory of the United Kingdom of Great Britain and Ireland: for the Year 1890* (Dublin: Alexander Thom, 1890), p.1515. Pollock, a magistrate, was patron of the club.

337. *Irish Cyclist*, 23 April 1890; *Sport*, 10 December 1892.

338. *Sport*, 16 April 1892; *Thom's Official Directory of the United Kingdom of Great Britain and Ireland: for the Year 1892* (Dublin: Alexander Thom, 1892), p.1360.

339. *Sport*, 18 May 1892. John Griffiths, the company director, was elected club president.

340. *Irish Wheelman*, 18 May 1897; *Thom's Official Directory of the United Kingdom of Great Britain and Ireland: for the Year 1897* (Dublin: Alexander Thom, 1897), p.1394.

341. *Irish Wheelman*, 5 June 1900.

342. *Freeman's Journal*, 4 July 1889; *Irish Wheelman*, 20 March 1900. The employees of Todd and Burns would have been keenly aware of the allure of cycling, as an advertisement for the firm in January 1897 claimed that the establishment was 'the largest bicycle costume designers and manufacturers in Ireland'. See *Irish Times*, 15 January 1897.

343. *Irish Cyclist*, 23 September 1891.

344. Details from *Sport*, 21 May 1892, 13 May 1893; *Irish Cyclist*, 10 May 1893. A cycling race under ICA rules was held at Ginnett's Circus in Belfast, which 'created considerable interest among local wheelmen'. It was comprised of a circuit of twenty times around the circus ring, for a prize of a silver cup. D. Rainey, secretary of the ICA, was the timekeeper. According to one observer, 'The course being very short, a considerable skill was necessary, and falls were pretty numerous, but as the sawdust minimised the risk of injury they were more a source of amusement than anxiety': *Irish Weekly Independent*, 9 January 1895.

345. *Irish Athletic and Cycling Record*, 4 March 1897; *The Belfast and Province of Ulster Directory for the Year 1897* (Belfast: *Belfast Newsletter*, 1897), p.742.

346. *Irish Cyclist*, 4 August 1897.

347. *Freeman's Journal*, 13 May 1887.

348. *Irish Cyclist*, 26 February 1890.

349. *Freeman's Journal*, 9 September 1889, 5 August 1890.

350. Ibid, 25 July 1890; *Irish Cyclist*, 13 August 1890.

351. *Sport*, 1 April 1893.
352. Ibid, 15 July 1893.
353. Ibid, 15 September 1894.
354. *Irish Weekly Independent*, 13 April 1895.
355. *Irish Cyclist*, 12 May 1886.
356. *Westmeath Examiner*, 24 May 1890.
356. *Leinster Leader*, 13 August 1892.
358. Ibid, 8 April 1893.
359. *Irish Cyclist*, 22 July 1896.
360. Ibid, 9 October 1889, 21 May 1890; *Irish Society*, 6 February 1897; Synge, *Letters to Molly*, p.51.
361. *Irish Cyclist*, 16 August 1893, 27 December 1893; *Drogheda Argus*, 30 May 1896; M.J. Daunton, *Royal Mail: The Post Office since 1840* (London and Dover, New Hampshire: Athlone Press, 1985).
362. *Weekly Irish Times*, 16 October 1897.
363. *Irish Cyclist*, 2 March 1892.
364. *Freeman's Journal*, 19 June 1888, 4 July 1888, 4 July 1889, 3 July 1890, 30 August 1890. Machines were often offered for sale as their owners had decided to emigrate: see ibid, 1 May 1886, 2 June 1886, 14 July 1890, 30 July 1890, 15 August 1890, 19 August 1890, 25 August 1890.
365. Ibid, 18 July 1890.
366. *Ulster Cycling News*, 26 July 1893.
367. *Kerry News*, 1 April 1898.
368. *Irish Cyclist*, 21 March 1894.
369. Ibid, 7 March 1894, 12 February 1896; *Ulster Football and Cycling News*, 8 May 1896; *Derry Journal*, 6 July 1896; *Irish Homestead*, 27 February 1897; *Weekly Irish Times*, 8 May 1897, 29 May 1897.
370. *Irish Athletic and Cycling Record*, 2 June 1899.
371. *Irish Cyclist*, 7 October 1891.
372. Ibid, 2 March 1892.
373. *Freeman's Journal*, 30 July 1890.
374. *Irish Cyclist*, 2 March 1892.
375. *Ulster Cycling News*, 9 August 1893; *Ulster Football and Cycling News*, 25 May 1894.
376. *Irish Cyclist*, 11 April 1894. In 1892 some Waterford cyclists came across 'an antiquated bicycle', which one of them felt 'must have been discarded in the ruins of Pompeii', being ridden by villagers in Glenmore. This machine's joints 'were made of ponderous iron girders, and the handle bar was of ungainly shape and gigantic proportions'. The villagers used the 'infernal machine' as a means of learning how to cycle: *Waterford News*, 2 April 1892.
377. *Sport*, 28 April 1888.
378. *Irish Athletic and Cycling Record*, 18 March 1898.
379. A.W. Rumney, *A Cyclist's Note Book* (London and Edinburgh: W. and A.K. Johnston, 1901), p.77.
380. *Irish Cyclist*, 20 June 1888.
381. Ibid, 5 September 1888.
382. *Freeman's Journal*, 18 June 1889; *Irish Athletic and Cycling News*, 25 June 1889. According to the *Freeman's Journal*, the accident was caused by Mackey's inexperience at cycling, rather than his being drunk.
383. *Irish News*, 3 July 1897.
384. *Freeman's Journal*, 27 September 1889; *Sport*, 24 September 1892, 18 November 1893. For police files on people convicted of stealing bicycles see Criminal Index Files, C-131-1896, C-8-1901, and B-37-1903 (National Archives).
385. Details of case of John Newton, 'alias Harry Hall &c', tried at Clonmel, 7 July 1902: notebook of Michael Gleeson, County Tipperary crown solicitor (M3049, National Archives).
386. *Sport*, 24 September 1892.
387. For newspaper comment to this effect see *Irish Cyclist*, 18 March 1895, 19 June 1895; *Ulster Football and Cycling News*, 10 May 1895; *Irish Wheelman*, 4 June 1895, 4 July 1899.
388. *Munster Life*, 17 April 1897.
389. *Irish Cyclist*, 11 April 1894.
390. Letter from 'Seamont' in *Irish Cyclist*, 15 July 1896.
391. *Constabulary Gazette*, 19 March 1898. The 'crowd of young roughs from the city, "out for a holiday", swarming over the place, shouting, indulging in horse-play, and breaking the shrubs', who had caused a favourite cyclists' resort at the Little Dargle to be closed to cyclists in April 1891

because of their 'caddishness', had probably hired their machines for their Easter Monday holiday: *Irish Cyclist*, 29 April 1891.

392. *Derry Journal*, 7 September 1896; *Irish Cyclist*, 10 March 1897, 2 August 1899; *Waterford News*, 1 March 1901.

393. *Irish Tourist*, July 1898.

394. *Irish Cyclist*, 18 March 1891.

395. Ibid, 26 July 1893.

396. *Drogheda Argus*, 20 June 1896.

397. *Irish Cyclist*, 26 June 1895. Italics in original.

398. *Social Review*, 9 July 1898.

399. *Midland Reporter and Westmeath Nationalist*, 18 November 1897.

400. Edward O'Malley, *Memories of a Mayoman* (Dublin: Foilseacháin Náisiúnta, 1981), p.10.

401. Patrick Kavanagh, *The Green Fool* (London: Penguin, 1971; first published 1938), p.53.

402. *Irish Cyclist*, 25 February 1891. 'Our Latest Hobby, and How We Rode It', an article by 'A Girl Correspondent' in the 31 March 1886 issue of the *Irish Cyclist*, tells of the attraction which riding tricycles and bicycles had for middle-class girls and boys in the Dublin suburb of Blackrock.

403. Ibid, 14 October 1885; *Irish Athletic and Cycling Record*, 7 April 1899. For a reference to a boy who won £60 in his Intermediate examination and bought 'a long-coveted treasure in the shape of a new bicycle', see *Irish Cyclist*, 12 December 1888.

404. *Irish Cyclist*, 3 April 1895.

405. *Irish Athletic and Cycling Record*, 19 May 1899.

406. For boys as 'scorchers' see *Irish Cyclist*, 27 September 1893.

407. *Irish Tourist*, July 1898, contains a nostalgic account of the club's activities by an erstwhile member, who was then in his adult years.

408. *Irish Wheelman*, 1 June 1892; *Irish Cyclist*, 11 April 1894; *Irish Weekly Independent*, 6 July 1895.

409. *Irish Cyclist*, 2 March 1892, 23 March 1892.

410. Ibid, 26 January 1887.

411. *Wheel World*, July 1881.

412. *Freeman's Journal*, 16 May 1887. For a biographical sketch of Knowles see *Irish Cyclist*, 25 April 1894. In 1897 a special bicycle 'stable' was built at the Royal Belfast Academical Institution to house pupils' machines: John Jamieson, *The History of the Royal Belfast Academical Institution 1810-1960* (Belfast: William Mullan, 1959), p.129n.

413. *Irish Cyclist*, 23 October 1889; Gogarty, *It Isn't*, pp 23-24; J.B. Lyons, *The Enigma of Tom Kettle: Irish Patriot, Essayist, Poet, British Soldier, 1880-1916* (Dublin: Glendale Press, 1983), pp 22, 24, 25, 27.

414. *Sport*, 10 October 1891; *Irish Cyclist*, 23 December 1896. Oliver St John Gogarty occasionally competed in races for the Al Fresco club: O'Connor, *Oliver St John Gogarty*, p.25.

415. *Irish Cyclist*, 25 December 1889; James H. Murphy (ed.), *Nos Autem: Castleknock College and Its Contribution* (Dublin: Gill and Macmillan, 1996), p.62. The fact that 'The Pleasures and Advantages of Cycling' was one of the two composition titles on the junior grade English Intermediate examination in 1891 is probably an indication of cycling's popularity with secondary school pupils: *Report of the Intermediate Education Board for Ireland for the Year 1891* H.C. 1892 [c.6619] xxix 1, p.17.

416. *Irish Cyclist*, 6 August 1890, 11 April 1892. The Coleraine club held its fourth annual meeting in May 1892: ibid, 11 May 1892.

417. *Sport*, 21 May 1892; Seán Farragher and Annraoi Wyer, *Blackrock College 1860-1995* (Blackrock: Paraclete Press, 1995), pp 91-92, 122; Coogan, *De Valera*, p.26.

418. *Sport*, 9 June 1894. Fr R. Collins, president of Thurles College, was president of the Rockwell Cycling Club.

419. *Derry Journal*, 7 September 1896.

420. Anne V. O'Connor and Susan M. Parkes, *Gladly Learn and Gladly Teach: Alexandra College and School 1866-1966* (Dublin: Blackwater Press, 1984), p.57.

421. *Alexandra College Magazine*, June 1896. I would like to record my gratitude to Mrs Margaret P. Lennon-Wynne of Rathmines for supplying me with this reference.

422. *Irish Figaro*, 10 July 1897. The day's events included a quarter-mile bicycle race, which was won by Miss Ethel Mercer.

423. *Alexandra College Magazine*, June 1898. My thanks to Mrs Margaret P. Lennon-Wynne for this reference.

424. *Lady's Herald*, June 1898.

425. C.S. Andrews, *Dublin Made Me: An Autobiography* (Dublin and Cork: Mercier Press, 1979), p.60.
426. *Irish Wheelman*, 24 May 1898.
427. *Irish Cyclist*, 25 November 1885.
428. Ibid, 12 December 1888.
429. Stanislaus Joyce, *My Brother's Keeper* (London: Faber and Faber, 1958), p.30.
430. *Ulster Football and Cycling News*, 10 May 1895.
431. *Irish Society*, 1 May 1897; *Londonderry Sentinel*, 8 July 1897.
432. See *Irish Cyclist*, 15 April 1891.

Chapter 4 (pp. 102–141)

1. The quotation is taken from a line of 'The Wheels', a poem about women's cycling in *The Lady of the House*, 14 September 1895.
2. Anna Parnell, *The Tale of a Great Sham* (Dublin: Arlen House, 1896), ed. Dana Hearne, p.139.
3. *Irish Wheelman*, 17 October 1899.
4. *Irish Society*, 15 May 1897.
5. *Irish Cyclist*, 19 March 1890.
6. Ibid.
7. Ibid, 2 July 1890.
8. See the comical illustration of women racing on Ordinaries in *The Jarvey*, 12 October 1889. For a discussion of the links between innovations in women's clothing and increased female participation in sport in the nineteenth and twentieth centuries see Janet Phillips and Peter Phillips, 'History from Below: Women's Underwear and the Rise of Women's Sports', *Journal of Popular Culture*, vol. 27, no. 2 (1993), pp 129–148.
9. *Social Review*, 16 January 1897.
10. *Irish Cyclist*, 22 September 1886.
11. R.J. Mecredy, *Health's Highway* (London: Yellon and Williams, 1909), p.29.
12. *Irish Cyclist*, 8 June 1887; Wilson, *Two Trips*, p.10.
13. Bassett, *Book of Antrim*, p.55.
14. George Henry Bassett, *The Book of County Armagh. A Manual and Directory for Manufacturers, Merchants, Traders, Professional Men, Land-Owners, Farmers, Tourists, Anglers and Sportsmen Generally* (Dublin: Sealy, Bryers and Walker, 1888), p.53.
15. *Irish Cyclist*, 9 June 1886, 22 September 1886. Italics in original.
16. Ibid, 30 May 1888, 2 February 1894.
17. *Ulster Cyclist and Football News*, 22 March 1889; *Irish Cyclist*, 9 April 1890. Italics in original.
18. *Irish Cyclist*, 16 May 1888, 22 April 1891.
19. See Griffin, 'Cycling and Gender'.
20. *Social Review*, 16 January 1897.
21. *Irish Cyclist*, 5 September 1888.
22. Mecredy (ed.), *Xmas Number 1886*, p.19.
23. *Irish Cyclist*, 3 June 1885. Italics in original.
24. Mecredy (ed.), *Xmas Number 1886*, pp 4, 7.
25. *Irish Cyclist*, 20 January 1886.
26. Ibid, 15 September 1886.
27. Ibid, 14 July 1886. The distance travelled was approximately thirty-seven miles.
28. Ibid, 22 September 1886. The newspaper added that the two cyclists (one of whom was married, and the other of whom was her sister-in-law) had only recently commenced cycling, and yet were able to ride from Dublin to Gorey, a distance of nearly seventy miles, 'without being unduly fatigued'.
29. Ibid, 10 July 1889.
30. Ibid, 23 April 1890.
31. Letter from 'Tricyclist' in ibid, 2 December 1885; James H. Cousins and Margaret E. Cousins, *We Two Together* (Madras: Ganesh, 1950), p.18.
32. The *Irish Cyclist* of 1 July 1885 contains an article, 'My First and Last', written by 'Dolly', in which she describes how she came to grief on her first tricycle ride as a result of her dress getting caught in her machine. The subject of Ireland's roads is discussed in pp 160–163.

33. *Social Review*, 16 January 1897. This feat was accomplished 'about 1886'.

34. *Irish Cyclist*, 3 March 1886, 29 September 1886.

35. Ibid, 14 July 1886.

36. *Sport*, 23 June 1888; *Irish Cyclist*, 1 January 1890, 18 June 1890.

37. See the leading article on 'Tricycling for Ladies' in *Irish Cyclist*, 30 March 1886.

38. Katherine Tynan, *Memories* (London: Eveleigh, Nash and Gryson, 1924), p.258; Beatrice Grimshaw, *Isles of Adventure* (London: Herbert Jackson, 1930), p.15.

39. *Irish Cyclist*, 3 June 1885.

40. Ibid, 2 December 1885, 12 May 1886.

41. *Wheel World*, October 1886.

42. *Irish Cyclist*, 3 December 1886, 18 June 1890; Lillias Campbell Davidson, *Handbook for Lady Cyclists* (London: Hay and Nisbet, 1896), p.65. See also 'A Midsummer Night's Dream', a poem about towing 'the belles' to Glencullen, in *Irish Cyclist*, 13 May 1891.

43. *Irish Cyclist*, 1 January 1890.

44. Ibid, 8 June 1887; *The Cyclist*, 8 June 1887.

45. *Irish Cyclist*, 23 April 1890, 15 April 1891.

46. Ibid, 9 March 1892.

47. *Sport*, 31 January 1891.

48. *Irish Cyclist*, 11 February 1891.

49. Ibid, 26 December 1888.

50. *Nenagh Guardian*, 26 May 1888, 30 May 1888. The *Irish Cyclist* of 10 July 1889 described the second Irish women's cycling club, the Ladies' Cycling Club, as the United Kingdom's only all-female cycling club then in existence.

51. *Nenagh Guardian*, 26 May 1888, 30 May 1888.

52. *Irish Cyclist*, 13 January 1892. Mrs Ross was sub-editor of the *Social Review*, and became a partner in the company in April 1894: *Social Review*, 21 April 1894.

53. *Irish Cyclist*, 17 October 1888, 24 October 1888.

54. Ibid, 22 October 1890.

55. Ibid, 17 September 1890, 15 June 1892.

56. Ibid, 17 September 1890.

57. Ibid, 10 September 1890.

58. Ibid, 10 July 1889.

59. Ibid, 24 July 1889.

60. Roberts, *Cycling History*, pp 42-43.

61. *Irish Cyclist*, 27 June 1888.

62. *Social Review*, 16 January 1897. Italics in original.

63. *Irish Athletic and Cycling News*, 16 July 1889. Having recovered from the shock of his first sight of a female bicyclist, the witness added that he was in favour of the novelty because bicycles were lighter than tricycles and were, therefore, 'the more appropriate machine for women, lovely women'. He stated that his 'Swift' safety bicycle was currently being ridden by a woman 'who can knock a good ten miles an hour out of it'.

64. *Irish Cyclist*, 10 July 1889.

65. Ibid, 15 October 1890.

66. Letter from 'The Crank' in ibid, 31 July 1889.

67. *Social Review*, 16 January 1897.

68. *Sport*, 19 November 1892.

69. *Irish Cyclist*, 25 October 1893.

70. Ibid, 21 February 1894.

71. Ibid, 4 April 1894; *Weekly Irish Times*, 13 July 1895.

72. *Irish Cyclist*, 5 April 1893, 27 December 1893.

73. Ibid, 13 September 1893; *Irish Wheelman*, 25 September 1894.

74. *Irish Cyclist*, 11 April 1894.

75. *The Wheelwoman*, 21 November 1896. For similar gloomy complaints from other parts of Ireland, see *Commission on Horse Breeding, Ireland. Minutes of Evidence taken before the Commissioners, with Appendices* H.C. 1898 [c.8652] xxxiii 295, pp 44, 213, 221, 258.

76. *Irish Cyclist*, 22 May 1895.

77. See p.104.

78. *The Wheelwoman*, 18 July 1896. On 9 August 1899 the *Irish Cyclist* stated that 'Now that cycling has become so very general, the bicycle is being used by ladies, not only for bona-fide cycling excursions, but as a means of transit to entertainments, garden parties, picnics, and even for paying afternoon calls, practically taking the place of a carriage or car'.

79. *Irish Cyclist*, 29 April 1896.

80. Ibid, 6 May 1896.

81. Ibid, 16 September 1896.

82. Ibid, 29 July 1896.

83. Ibid, 6 May 1896, 13 May 1896.

84. *Irish Wheelman*, 7 April 1896.

85. *Social Review*, 16 January 1897.

86. *Munster Life*, 27 March 1897.

87. *Weekly Irish Times*, 5 June 1897.

88. *Irish Athletic and Cycling Record*, 18 February 1897.

89. *Irish Cyclist*, 17 February 1897.

90. *Irish Athletic and Cycling Record*, 11 March 1897, 1 April 1897, 13 May 1897; *The Wheelwoman*, 3 April 1897.

91. *Irish Cyclist*, 19 May 1897; *Irish Society*, 22 May 1897; *The Lady Cyclist*, 5 June 1897; *The Wheelwoman*, 1 January 1898. In 1896 Lady Glentworth, 'a very ardent cyclist', who was taught how to cycle by her famous cricketing relative, Lawrence Bathurst, was reported as being 'keenly anxious for the establishment of a fashionable cycle ride in the Phoenix [Park], such as there is in Hyde Park', but this scheme does not appear to have taken off: *Irish Cyclist*, 19 February 1896; *The Wheelwoman*, 30 January 1897.

92. *Irish Cyclist*, 9 August 1893.

93. *Irish Wheelman*, 31 May 1898; *Irish Athletic and Cycling Record*, 5 April 1900.

94. *Irish Athletic and Cycling Record*, 2 June 1899.

95. *Irish Cyclist*, 24 August 1898; *Irish Athletic and Cycling Record*, 26 August 1898.

96. For instance, in April 1894 the Athy Cycling Club decided to admit female members on payment of half of the fee charged to men, by which date there were already several women in the Portarlington, Mountmellick and Killeigh clubs: *Irish Cyclist*, 11 April 1894, 18 April 1894.

97. Ibid, 29 April 1896.

98. Ibid, 5 July 1899.

99. The Ixion club, started in April 1897 in Dublin, was an unusual mixed outfit as it was established by a woman, Mrs Graham, the wife of the master of Rutland College: *Weekly Irish Times*, 10 April 1897.

100. For more on this subject see Brian Griffin, 'Cycling Clubs in Victorian Ireland', in William Murphy and Paul Rouse (eds.), *Sport and History in Ireland* (forthcoming).

101. *Irish Wheelman*, 7 August 1894.

102. *Irish Figaro*, 5 June 1897.

103. *Irish Athletic and Cycling Record*, 5 May 1899.

104. Ibid, 2 June 1899.

105. Ibid, 9 June 1899.

106. Ibid, 4 August 1899.

107. *Irish Cyclist*, 6 June 1886.

108. *Sport*, 30 January 1892.

109. *Irish Cyclist*, 27 September 1893.

110. Ibid, 26 February 1896.

111. *Weekly Irish Times*, 1 August 1896.

112. *Irish Cyclist*, 25 March 1891. Isabel J. Lough of Drummully House, Killeshandra, wrote in July 1898, 'Can we believe that anyone who really enjoys cycling, who knows what it is to put two feet on two rests and fly down a hill, "made for coasting", will ever allow such a joy to go? Believe me. No!': *The Lady of the House*, 15 July 1898.

113. *The Wheelwoman*, 14 November 1896. The case of a Dublin woman who died of tuberculosis in 1899, which she contracted by lying on damp grass after she was 'overheated' as a result of cycling, was treated as a salutary lesson on the dangers of women overexerting themselves on bicycles: *Irish Cyclist*, 5 July 1899.

114. *Weekly Irish Times*, 1 August 1896.

115. Máiréad ní Chinnéide, *Máire de Buitléir: Bean Athbheochana* (Dublin: Comhar, 1993), p.34. The girls of Alexandra College were also warned about the danger of developing a 'bicycle back', from leaning too far forwards on their machines: *Alexandra College Magazine*, 1893, p.95. My thanks to Mrs Margaret P. Lennon-Wynne for this reference.

116. *Social Review*, 10 April 1897.

117. *Weekly Irish Times*, 25 April 1896.

118. *Irish Cyclist*, 3 June 1896; *Social Review*, 22 June 1896.

119. *Drogheda Argus*, 20 June 1896.

120. *Nenagh Guardian*, 13 May 1896; *Irish Cyclist*, 21 April 1897; Davidson, *Handbook*, p.29.

121. *Irish Cyclist*, 18 April 1894.

122. Ibid, 29 July 1896; *Irish Wheelman*, 27 April 1897.

123. *Derry Journal*, 31 July 1896, 31 July 1897.

124. *Social Review*, 16 January 1897; *Weekly Irish Times*, 24 July 1897.

125. *Irish Times*, 7 January 1897.

126. Ibid, 13 January 1897. For a discussion of American manufacturers' efforts to emphasise the feminine nature of cycling to prospective female customers see Ellen Gruber Garvey, 'Reframing the Bicycle: Advertising-Supported Magazines and Scorching Women', *American Quarterly*, vol. 47, no. 1 (March 1995), pp 66-101. My thanks to Joe Casey of H.W. Wilson, Dublin, for this reference.

127. *Derry Journal*, 27 July 1896.

128. *Irish Society*, 22 May 1897.

129. Ibid, 23 April 1898.

130. *Meath Chronicle, One Hundred Years of Life and Times in North Leinster* (Navan: *Meath Chronicle*, 1997), p 13

131. Information supplied to the author by Dr Austin M. O'Sullivan, curator of the Irish Agricultural Museum, Johnstown Castle, Wexford.

132. *Irish Wheelman*, 27 April 1897.

133. *Social Review*, 23 January 1897, 13 August 1898; *Weekly Irish Times*, 6 March 1897; *Irish Society*, 22 May 1897; Belfast and County Down Railway Company, *Guide and Handbook of Seaside, Farmhouse and Country Lodgings, Boarding Houses and Hotels, 1899* (Belfast: Fairbarn, 1899), advertisement for Thomas Edens Osborne, unnumbered page.

134. *Social Review*, 3 April 1897; *Irish Society*, 10 April 1897; *Weekly Irish Times*, 26 June 1897. Another innovation was that the Griffiths depot employed a saleswoman in its cycling department.

135. *Irish Cyclist*, 20 January 1897.

136. *Irish Society*, 24 April 1897.

137. Walter Carson had a cycling school at his Bachelor's Walk depot in Dublin in the 1880s. His example was followed in the 1890s by the John Griffiths Cycle Company, which opened a cycling school in 1895 at Oriel House, Westland Row and at Parkgate Street, Dublin, and at Donegall Street, Belfast. In 1896 W.R. McTaggart ran a cycling school on the first floor of his Grafton Street, Dublin, premises. Rudge-Whitworth's Dublin cycling school was at the Earlsfort Terrace skating rink, in a room measuring 85 yards by 50, where five instructors put novice riders – mostly women – through their paces; its Belfast school was opened in January 1897 in a newly opened Young Men's Christian Association gymnasium, while its Cork school was operated by its agent, J.T. Mulligan of King Street, in a disused corn store, in a room measuring 130 feet by 40 feet. Details from *Irish Cyclist*, 27 January 1886, 10 March 1897, 8 June 1898; *Irish Athletic and Cycling News*, 15 October 1889; *Social Review*, 16 November 1895; *Irish Wheelman*, 21 April 1896, 19 June 1897; *Irish Athletic and Cycling Record*, 7 January 1897, 11 March 1897; *Irish Times*, 17 March 1897; *Belfast Newsletter*, 14 June 1897; Alan Hayes (ed), *The Years Flew By: The Recollections of Madame Sidney Gifford Czira* (Galway: Arlen House, 2000), p.8.

138. *Irish Wheelman*, 24 March 1896. Lord Ardilaun was one of the aristocratic novices who learned to cycle in Dublin: *Irish Society*, 15 May 1897.

139. *Social Review*, 2 May 1896. For another description of a visit to a riding school where 'two young ladies and one elderly gentleman were wobbling around' to the accompaniment of music from a piano that was being played by 'a not very talented performer', see *Irish Cyclist*, 13 May 1896.

140. Lady Augusta Gregory made doubly sure that she was away from the prying eyes of locals when she learned to cycle, by undergoing instruction at the Queen's Club in London in February and March 1897: Pethica (ed.), *Lady Gregory's Diaries*, pp 126, 128, 129, 131, 132, 133. According to the *Irish Cyclist* in 1896, John Russell of Glenageary, a 'veteran rider', taught some fifty-three women

how to cycle. As a mark of their gratitude the women presented him with 'a very fine oak frame clock, with quarter chime': *Irish Cyclist*, 17 June 1896, 24 June 1896.

141. David Rubinstein, 'Cycling Eighty Years Ago', *History Today*, vol. 28, no. 8 (August 1978), pp 546-547; Patricia Marks, *Bicycles, Bangs and Bloomers: The New Woman in the Popular Press* (Lexington: University Press of Kentucky, 1990), pp 174-203; Penny Russell, 'Recycling Femininity: Old Ladies and New Women', *Australian Cultural History*, vol. 13 (1994), pp 31-51; Denis Pye, *Fellowship is Life: The National Clarion Cycling Club 1895-1995* (Bolton: Clarion Publishing, 1995), pp 35-36; Robert A. Smith, *Merry Wheels and Spokes of Steel: A Social History of the Bicycle* (San Bernardino: Bargo Press, 1995), pp 75-78, 97-109; Sarah Wintle, 'Horses, Bikes and Automobiles: New Woman on the Move', pp 66-78 of Angelique Richardson and Chris Willis (eds.), *The New Woman in Fiction and in Fact: Fin-de-Siècle Feminisms* (Basingstoke and New York: Palgrave, 2001).

142. *Irish Cyclist*, 14 February 1894. Mecredy could hardly have opposed the idea of rational dress for female cyclists, as his wife was one of the few Irish women to adopt the innovative form of clothing: *Irish Athletic and Cycling Record*, 7 April 1899.

143. *Irish Cyclist*, 4 April 1894; du Cros, *Wheels of Fortune*, p.28. Du Cros was in favour of women wearing rational clothes, and felt that this pioneer's name 'should appear on the tablets of fame'. He records that 'It is possible that none of the consciously elite of Dublin ever spoke to her again, yet in her own way she helped to loosen the shackles from women's freedom and gave a sporting lead to the feminine world, which was to be emulated by the Lenglens and Earharts, the Mollisons and Battens, and all those others who, by their initiative and enterprise, were to expand the outlook of women and advance their status'.

144. Grimshaw, *Isles of Adventure*, p.14.

145. *Irish Cyclist*, 24 April 1895; *Irish Wheelman*, 4 June 1895.

146. *Irish Wheelman*, 14 April 1896.

147. *Sport*, 28 April 1894.

148. *Irish Wheelman*, 27 August 1895. One can probably discount the claim that a horse became so frightened at the sight of one of the women that it could only be restrained with difficulty from jumping through a window in Wine Street.

149. Letter to J. or T. Hudson from his brother or sister, 19 April 1898 (Kilmainham Jail Archives, 10LR-1B11-19). My thanks to Niamh O'Sullivan of the Kilmainham Jail Archives Department for this reference.

150. For some examples see *Irish Cyclist*, 25 October 1893; *Irish Figaro*, 22 June 1895.

151. *Irish Weekly Independent*, 21 September 1895; *The Lady of the House*, Christmas 1895 issue.

152. *Derry Journal*, 20 July 1896.

153. *Weekly Irish Times*, 26 January 1895.

154. Letter from F. Gahan in *Irish Cyclist*, 11 March 1896.

155. Ibid, 18 March 1896.

156. *Irish Wheelman*, 16 October 1894.

157. *Irish Cyclist*, 13 February 1895.

158. *Irish Wheelman*, 22 August 1899, reprinting undated *Cork Constitution* article; *Irish Cyclist*, 23 August 1899.

159. *Irish Cyclist*, 14 March 1894, 18 April 1894, 27 March 1895, 19 February 1896.

160. *Irish Weekly Independent*, 19 January 1895, 16 February 1895.

161. *Irish Cyclist*, 11 March 1896, 18 March 1896, 25 March 1896.

162. *Social Review*, 27 February 1897.

163. *Irish Cyclist*, 25 April 1894.

164. Ibid, 25 June 1890.

165. Ibid, 16 August 1893, 20 September 1893. The spoof race was won by 'Miss Angelina Prim', who wore a white bodice, collar and tie, a black hat and veil, and a striped fringe skirt for the occasion.

166. Ibid, 16 August 1893; *Sport*, 29 September 1894. Italics in original.

167. Letter from 'Woman Cyclist' in *Irish Cyclist*, 4 October 1893.

168. *Weekly Irish Times*, 25 April 1896; *Irish Cyclist*, 24 June 1896, 1 July 1896, 8 July 1896, 2 September 1896.

169. *Irish Cyclist*, 2 September 1896.

170. *Irish Wheelman*, 14 September 1897, 10 April 1900; *Irish Cyclist*, 29 June 1898, 31 August 1898, 16 September 1898; *Irish Athletic and Cycling Record*, 5 April 1900.

171. *Irish Cyclist*, 24 June 1896.

172. *Enniscorthy Guardian*, 26 June 1897.

173. Ibid, 3 July 1897, 10 July 1897, 17 July 1897; *Irish Wheelman*, 6 July 1897; *Irish Cyclist*, 8 July 1897.

174. Letter from W.H. Grattan Flood in *Enniscorthy Guardian*, 17 July 1897.

175. *Irish Cyclist*, 24 August 1898.

176. Ibid, 31 August 1898.

177. *Irish Weekly Independent*, 21 December 1895; *Kerry Sentinel*, 1 April 1896.

178. For accounts of races in Downpatrick, Derrygonnelly, Newtownards, Ballymena and Lisburn, respectively, see *Irish News*, 23 August 1897; *Irish Wheelman*, 14 September 1897; *Irish Athletic and Cycling Record*, 7 July 1899, 14 July 1899, 31 August 1899.

179. *Irish Athletic and Cycling Record*, 28 April 1899.

180. *Irish Cyclist*, 14 September 1898.

181. *Irish Wheelman*, 20 March 1900.

182. *Irish Athletic and Cycling Record*, 7 April 1899; *Irish Cyclist*, 11 October 1899. Carrie Ferret, the race winner, had applied for an ICA racing licence but failed to obtain one, as her club, the Bloomfield Cycling Club, was not affiliated to the ICA. The Ulster Cricket Club's cycling club made the seven contestants honorary members 'for the time being'. In July 1899 Carrie Ferret won a women's bicycle race at Ballycastle: *Irish Cyclist*, 12 July 1899.

183. Details from *Irish Athletic and Cycling Record*, 8 March 1900, 15 March 1900, 5 April 1900; *Irish Wheelman*, 10 April 1900.

184. *Irish Cyclist*, 24 August 1898; *Irish Wheelman*, 20 March 1900; *Irish Athletic and Cycling Record*, 5 April 1900.

185. *Irish Cyclist*, 5 October 1898, 13 September 1899; *Irish Athletic and Cycling Record*, 15 March 1900.

186. Grimshaw's route was from Sandycove to Stillorgan, Dundrum, Clondalkin, Rathcoole, Kill, Straffan, Celbridge, Maynooth, Enfield, Kinnegad, Rochfortbridge, 'to a point some miles beyond Athlone', and then back via Rochfortbridge, Rhode, Edenderry, Moyvalley, Enfield, Maynooth, Clondalkin, Dundrum and Monkstown. The previous record holder, a married woman, had been paced by her husband; as Grimshaw was unmarried, it was considered 'impossible' for her to be accompanied by men on her ride. Nevertheless, she was paced occasionally by 'various enthusiastic friends', an aspect of her record-breaking ride about which newspapers retained a 'discrete silence': *Irish Cyclist*, 13 September 1893; Grimshaw, *Isles of Adventure*, pp 16-17. Grimshaw was elected an honorary member of Ireland's premier cycling club, the Irish Road Club, and awarded its silver medal in recognition of her exploit: *Irish Weekly Independent*, 16 November 1895.

187. *Social Review*, 16 January 1897. Writing in 1974, Sidney Gifford Czira recalled that two girls from the Rathmines neighbourhood who cycled a distance of around eighteen miles, with a long rest in the middle of their ride, 'gained a reputation comparable to any astronaut of today'. This occurred at some time in the 1890s: Hayes (ed.), *The Years Flew By*, p.8.

188. *Social Review*, 23 January 1897.

189. *Irish Athletic and Cycling News*, 1 January 1889.

190. *Ulster Football and Cycling News*, 22 March 1889.

191. *Weekly Irish Times*, 23 March 1895.

192. Ibid, 21 August 1897.

193. Ibid, 29 May 1897.

194. Beatrice Grimshaw made this claim in *Irish Cyclist*, 3 August 1898.

195. Russell, 'Recycling Femininity', pp 33, 40-42; Garvey, 'Reframing the Bicycle', pp 74, 78-81; Richard Harmond, 'Progress and Flight: An Interpretation of the American Cycling Craze of the 1890s', *Journal of Social History*, vol. 5 (Winter 1971-1972), pp 243-244.

196. *Irish Cyclist*, 16 April 1890.

197. Ibid, 8 January 1890. It is relevant here to point out that Margaret Cousins felt that the bicycle had trebled her enjoyment of life: Cousins, *We Two*, p.53.

198. *Today's Woman*, 1 June 1895.

199. Margaret Ward, *Hanna Sheehy Skeffington: A Life* (Cork: Attic Press, 1997), pp 25, 27-28. 'Bicycle weddings', in which the bride, groom, best man and bridesmaid travelled to church on bicycles decorated with flowers, were popular in the late nineteenth and early twentieth centuries: Linda May Ballard, *Forgetting Frolic: Marriage Traditions in Ireland* (Belfast: Institute of Irish Studies, Queen's University of Belfast, 1998), pp 61-62.

200. *Irish Homestead*, 3 February 1900.

201. *Irish Cyclist*, 17 December 1890. Italics in original.

Chapter 5 (pp 142-185)

1.   Ball (ed.), *A Policeman's Ireland*, p.68; *Irish Cyclist*, 25 January 1888, 24 July 1889; *Weekly Irish Times*, 16 May 1896.

2.   *Irish Cyclist*, 18 April 1888; Paul Rouse, '1888: The First All-Ireland Hurling Final', paper presented at the Sports Ireland History Second Annual Conference, NUI Maynooth, 18 February 2006. Protestants tended to use the Plantation-era name of 'Parsonstown', while Catholics tended to use the pre-Plantation 'Birr' when referring to their town.

3.   Details from *Irish Wheelman*, 4 December 1894; *Irish Cyclist*, 23 September 1896.

4.   *Sport*, 10 February 1894.

5.   *Irish Cyclist*, 28 August 1896.

6.   Ibid, 3 December 1890, 15 April 1891, 10 May 1893.

7.   Ibid, 11 March 1891, 17 February 1892. The YMCA's clubhouse at Wellington Place was considered to be one of the best appointed in Ulster, consisting of a 'splendidly-furnished parlour, reading rooms, gymnasium, committee rooms, baths, etc'.

8.   Ibid, 2 April 1890, 23 March 1892, 30 March 1892, 15 April 1896.

9.   Hunt, 'Sport in Westmeath', p.162; *Irish Cyclist*, 2 May 1894.

10.   *Irish Athletic and Cycling Record*, 14 December 1899.

11.   *Irish Cyclist*, 3 April 1895. Rutland Square is now called Parnell Square.

12.   Ibid, 11 February 1891.

13.   *Irish Athletic and Cycling Record*, 15 April 1897.

14.   *Irish Cyclist*, 16 April 1890.

15.   *Westmeath Nationalist*, 5 March 1896; *Irish Cyclist*, 4 May 1898; *Irish Wheelman*, 22 May 1900.

16.   *Irish Wheelman*, 8 May 1900. Unfortunately, the author was unable to ascertain when the Cork CYMS Cycling Club was established.

17.   *Irish Weekly Independent*, 26 January 1895; *The Cycle*, 23 January 1897. The National Cycling Club was one of the most successful racing outfits in Ireland in the 1890s. Its members included such 'crack' riders as J.A. Healy of Drogheda and Harry Reynolds of Balbriggan. The Dundalk Young Ireland Cycling Club, which was formed in 1893 or 1894 and affiliated to the ICA in April 1896, is another example of a Nationalist cycling club in this period: *Irish Weekly Independent*, 30 November 1895; *Irish Wheelman*, 14 April 1896.

18.   *Irish Weekly Independent*, 26 January 1895.

19.   *Irish Wheelman*, 31 July 1894; *Irish Weekly Independent*, 3 August 1895; *Irish News*, 3 July 1897, 20 July 1897. The club often raised funds for Belfast's Mater Hospital.

20.   *Irish Cyclist*, 9 August 1893; *Irish Weekly Independent*, 3 August 1895.

21.   Details of the Central Catholic Club from A.C. Hepburn, *A Past Apart: Studies in the History of Catholic Belfast 1850-1950* (Belfast: Ulster Historical Foundation, 1996), p.131.

22.   *Irish Cyclist*, 17 February 1897; *Irish News*, 7 August 1897.

23.   For some of the activities of the club see *Irish Cyclist*, 22 April 1891; *Irish Times*, 2 July 1891; *Daily Express*, 5 May 1892.

24.   *Irish Wheelman*, 27 March 1900.

25.   *Irish Cyclist*, 23 April 1890.

26.   Pádraig Ó Fearáil, *The History of Conradh na Gaeilge* (Dublin: Clódhanna, 1975), p.17.

27.   *Irish Cyclist*, 15 October 1890.

28.   Ibid, 15 June 1887.

29.   Ibid, 14 May 1890.

30.   Ibid, 29 April 1891.

31.   Ibid, 28 January 1891; *Sport*, 14 May 1892. For a good description of the facilities of the Elysian Harriers Cycling Club's clubhouse at Ringsend, which was considered the best equipped in Dublin, see *Sport*, 27 August 1892.

32.   See, for example, the comments of the *Irish Wheelman* of 23 April 1895 on the spectators at the hurling match between Kerry and Cork at Laccabawn, Killarney, earlier in the same month.

33.   W.F. Mandle, *The Gaelic Athletic Association and Irish Nationalist Politics 1884-1924* (Dublin: Gill and Macmillan, 1987), p.23.

34.   *Irish Cyclist*, 30 September 1885.

35.   Mandle, *Gaelic Athletic Association*, pp 22-25.

36. Ibid, p.25; Marcus de Búrca, *The Story of the GAA to 1990* (Dublin: Wolfhound Press, 1990), p.68.

37. *Sport*, 6 March 1886; *Irish Cyclist*, 25 June 1890.

38. Wilson, *Two Trips*, pp 26-27.

39. For examples, see *Irish Cyclist*, 19 August 1885; *Freeman's Journal*, 5 August 1886, 10 August 1886, 17 August 1886, 23 May 1887, 30 May 1887, 18 July 1887, 6 September 1887, 30 July 1888, 27 August 1889, 19 September 1889, 27 September 1889, 3 October 1889, 8 October 1889, 18 August 1890, 22 August 1890, 26 August 1890, 1 September 1890, 8 September 1890, 10 September 1890, 15 September 1890.

40. For the examples of the Clonmel GAA sports in August 1889, where the crowd was entertained by the Manchester Regiment's band, and the Balbriggan GAA sports in July 1890, where the band of the Seaforth Highlanders provided the musical entertainment, and the 'Wexford Sporting Festival' held under joint GAA/ICA rules in September 1892, where a military band performed for the spectators, see *Freeman's Journal*, 6 August 1889, 30 July 1890; *Sport*, 17 September 1892.

41. Details from *Irish Cyclist*, 19 August 1885, 21 April 1886; *United Ireland*, 15 May 1886. In March 1887 the new mayor of Limerick, Francis O'Keefe, was elected president of the club: *Irish Cyclist*, 9 March 1887.

42. Details from *Irish Cyclist*, 18 May 1887, 13 June 1888, 25 June 1889, 7 May 1890. In January 1890 the president of the Cork Gaelic Cycle Club, Daniel Horgan, was elected as Mayor of the city of Cork: ibid, 8 January 1890.

43. Ibid, 21 March 1893.

44. Ibid, 20 December 1893.

45. *Gaelic Journal*, March 1896.

46. Details from *Irish Cyclist*, 20 November 1889, 3 December 1890, 2 June 1897; Dublin Corporation Reports, 1891, vol. 2, no. 97 (Dublin Civic Museum); *Dunlop Gazette*, 7 December 1921; John Moore, *Motor Makers in Ireland* (Belfast: Blackstaff, 1982), pp 140-144; David Higman, 'Founding of the Dunlop Tyre Company', pp 91-94 of Rob van der Plas (ed), *Cycle History: Proceedings of the 5th International Cycle History Conference* (San Francisco: Bicycle Books, 1995).

47. *Irish Wheelman*, 15 June 1897, 29 June 1897; Henry Morris correspondence, Gaelic 1897, envelope 6, no. 11 (University College Dublin Special Collections) By the end of the decade there were also Gaelic League cycling clubs in Passage West and Cork: *Irish Cyclist*, 14 April 1897; *Irish Wheelman*, 29 May 1900.

48. *All Ireland Review*, 23 June 1900, 30 June 1900, 21 July 1900, 28 July 1900, 3 August 1900, 11 August 1900, 18 August 1900, 15 September 1900, 22 September 1900, 29 September 1900, 3 November 1900, 24 November 1900, 8 December 1900, 15 December 1900.

49. Donncha Ó Súilleabháin, *Na Timirí i Ré Tosaigh an Chonartha 1893-1927* (Dublin: Conradh na Gaeilge, 1990), pp 14-15, 98; Georg Grote, *Torn Between Politics and Culture: The Gaelic League 1893-1993* (Münster and New York: Waxmann, 1994), pp 69-72.

50. Poem from Milligan's *Hero Lays*, published in *Sinn Féin*, 8 February 1908.

51. For the example of Modeligo, Co. Waterford, in August 1899 see *Cork Examiner*, 18 August 1899. See also *United Irishman*, 13 September 1902.

52. Augusta Gregory, *Our Irish Theatre: A Chapter of Autobiography* (Gerrards Cross: Colin Smythe, 1972), p.49.

53. Hilary Pyle, *Red-Headed Rebel: Susan L. Mitchell, Poet and Mystic of the Irish Cultural Renaissance* (Dublin: Woodfield Press, 1998), p.102.

54. *United Irishman*, 18 October 1902, 25 October 1902; Cousins, *We Two*, pp 142-143; Bridget Boland, *At My Mother's Knee* (London, Sydney and Toronto: The Bodley Head, 1978), p.38.

55. Ruth Dudley Edwards, *Patrick Pearse: The Triumph of Failure* (London: Victor Gollancz, 1977), pp 56-57.

56. Arthur Clery, *Dublin Essays* (Dublin and London: Maunsel, 1919), p.133.

57. *Irish Cyclist*, 2 July 1890.

58. Ibid, 22 April 1891.

59. *Sport*, 28 May 1892.

60. Ibid, 28 October 1893.

61. *Irish Wheelman*, 11 September 1894.

62. *Irish Cyclist*, 20 February 1895, 27 February 1895.

63. *Meath Herald*, 22 May 1897.

64. *Irish Athletic and Cycling Record*, 23 June 1899.

65. Jim Gilligan, 'Murray's of Dunshaughlin, 1896-1910', in Denis A.Cronin, Jim Gilligan and Karina Holton (eds.), *Irish Fairs and Markets: Studies in Local History* (Dublin: Four Courts Press, 2001), p.239.

66. For some of the myriad examples see *Bicycling News*, 1 September 1876, 8 September 1876, 15 September 1876, 20 October 1876, 26 April 1878, 1 November 1878, 29 November 1878, 30 January 1880; *Bicycling Times*, 28 June 1877; *Irish Cyclist*, 4 August 1886, 30 April 1890; *Nenagh Guardian*, 26 May 1888, 30 May 1888; *Sport*, 31 March 1894; *Derry Journal*, 10 August 1896; *Irish Athletic and Cycling Record*, 28 April 1899.

67. Examples may be found in *Bicycling News*, 27 October 1876, 3 November 1876, 10 November 1876, 17 November 1876, 24 November 1876, 1 December 1876, 15 December 1876, 22 December 1876, 5 January 1877, 12 January 1877, 26 January 1876, 16 February 1877, 2 March 1877, 9 March 1877, 23 March 1877, 6 April 1877, 20 April 1877, 16 August 1878, 20 September 1878, 25 October 1878, 27 December 1878; *Limerick Chronicle*, 30 September 1880; *Wheel World*, June 1883, July 1883, September 1883, November 1883; *Irish Cyclist*, 25 January 1888, 12 May 1897, 25 August 1897, 13 July 1898.

68. *Wheel World*, February 1883; *Irish Cyclist*, 5 September 1888.

69. *The Country*, 8 July 1875; *Bicycling News*, 27 October 1876, 3 November 1876, 26 January 1877, 25 October 1878; *Irish Cyclist*, 29 September 1886.

70. *Irish Cyclist*, 4 August 1886.

71. *Morning Mail*, 4 February 1881; *Irish Cyclist*, 24 July 1889, 23 April 1890; *Today's Woman*, 1 June 1895; *The Wheelwoman*, 12 December 1896; *Irish Athletic and Cycling Record*, 4 February 1897; *Weekly Irish Times*, 19 June 1897; Mecredy and Stoney, *Art and Pastime*, p.157.

72. Synge, *Letters to Molly*, p.211.

73. *Sport*, 17 March 1894; *Nenagh Guardian*, 13 May 1896; *Midland Reporter*, 14 April 1898.

74. *Wheel World*, May 1882, April 1884; *Irish Cyclist*, 16 April 1890, 5 April 1893, 28 March 1894; *Sport*, 31 March 1894, 8 April 1893; *Irish Wheelman*, 7 April 1896.

75. *Irish Cyclist*, 5 February 1890.

76. Ibid, 29 October 1890.

77. *Ulster Football and Cycling News*, 25 January 1895.

78. Dal Riada Cycling Club rules and regulations, 1898 (PRONI, D2800/13).

79. *Irish Cyclist*, 28 April 1886, 25 January 1888, 28 May 1890, 21 March 1894, 20 September 1899; Wilson, *Two Trips*, pp 6-7, 11; Mecredy and Stoney, *Art and Pastime*, pp 150-156; *Weekly Irish Times*, 19 June 1897.

80. *Irish Cyclist*, 7 April 1886, 4 May 1887, 25 January 1888.

81. Ibid, 3 November 1886, 23 April 1890, 14 March 1894.

82. *Irish Athletic and Cycling News*, 19 March 1889.

83. Griffin, 'Early History', pp 129-130.

84. *Irish Cyclist*, 9 June 1886, 3 December 1890; *Irish Wheelman*, 25 May 1897; *Irish Athletic and Cycling Record*, 28 April 1899.

85. *Irish Athletic and Cycling Record*, 25 March 1897, 17 June 1897.

86. *Irish Cyclist*, 29 June 1898.

87. *Sport*, 21 April 1888. In February 1890 Richard Edward Brenan gave a lecture to the Mechanics Insitute in Lismore on 'A Day with my Camera', an account of a day's cycling in Co. Waterford: *Irish Cyclist*, 5 February 1890.

88. *Irish Cyclist*, 14 April 1886, 23 April 1890, 18 February 1891; *Freeman's Journal*, 29 May 1890.

89. *Irish Cyclist*, 15 January 1890, 22 April 1891, 2 March 1893. Mayne, a keen cyclist, had been a Liberal MP for Portarlington in 1883 and then a Home Rule MP for two Tipperary constituencies from 1883 to 1890.

90. Ibid, 16 March 1892. The captain of the Pathfinders Cycling Club, who photographed club members at Glen of the Downs and Delgany, was described as a 'photographic fiend': *Sport*, 14 April 1894.

91. See the examples in *Irish Cyclist*, 11 March 1891, 9 January 1895, 23 February 1896, 15 April 1896, 29 April 1896, 20 May 1896, 27 May 1896, 26 August 1896, 23 December 1896, 7 April 1897; *Irish Wheelman*, 31 July 1894, 14 August 1894, 29 June 1897, 6 July 1897, 5 October 1897, 23 November 1897, 31 May 1898, 26 September 1899, 5 June 1900; *The Cycle*, 23 January 1897; *Munster Life*, 3 April 1897; *Irish Athletic and Cycling Record*, 12 May 1899; W.A. Maguire, *Belfast* (Keele: Ryburn Publishing, 1993), p.101.

92. G. Lacy Hillier and William Coutts Keppel (Viscount Bury), *Cycling* (London: Longmans and Green, 1887), pp 34-35; William Oakley, *Winged Wheel: The History of the First Hundred Years of the Cyclists' Touring Club* (Godalming: Cyclists' Touring Club, 1977), pp 3-6.

93. See Griffin, 'Cycling Clubs'.

94. *Irish Cyclist*, 21 November 1888.

95. *Bicycling*, August 1878.

96. *Irish Cyclist*, 23 April 1890; A.W. Rumney, *A Hank of Cycling Yarn* (Keswick: A.W. Rumney, 1935), pp 18-19. An Italian bicyclist preceded the Irishmen in achieving this feat. The other Irish CTC consuls in 1879 were Professor Everett and H.H. Law of Belfast, James Foley of Cork, H.S. Butler of Dublin, Richard Edward Brenan of Dungarvan and W. Lysaght of Limerick: *Irish Cyclist*, 30 April 1890.

97. *Cyclists' Touring Club Gazette*, March 1884, July 1884.

98. *Irish Cyclist*, 30 September 1885, 10 October 1888, 8 October 1890, 21 October 1896.

99. *Irish Tourist*, July 1898. For a brief discussion of the CTC in Ireland in the late nineteenth and early twentieth centuries see James J. Lightwood, *The Cyclists' Touring Club, being the Romance of Fifty Years' Cycling* (London: Cyclists' Touring Club, 1928), pp 167-168.

100. *Ulster Cycling News*, 24 May 1893.

101. A.W. Rumney, *Fifty Years a Cyclist* (Penrith: *Cumberland and Westmoreland Herald*, n.d.), p.21.

102. *Irish Wheelman*, 17 October 1899. For cyclists' accounts of ghastly accommodation or catering in Irish hotels and inns see *Bicycling News*, 8 September 1876; *Wheel World*, December 1883; *Cyclists' Touring Club Monthly Gazette*, April 1884; *Irish Cyclist*, 8 May 1895; Dawson, *Incidents*, pp 47-48.

103. *Irish Cyclist*, 16 September 1885; Wilson, *Two Trips*, p.15.

104. G.W. Hurston and H.R. Stokes, *Round the World on Bicycles* (Melbourne, Sydney and Adelaide: George Robertson, 1890), p.264.

105. Mecredy and Stoney, *Art and Pastime*, p.108.

106. R.J. Mecredy, *The 'Irish Cyclist' Third Annual Tour (1888) through the North on a Ten-in-Hand* (Dublin: Irish Cyclist, 1888); *Irish Cyclist*, 28 May 1890, 9 May 1894; *Irish Tourist*, July 1898; *Irish Wheelman*, 7 August 1894, 4 June 1895; Thomas Hiram Holding, *Cycle and Camp* (London: L. De Vere, 1898), pp 21-22.

107. *Bicycling News*, 3 November 1876, 21 September 1877; Howard (ed), 'Man on a Tricycle', p.256; *Wheel World*, March 1884; Hurston and Stokes, *Round the World*, p.265; Mecredy and Stoney, *Art and Pastime*, p.109; Holding, *Cycle and Camp*, pp 53-54, 91, 96, 100-101; Rumney, *Hank of Yarn*, p.18.

108. Holding, *Cycle and Camp*, pp 11-12, 120.

109. *Weekly Irish Times*, 1 May 1897.

110. Robert Lloyd Praeger, *Belfast and County Down Railway Company. Official Guide to County Down and the Mourne Mountains* (Belfast: Marcus Ward, 1898); John O'Mahony, *The Sunny Side of Ireland. How to See It, by the Great Southern and Western Railway* (Dublin: Alexander Thom, 1898).

111. For a discussion of Bulfin's work see Patrick Callan, 'Rambles in Eirinn, by William Bulfin', *Studies* (1982), pp 391-398.

112. *Freeman's Journal*, 21 July 1889; *Irish Cyclist*, 10 August 1898.

113. *Irish Cyclist*, 9 August 1893.

114. *Leinster Leader*, 10 June 1893; *Irish Cyclist*, 5 August 1896; *Belfast Newsletter*, 5 June 1897, 7 June 1897; *Weekly Irish Times*, 12 June 1897.

115. *Irish Figaro*, 10 July 1897; *Weekly Irish Times*, 17 July 1897. See also Gorham, *Ireland from Old Photographs*, illustration 182.

116. *Weekly Irish Times*, 12 June 1896; John Cooke, *Handbook for Travellers in Ireland* (London: John Murray, 1896), pp 11-12; *Lady Cyclist*, 31 July 1897; *Weekly Irish Times*, 14 August 1897; *Irish Tourist*, July 1898, May 1899; *Cork Examiner*, 14 August 1899, 16 August 1899; *Irish Wheelman*, 29 August 1899; Donal Horgan, *The Victorian Visitor in Ireland: Irish Tourism 1840-1910* (Cork: Imagimedia, 2002).

117. *Irish Weekly Independent*, 14 December 1895; *The Wheelwoman*, 5 September 1896, 12 December 1896.

118. *Irish Wheelman*, 4 July 1899; Gwynn, *Highways and Byways*, pp 18, 69; idem, *Experiences of a Literary Man* (London: Thornton Butterworth, 1926), p.220.

119. Colum, *Life and the Dream*, p.69.

120. *Bicycling: Its Rise and Development, a Text Book for Riders* (London: Tinsley Brothers, 1874), p.29; *Bicycling News*, 15 September 1876, 20 April 1877; Mecredy (ed), *Xmas Number 1886*, p.5; R.J.

Mecredy, *Mecredy's Road Book of Ireland* (Dublin: R.J. Mecredy and S. Kyle, 1892), p.85.

121. Bassett, *County Down Guide*, p.17; Mecredy, *Road Book*, p.85; Praeger, *Belfast and Down*, p.17. See also Fred Hamond, 'Communications in County Down', in Lindsay Proudfoot (ed.), *Down History and Society: Interdisciplinary Essays on the History of an Irish County* (Dublin: Geography Publications, 1997), pp 602–605.

122. *Wheel World*, November 1883; Wilson, *Two Trips*, p.56; *Irish Cyclist*, 16 April 1890, 23 April 1890, 11 May 1892; *Irish Times*, 22 January 1897, 12 February 1897; *Weekly Irish Times*, 26 June 1897, 10 July 1897, 31 July 1897; *Irish Tourist*, May 1898; Séamas Ó Maitiú, *Dublin's Suburban Towns 1834-1930* (Dublin: Four Courts Press, 2003), pp 80–81.

123. *Bicycling News*, 28 September 1877; *Wheel World*, December 1883, January 1884; *Irish Cyclist*, 30 September 1885, 14 October 1885, 18 June 1890, 20 May 1896, 17 February 1897; Wilson, *Two Trips*, p.17; *Sport*, 24 March 1894; *Irish Weekly Independent*, 23 February 1895; *Meath Herald*, 27 February 1897; Holding, *Cycle and Camp*, pp 114, 122.

124. *Wheel World*, December 1883; *Sport*, 26 November 1892; *Irish Cyclist*, 5 February 1896.

125. *Dunlop Gazette*, August 1919, February 1926; Grew, *Cycle Industry*, pp 54–55.

126. *Irish Cyclist*, 15 June 1898.

127. *Irish Athletic and Cycling Record*, 13 January 1899. Brown was president of the Irish Roads Improvement Association, an organisation formed in 1897 by the Irish Tourist Association to pressurize Grand Juries and other public bodies to provide better roads: *Weekly Irish Times*, 24 April 1897; Kate Newman (ed.), *Dictionary of Ulster Biography* (Belfast: Institute of Irish Studies, Queen's University of Belfast, 1993), p.24. R.J. Mecredy was one of the Irish Roads Improvement Association's two honorary secretaries.

128. J.D. Williamson, *Donegal County Council 75 Years* (Lifford: Donegal County Council, 1974), pp 33–34.

129. W. Fitzwalter Wray, *A Vagabond's Note Book* (London: *Daily News*, 1908), pp 200–201. Cycling tourists frequently commented on the scarcity of finger posts in Ireland; according to W.H. Duignan in 1883, 'Travellers in Ireland are left to find their own way, and guide posts are unknown; I was told there was one in the county of Carlow, the arms of which had long ago disappeared, and it was known for a hundred miles round as "the guide post"': *Wheel World*, November 1883.

130. Wray, *Note Book*, p.206.

131. Ibid, p.217.

132. Ibid, p.220.

133. R.T. Lang (ed.), *Irish Road Book (Part 1 – South)* (London: E.R. Shipton, 1899), p.vii.

134. *Bicycling News*, 15 September 1876, 28 September 1877, 27 December 1878. Bayliss and Thomas were supplying most of Dublin's cyclists with their machines in the late 1870s: *Irish Cyclist*, 6 January 1886, 2 July 1890.

135. *Irish Cyclist*, 16 February 1887; advertisement in unnumbered page of Wilson, *Two Trips*.

136. *Irish Cyclist*, 16 February 1887, 11 March 1891.

137. *Irish Times*, 10 July 1888, 14 July 1888.

138. *Irish Cyclist*, 12 February 1890, 19 February 1890, 5 March 1890.

139. *Sport*, 26 November 1892.

140. *Irish Wheelman*, 19 January 1897.

141. *Cyclists' Touring Club Monthly Gazette*, April 1884; *Sport*, 20 March 1886, 16 January 1892; *Irish Cyclist*, 22 August 1888, 5 September 1888; *Irish Wheelman*, 11 September 1894; *Weekly Irish Times*, 22 May 1897. For T. Roy Fraser's 'A Narrow Escape', a fictional account of an attack on an Ordinary rider by a rabid dog in Co. Mayo, see *Irish Wheelman*, 25 September 1894.

142. *Irish Cyclist*, 3 June 1885.

143. *Bicycling News*, 7 January 1881.

144. *Cyclists' Touring Club Monthly Gazette*, November 1884; *Irish Cyclist*, 5 March 1890. Trench later patented a tubeless tyre in 1896 and began manufacturing his invention in a London factory in 1897. For an account of his invention and an interview with his manager see *The Wheelwoman*, 22 January 1898.

145. *Weekly Irish Times*, 5 October 1895, 21 August 1897.

146. *Leinster Leader*, 17 June 1893.

147. Charles Jarrott, *Ten Years of Motors and Motor Racing* (London: Grant Richards, 1906), p.185. For a good description of the hazards posed to cyclists by dogs, poultry and farm animals in the Midlands, see article by 'Rural' in *Irish Cyclist*, 12 August 1896.

148. *Irish Cyclist*, 21 April 1886, 25 March 1891, 24 April 1895.

149. Ibid, 24 January 1893; Holding, *Cycle and Camp*, pp 40-41.

150. *Wheel World*, February 1883; *Irish Wheelman*, 25 September 1894; Carpenter (ed.), *My Uncle John*, p.161.

151. *Bicycling News*, 26 January 1877; Wilson, *Two Trips*, p.25.

152. *Irish Cyclist*, 16 September 1891.

153. *Rathmines News*, 25 April 1896; *Weekly Irish Times*, 12 June 1897; *Hansard's Parliamentary Debates*, 4th series, vol. lxi, July 1898, col. 182; *Midland Reporter*, 25 August 1898.

154. *Bicycling News*, 30 January 1880, 2 September 1881.

155. *Irish Cyclist*, 23 April 1890.

156. *Limerick Chronicle*, 7 October 1890. My thanks to Tom Hayes for this reference.

157. William Bulfin, *Rambles in Eirinn. Volume I* (London: Sphere Books, 1981; first published 1907), p.66.

158. Ibid.

159. *Leinster Leader*, 8 September 1892.

160. *Irish Cyclist*, 11 April 1890.

161. *Freeman's Journal*, 13 September 1890; *Sport*, 7 May 1892; Holding, *Cycle and Camp*, p.164.

162. *Bicycling News*, 29 November 1878. Larkin's prosperous status may be gauged from the fact that he had recently built a house at a cost of £90 in Lisdoonvarna, which was to be let to lodgers in the holiday season.

163. *Drogheda Argus*, 19 May 1894; *Sport*, 9 June 1894.

164. *Irish Cyclist*, 25 June 1890, 11 April 1894; *Sport*, 24 February 1894; *Irish Wheelman*, 16 March 1897; Rumney, *Hank of Yarn*, p.19.

165. *Waterford Mail*, 9 May 1895.

166. Ibid, 18 April 1895; *Irish Wheelman*, 23 April 1895.

167. *Wheel World*, October 1881; *Irish Times*, 18 April 1888; *Donegal Independent*, 21 April 1888.

168. *Weekly Irish Times*, 11 September 1897, 27 November 1897.

169. *Nenagh Guardian*, 20 May 1896.

170. *Weekly Irish Times*, 15 May 1897, 4 December 1897.

171. *Irish Cyclist*, 7 May 1902.

172. Chief Crown Solicitor's papers, 1869/158 (National Archives); *Irish Cyclist*, 17 June 1885, 9 September 1886; *Irish Times*, 10 September 1888; *Freeman's Journal*, 3 September 1890; *Sport*, 26 September 1891; Inspectors Thomas Grant and Patrick Byrne, Irishtown, to Superintendent Peter Hughes, DMP 'E' Division, 6 May 1894, Chief Secretary's Office Registered Paper [hereafter CSORP] 1894/5786 (National Archives); *Constabulary Gazette*, 5 February 1898.

173. *Bicycling News*, 30 January 1880, 2 September 1881; *Cork Examiner*, 23 August 1888; Wilson, *Two Trips*, p.55; Hurston and Stokes, *Round the World*, p.272; *Irish Cyclist*, 25 June 1890; *Drogheda Argus*, 11 July 1896; *Weekly Irish Times*, 3 April 1897; *Kerry News*, 23 July 1897, 30 July 1897; Holding, *Cycle and Camp*, p.163; Lang (ed), *Irish Road Book*, p.xiii; Wray, *Vagabond's Note Book*, p.196.

174. *Sport*, 6 February 1892, 20 February 1892.

175. *Irish Cyclist*, 24 June 1896; *Drogheda Argus*, 25 July 1896; *Weekly Irish Times*, 3 April 1897; *Irish Wheelman*, 24 May 1898.

176. *Midland Tribune*, 16 October 1897; *Constabulary Gazette*, 23 October 1897; *Weekly Irish Times*, 23 October 1897.

177. *Londonderry Sentinel*, 15 July 1897. For examples of policemen, judges and magistrates cycling on footpaths, see *Irish Wheelman*, 1 June 1897; *Constabulary Gazette*, 18 September 1897; Thomas Miller, The Crescent, Lucan, to the Irish Privy Council, 18 March 1898, and District Inspector W.J. O'Hara, Abbeyleix, to County Inspector Babbage, 26 March 1898, CSORP 1898/6081 (National Archives); Dawson, *Incidents*, p.9.

178. *Irish Wheelman*, 30 November 1897.

179. *Constabulary Gazette*, 27 November 1897.

180. *Weekly Irish Times*, 23 October 1897, 25 November 1897; *Irish Wheelman*, 19 October 1897.

181. *Midland Reporter*, 17 March 1898.

182. Ibid, 23 June 1898.

183. *Irish Cyclist*, 25 June 1890, 14 September 1898; *Freeman's Journal*, 3 September 1890; *Sport*, 28 February 1891, 7 May 1892, 27 October 1894; *Derry Journal*, 18 May 1892; *Irish Wheelman*, 28 May

1895; *Weekly Irish Times*, 3 April 1897, 5 June 1897; *Irish News*, 19 August 1897; Edward Glover, 'The Bicycle and Common Roads', *Transactions of the Institution of Civil Engineers of Ireland*, vol. xxvi (1897), p.86.

184. For examples from Portadown, Naas, Dublin and Portaferry, respectively, see *Wheel World*, November 1884; *Weekly Irish Times*, 17 August 1895, 30 October 1897; *Irish Cyclist*, 2 August 1899.

185. *Bicycling Times*, 19 July 1877.

186. *Irish Cyclist*, 29 December 1886; *Irish Society*, 19 June 1897; Horgan, *Victorian Visitor*, p.63.

187. *Irish Cyclist*, 8 July 1896, 4 May 1898. A Cork by-law of July 1896 imposed an upper speed limit of six miles per hour on cyclists, and required them to walk their machines through Wintrop Street and Pembroke Street.

188. Ibid, 14 March 1894.

189. *Londonderry Sentinel*, 17 August 1897.

190. *Irish Cyclist*, 26 December 1888.

191. *Weekly Irish Times*, 9 January 1897, 23 January 1897.

192. *Irish Wheelman*, 24 May 1898.

193. Ibid, 29 May 1900.

194. *The Cyclist*, 7 May 1884; *Irish Times*, 10 October 1888; *Irish Cyclist*, 29 July 1896; *Weekly Irish Times*, 18 September 1897.

195. *Weekly Irish Times*, 31 August 1895, 10 July 1897, 31 July 1897, 16 October 1897, 13 November 1897, 20 November 1897.

196. *Sport*, 1 October 1892, 24 June 1893, 15 September 1894, 6 October 1894; *Irish Wheelman*, 18 September 1894, 25 September 1894.

197. *Sport*, 9 September 1893.

198. *Weekly Irish Times*, 21 September 1895.

199. *Sport*, 15 September 1895. C.F. Brenan of Kilkenny, a member of the Irish Road Club, was the first person to accomplish this ride, in a time of thirty-eight hours and forty minutes.

200. *Irish Cyclist*, 23 April 1890.

201. *Wheel World*, March 1885; *Irish Cyclist*, 20 May 1885, 21 March 1888.

202. *Sport*, 4 June 1892, 3 February 1894; *Ulster Cycling News*, 15 March 1893.

203. *Ulster Cycling News*, 12 April 1893.

204. O'Toole, *Whist*, p.94.

205. *Leinster Leader*, 13 August 1892; *Sport*, 15 October 1892; Griffin, 'Early History', pp 129-133.

206. *Leinster Leader*, 13 August 1892; *Sport*, 19 November 1892; *Irish Weekly Independent*, 28 September 1895.

207. *Limerick Chronicle*, 17 August 1869. My thanks to Tom Hayes for this reference. Ensign M.N.G. Kane won the race, Inspector of Musketry Reginald Garrett came second, Assistant Surgeon R.W. Davies came third, and Ensign C.L. Hamilton came fourth: *Thom's Irish Almanac 1869*, p.617.

208. *Irish Times*, 6 June 1870; *Ixion*, January 1875. Black's Capel Street business specialised in 'Ariel' and Coventry Machinists' Company bicycles.

209. Walsh's reminiscences in *Irish Wheelman*, 25 September 1894.

210. Details from *Waterford News*, 23 September 1870; *Irish Cyclist*, 12 March 1890, 7 March 1894; *Irish Wheelman*, 5 February 1901.

211. 'J.T.H' (ed.), *John Lawrence's Handbook of Cricket in Ireland, and Record of Athletic Sports, Football, &c. Sixth Number, 1870-71* (Dublin: John Lawrence, 1870), pp 222, 226, 228; Bassett, *Book of Armagh*, p.285; *Irish Cyclist*, 7 February 1894. My thanks to Neal Garnham for the *John Lawrence's Handbook* reference.

212. Reminiscences of Harry Hewitt Griffin in *Irish Cyclist*, 7 February 1894.

213. *Bicycling News*, 7 January 1881.

214. Ibid, 21 July 1876.

215. Ibid, 21 June 1878.

216. *Irish Cyclist*, 26 August 1891.

217. For descriptions of large turnouts at provincial race gatherings see *Bicycling News*, 21 September 1877; *Freeman's Journal*, 24 June 1886, 8 June 1888, 21 June 1889; *Sport*, 30 April 1892, 21 May 1892, 17 June 1893, 29 July 1893, 12 August 1893, 16 September 1893, 25 August 1894; *Impartial Reporter*, 10 May 1894; *Irish Cyclist*, 16 May 1894; *Irish Wheelman*, 13 July 1897; Hunt, 'Sport in Westmeath', p.165.

218. Letter from 'A Countryman' in *Irish News*, 7 July 1897.

219. *Irish Cyclist*, 31 May 1893.

220. *Leinster Leader*, 28 April 1894.

221. *Drogheda Argus*, 1 August 1896.

222. Mecredy (ed.), *Xmas Number 1886*, p.19; Mecredy and Stoney, *Art and Pastime*, p.194.

223. *United Ireland*, 22 May 1886; *Irish Times*, 5 July 1888, 1 September 1888, 3 September 1888; *Cork Examiner*, 20 August 1888; William Cunningham, honorary secretary of Elysian Harriers Cycling Club, to DMP Chief Commissioner David Harrel, 7 May 1891, DMP files 1891/2522 (National Archives); *Irish Wheelman*, 31 July 1894, 30 July 1895.

224. Wilson, *Two Trips*, p.47; *Copy of Report to the Board of Trade by Major Francis Arthur Marindin, R.E, C.M.G, with Michael Adams, Esq, Q.C, Legal Assessor, of the Inquiry into the Accident at Camp on May 22, 1893, held in Tralee Court House on June 7th, 8th, 9th, 10th, 1893, together with the Evidence and Appendix* H.C. 1893-94 [c.7074-1] lxxix 621, p.28.

225. *Irish Cyclist*, 18 February 1891; *Sport*, 28 May 1892; *Irish Cyclist*, 7 September 1898; Redmond, *Beauty Spots*, pp 32-33.

226. *Irish Cyclist*, 23 August 1893, 2 June 1897.

227. *Irish Wheelman*, 29 June 1897.

228. *Irish Cyclist*, 17 June 1885, 4 August 1886, 3 September 1890, 25 March 1891, 23 August 1893, 25 October 1893, 21 March 1894, 18 March 1896, 12 May 1897; *Sport*, 30 June 1888, 9 September 1893, 11 November 1893, 28 July 1894; *Ulster Cycling News*, 22 February 1893, 26 April 1893; *Londonderry Sentinel*, 6 July 1897, 20 July 1897.

229. Undated *Scottish Cyclist* extract in *Irish Cyclist*, 25 April 1894; *Weekly Independent*, 9 March 1895, 6 July 1895.

230. *Weekly Irish Times*, 16 October 1897.

231. *Irish Cyclist*, 25 March 1891.

232. For examples see *Sport*, 5 March 1892; *Irish Wheelman*, 11 September 1894, 21 April 1896, 23 February 1897, 9 March 1897, 8 June 1897, 22 June 1897, 17 October 1899, 15 January 1901, 19 February 1901; *Irish Cyclist*, 10 April 1895; *Westmeath Nationalist*, 9 January 1896; *Irish Athletic and Cycling Record*, 1 April 1898.

233. *Irish Cyclist*, 19 June 1895. Maxwell and Harding, who started in business in 1889, were the first Irishmen to ride a tandem safety bicycle.

234. Details from Michael Killeen, 'Harry Reynolds World Cycling Champion', *Dublin Historical Record*, vol. xli (December 1987-September 1988), pp 70-81.

235. *The Leader*, 9 March 1901.

List of Illustrations

(Page 133)

76. Source: *Irish Cyclist*, 30 January 1895, courtesy of the National Library of Ireland. (Page 134)

77. Source: *The Lady Cyclist*, 10 July 1897, by permission of the British Library: shelf mark 718. (Page 136)

78. Source: *Social Review*, 23 January 1897, by permission of the British Library: shelf mark s20. (Page 137)

79. Source: *Irish Cyclist*, 20 July 1898, courtesy of the National Library of Ireland. (Page 143)

80. Source: *Irish Cyclist*, 26 August 1896, courtesy of the National Library of Ireland. (Page 144)

81. Source: *Irish Wheelman*, 23 November 1897, courtesy of the National Library of Ireland. (Page 146)

82. Source: *Irish Cyclist*, 21 April 1897, courtesy of the National Library of Ireland. (Page 148)

83. Source: *Irish Cyclist*, 12 May 1897, courtesy of the National Library of Ireland. (Page 149)

84. Source: *Sport*, 11 July 1891, courtesy of the National Library of Ireland. (Page 151)

85. Source: *Irish Wheelman*, 27 August 1895, courtesy of the National Library of Ireland. (Page 152)

86. Source: *All Ireland Review*, 7 December 1901, courtesy of the National Library of Ireland. (Page 153)

87. Source: *Irish Cyclist*, 3 December 1890, courtesy of the National Library of Ireland. (Page 154)

88. Source: *Irish Cyclist*, 18 February 1891, courtesy of the National Library of Ireland. (Page 155)

89. Source: *Irish Cyclist*, 22 April 1891, courtesy of the National Library of Ireland. (Page 156)

90. Source: *Irish Cyclist*, 3 July 1889, courtesy of the National Library of Ireland. (Page 157)

91. Courtesy of the National Library of Ireland. (Page 158)

92. Source: *Irish Wheelman*, 12 October 1897, courtesy of the National Library of Ireland. (Page 159)

93. Source: *Irish Cyclist*, 2 May 1888, courtesy of the National Library of Ireland. (Page 161)

94. *Irish Cyclist*, 16 February 1887, courtesy of the National Library of Ireland. (Page 162)

95. Source: *Irish Cyclist*, 19 March 1890, courtesy of the National Library of Ireland. (Page 164)

96. Source: *The Jarvey*, 22 November 1890, courtesy of the National Library of Ireland. (Page 164)

97. Source: *Irish Cyclist*, 25 April 1894, courtesy of the National Library of Ireland. (Page 165)

98. Source: *The Jarvey*, 25 October 1890, courtesy of the National Library of Ireland. (Page 166)

99. Source: *The Jarvey*, 7 December 1889, courtesy of the National Library of Ireland. (Page 167)

100. Source: A.J. Wilson, *Two Trips to the Emerald Isle* (London: Iliffe, 1888), p.20, by permission of the British Library: shelf mark 10390.c.24. (Page 168)

101. Source: *The Jarvey*, 15 November 1890, courtesy of the National Library of Ireland. (Page 171)

102. Source: *Irish Tourist*, July 1898, courtesy of the National Library of Ireland. (Page 172)

103. Source: *Irish Cyclist*, 3 April 1895, courtesy of the National Library of Ireland. (Page 173)

104. Source: *Irish Cyclist*, 8 January 1896, courtesy of the National Library of Ireland. (Page 174)

105. Source: *Irish Wheelman*, 18 September 1894, courtesy of the National Library of Ireland. (Page 174)

106. Source: *Irish Wheelman*, 25 September 1894, courtesy of the National Library of Ireland. (Page 177)

107. Source: *Wheel World*, November 1885, by permission of the British Library: shelf mark pp.1873.g. (Page 179)

108. Source: *Irish Cyclist*, 17 February 1886, courtesy of the National Library of Ireland. (Page 181)

109. Source: *Irish Cyclist*, 13 April 1887, courtesy of the National Library of Ireland. (Page 182)

110. Source: *Irish Cyclist*, 18 March 1896, courtesy of the National Library of Ireland. (Page 183)

111. Source: *Irish Wheelman*, 27 February 1900, courtesy of the National Library of Ireland. (Page 184)

Bibliography

Primary Sources

Manuscripts

Ireland:

Dublin Civic Museum:
Dublin Corporation reports, 1891

Kilmainham Jail:
Ms 10 LR 1B11 19: letter to Prisoner J464 from his brother or sister, 19 April 1898

National Archives:
Chief Crown Solicitor's Papers
Chief Secretary's Office Registered Papers
Criminal Index Files
DMP Files
M3049: Notebooks of Michael Gleeson, Crown Solicitor for Co. Tipperary, 1901-1903 assizes
National Library of Ireland:
Ms 32624: scrapbook of newspaper cuttings relating to cycling, mid-1890s
Ms 34233: diary of cycling trips in Co. Waterford by member of Bonaparte-Wyse family, possibly A.N. Bonaparte-Wyse, 1886
Royal Irish Constabulary circulars, August 1882-July 1900 (IR 5322 r 3)
Public Record Office of Northern Ireland:
D2800/13: Dal Riada Cycling Club rules and regulations, 1898
Trinity College Dublin:
Ms3918a: David Harrel's manuscript autobiography
University College Dublin:
Special Collections: Henry Morris correspondence

Britain:

British Library:
Patent Library cycling industry patents

Published primary sources

Newspapers and periodicals (published in Dublin, unless stated otherwise):

Alexandra College Magazine
All Ireland Review
Belfast Newsletter (Belfast)
Bicycling (Newcastle-upon-Tyne)
Bicycling News (Birmingham)
Bicycling Times (London)
Constabulary Gazette
Cork Examiner (Cork)
The Country (London)
The Cycle (London)
The Cyclist (London)
Cyclists' Touring Club Monthly Gazette (London)
Daily Express
Daily Graphic (London)
Derry Journal (Derry)
Donegal Independent (Ballyshannon)
Drogheda Argus (Drogheda)
Dublin Figaro
Dunlop Gazette (Birmingham)
Enniscorthy Guardian (Enniscorthy)
Freeman's Journal
Gaelic Journal
Icycles (London)
Illustrated London News (London)
Impartial Reporter (Enniskillen)
Irish Athletic and Cycling News
Irish Athletic and Cycling Record (Belfast)
Irish Catholic
Irish Cyclist
Irish Figaro
Irish Homestead
Irish News (Belfast)
Irish Society
Irish Sportsman and Farmer
Irish Teachers' Journal
Irish Times
Irish Tourist
Irish Weekly Independent

Irish Wheelman
Ixion (London)
The Jarvey
Kerry News (Tralee)
Kerry Sentinel (Tralee)
Lady Cyclist (London)
Lady's Herald
Lady of the House
The Leader
Leinster Leader (Naas)
Limerick Chronicle (Limerick)
Londonderry Sentinel (Derry)
Meath Herald (Kells)
Midland Reporter (Mullingar)
Midland Tribune (Birr)
Morning Mail
Munster Life (Tralee)
Nenagh Guardian (Nenagh)
Q.C.B. (Belfast)
Rathmines News
Sinn Féin
Sligo Champion (Sligo)
Social Review
Sport
Today's Woman
Tuam Herald (Tuam)
Ulster Cycling News (Belfast)
Ulster Football and Cycling News (Belfast)
United Ireland
United Irishman
Waterford Mail (Waterford)
Waterford News (Waterford)
Weekly Irish Times
Westmeath Examiner (Mullingar)
Westmeath Nationalist (Mullingar)
The Wheelwoman (London)
Wheel World (London)
Zozimus

Parliamentary Publications and Proceedings:

Hansard's Parliamentary Debates

Report of the Intermediate Education Board for Ireland for the Year 1891 H.C. 1892 [c.6619] xxix 1

The Fifty-Eighth Report of the Commissioners of National Education in Ireland for the Year 1891 H.C. 1892 [c.6788-1] xxx 63

Copy of Report to the Board of Trade by Major Francis Arthur Marindin, RE, C.M.G, with Michael Adams, Esq, Q.C, Legal Assessor, of the Inquiry into the Accident at Camp on May 22, 1893, held in Tralee Court House of June 7th*, 8*[th]*, 9*[th]*, 10*[th]*, 1893, together with the Evidence and Appendices* H.C. 1893-94 [c.7074-1] lxxix 621

Royal Commission on Liquor Licensing Laws. Minutes of Evidence taken before the Royal Commission on Liquor Licensing Laws, with Appendix. Vol. VII. [Ireland] *H.C. 1898 [c.8980] xxxviii 527*

Commission on Horse Breeding, Ireland. Minutes of Evidence taken before the Commissioners, with Appendices H.C. 1898 [c.8652] xxxiii 295

Royal Irish Constabulary. Evidence taken before the Committee of Enquiry, 1901. With Appendix H.C. 1902 Cd. 1094 xlii 313

Guides and Works of Reference:

George Henry Bassett, *Louth County Guide and Directory, Including the Town and County Guide of the Town of Drogheda* (Dublin: Sealy, Bryers and Walker, 1886)

George Henry Bassett, *The Book of Antrim. A Manual and Directory for Manufacturers, Merchants, Traders, Professional Men, Land-Owners, Farmers, Tourists, Anglers and Sportsmen Generally* (Dublin: Sealy, Bryers and Walker, 1888)

George Henry Bassett, *The Book of Armagh. A Manual and Directory for Manufacturers, Merchants, Traders, Professional Men, Land-Owners, Farmers, Tourists, Anglers and Sportsmen Generally* (Dublin: Sealy, Bryers and Walker, 1888)

George Henry Bassett, *The Book of Tipperary. A Manual and Directory for Manufacturers, Merchants, Traders, Professional Men, Land-Owners, Farmers, Tourists, Anglers and Sportsmen Generally* (Dublin: Sealy, Bryers and Walker, 1889)

Belfast and County Down Railway Company, *Guide and Handbook of Seaside, Farmhouse and Country Lodgings, Boarding Houses and Hotels, 1899* (Belfast: Fairbarn, 1899)

Belfast and Province of Ulster Directory for 1865-66 (Belfast: *Belfast Newsletter*, 1865)

Belfast and Province of Ulster Directory for 1884 (Belfast: *Belfast Newsletter*, 1884)

Belfast and Province of Ulster Directory for 1897 (Belfast: *Belfast Newsletter*, 1897)

John Cooke, *Handbook for Travellers in Ireland* (London: John Murray, 1896, fifth edition)

George Amyralde de Montmorency Edwin Dagg, *'Devia Hibernia'. The Road and Route Guide for the Ireland of the Royal Irish Constabulary* (Dublin: Hodges and Figgis, 1893)

'J.T.H.' (ed), *John Lawrence's Handbook of Cricket in Ireland, and Record of Athletic Sports, Football, &c. Sixth Number, 1870-71* (Dublin: John Lawrence, 1870)

Weston St John Joyce, *Rambles around Dublin* (Dublin: *Evening Telegraph*, 1890)

Weston St John Joyce, *Rambles near Dublin* (Dublin: *Evening Telegraph*, 1890)

R.T. Lang (ed), *Irish Road Book (Part 1–South)* (London: E.R. Shipton, 1899)

R.J. Mecredy, *Mecredy's Road Book of Ireland* (Dublin: R.J. Mecredy and S. Kyle, 1892)

John O'Mahony, *The Sunny Side of Ireland. How to see it by the Great Southern and Western Railway* (Dublin: Alexander Thom, 1898)

Robert Lloyd Praeger, *Belfast and County Down Railway Company. Official Guide to County Down and the Mourne Mountains* (Belfast: Marcus Ward, 1898)

C.P. Redmond, *Beauty Spots in the South-East of Ireland and How to See them by Car and Cycle* (London and Dublin: Henry Gaze, 1901)

Thom's Irish Almanac and Official Directory of the United Kingdom of Great Britain and Ireland: for the Year 1867 (Dublin: Alexander Thom, 1867)

Thom's Irish Almanac and Official Directory of the United Kingdom of Great Britain and Ireland: for the Year 1869 (Dublin: Alexander Thom, 1869)

Thom's Irish Almanac and Official Directory of the United Kingdom of Great Britain and Ireland: for the Year 1870 (Dublin: Alexander Thom, 1870)

Thom's Irish Almanac and Official Directory of the United Kingdom of Great Britain and Ireland: for the Year 1872 (Dublin: Alexander Thom, 1872)

Thom's Irish Almanac and Official Directory of the United Kingdom of Great Britain and Ireland: for the Year 1890 (Dublin: Alexander Thom, 1890)

Thom's Official Directory of the United Kingdom of Great Britain and Ireland: for the Year 1892 (Dublin: Alexander Thom, 1892)

Thom's Official Directory of the United Kingdom of Great Britain and Ireland: for the Year 1897 (Dublin: Alexander Thom, 1897)

Other Published Primary Sources:

R.A. Anderson, *With Plunkett in Ireland: The Co-Op Organiser's Story* (London: Macmillan, 1935)

C.S. Andrews, *Dublin Made Me: An Autobiography* (Dublin and Cork: Mercier Press, 1979)

Lombe Atthill, *Recollections of an Irish Doctor* (London: Religious Tract Society, 1911)

Stephen Ball (ed), *A Policeman's Ireland: Recollections of Samuel Waters, RIC* (Cork: Cork University Press, 1999)

Bicycling: Its Rise and Development, a Text Book for Riders (Newton Abbot: David and Charles, 1970 reprint; first published in 1874)

Matthias McDonnell Bodkin, *Recollections of an Irish Judge: Press, Bar and Parliament* (London: Hurst and Blackett, 1914)

Bridget Boland, *At My Mother's Knee* (London, Sydney and Toronto: Bodley Head, 1978)

Joseph Firth Bottomley, *The Velocipede, Its Past, Its Present, and Its Future* (London: Simpkin and Marshall, 1869)

William Bulfin, *Rambles in Eirinn. Volume 1* (London: Sphere Books, 1981; first published 1907)

William Bulfin, *Rambles in Eirinn. Volume 2* (London: Sphere Books, 1981; first published 1907)

Andrew Carpenter (ed), *My Uncle John: Edward Stephens's Life of J.M. Synge* (London: Oxford University Press, 1974)

Arthur Clery, *Dublin Essays* (Dublin and London: Maunsel, 1919)

Blanche Cole and Grenville Arthur James Cole, *As We Ride* (Dublin: Royal City of Dublin Hospital, 1902)

Mary Colum, *Life and the Dream* (London: Macmillan, 1947)

James H. Cousins and Margaret E. Cousins, *We Two Together* (Madras: Ganesh, 1950)

Lillias Campbell Davison, *Hints to Lady Travellers at Home and Abroad* (London: 1889)

Lillias Campbell Davison, *Handbook for Lady Cyclists* (London: Hay and Nisbet, 1896)

Samuel Dawson, *Incidents in the Course of a Long Cycling Career* (Lancaster: Beeley Brothers, 1906)

Arthur du Cros, *Wheels of Fortune: A Salute to Pioneers* (London: Chapman and Hall, 1938)

Thomas Fennell, *The Royal Irish Constabulary: A History and Personal Memoir* (ed. Rosemary Fennell) (Dublin: University College Dublin Press, 2003)

Edward Glover, 'The Bicycle and Common Roads', *Transactions of the Institution of Civil Engineers of Ireland*, vol. xxvi (1897), pp 80–93

Oliver St John Gogarty, *Tumbling in the Hay* (London: Sphere Books, 1982; first published 1939)

Oliver St John Gogarty, *It Isn't This Time of Year at All!* (London: Sphere Books, 1983; first published 1954).

Augusta Gregory, *Our Irish Theatre: A Chapter of Autobiography* (Gerrards Cross: Colin Smythe, 1972)

Harry Hewitt Griffin, *Bicycles and Tricycles of the Year 1879-80* (London: The Bazaar Office, 1880)

Beatrice Grimshaw, *Isles of Adventure* (London: Herbert Jenkins, 1930)

Stephen Gwynn, *Highways and Byways in Donegal and Antrim* (London: Macmillan, 1899)

Stephen Gwynn, *Today and Tomorrow in Ireland: Essays on Irish Subjects* (Dublin: Hodges and Figgis, 1903)

Stephen Gwynn, *Experiences of a Literary Man* (London: Thornton Butterworth, 1926)

James Owen Hannay ('George A. Birmingham'), *Pleasant Places* (London: William Heinemann, 1934)

Alan Hayes (ed), *The Years Flew By: Recollections of Madame Sidney Gifford Czira* (Galway and Dublin: Arlen House, 2000)

G. Lacy Hiller and William Coutts Keppel (Viscount Bury), *Cycling* (London: Longmans and Green, 1887)

T.H. Holding, *Cycle and Camp* (London: L. de Vere, 1898)

C.H.D. Howard (ed), 'Select Documents XXVI. "The Man on a Tricycle": W.H. Duignan and Ireland, 1881-5', *Irish Historical Studies*, vol. xiv, no. 55 (May 1965), pp 246-260

G.W. Hurston and H.R. Stokes, *Around the World on Bicycles* (Melbourne, Sydney and Adelaide: George Robertson, 1890)

Charles Jarrott, *Ten Years of Motors and Motor Cycling* (London: Grant Richards, 1906)

Stanislaus Joyce, *My Brother's Keeper* (London: Faber and Faber, 1958)

Patrick Kavanagh, *The Green Fool* (London: Penguin Books, 1975; first published 1938).

Christopher Lynch-Robinson, *The Last of the Irish R.M.s* (London: Cassell, 1951)

Michael J.F. McCarthy, *Five Years in Ireland 1895-1900* (London: Simpkin, Marshall, Hamilton and Kent, 1901)

R.J. Mecredy (ed), *Xmas Number of the Irish Cyclist and Athlete* (Dublin: A. and E. Cahill, 1885)

R.J. Mecredy (ed), *Xmas Number of the Irish Cyclist and Athlete* (Dublin: A. and E. Cahill, 1886)

R.J. Mecredy, *'The Irish Cyclist' Tour to Connemara* (Dublin: Abbey Printing Works, 1887)

R.J. Mecredy (ed), *The 'Irish Cyclist' Third Annual Tour (1888) Through the North on a Ten-in-Hand* (Dublin: *Irish Cyclist and Athlete*, 1888)

R.J. Mecredy, *Health's Highway* (Dublin: Mecredy and Percy, 1909)

R.J. Mecredy and A.J. Wilson, *The Art and Pastime of Cycling* (Dublin: Mecredy and Kyle, 1890)

George Moore, *Hail and Farewell: Ave, Salve, Vale* (Gerrards Cross: Colin Smythe, 1976)

Sean O'Casey, *Autobiography Book 3: Drums under the Windows* (London: Pan Books, 1972; first published 1945).

Edward O'Malley, *Memories of a Mayoman* (Dublin: Foilseacháin Náisiúnta Teoranta, 1981).

Edward O'Toole, *Whist for Your Life, That's Treason: Recollections of a Long Life* (Dublin: Ashfield Press 2003)

Anna Parnell, *The Tale of a Great Sham* (Dublin: Arlen House, 1986) ed. Dana Hearne

James Pethica (ed), *Lady Gregory's Diaries 1892-1902* (Gerrards Cross: Colin Smythe, 1996)

Elizabeth Plunkett (Countess Fingall), *Seventy Years Young: Memories of Elizabeth, Countess of Fingall as told to Pamela Hinkson* (Dublin: Lilliput Press; first published 1937)

Windham Thomas Wyndham Quin (4th Earl of Dunraven), *Past Times and Pastimes* (London: Hodder and Stoughton, 1922)

Marian Raiswell (ed), 'Private Notes of George McKee, Royal Irish Constabulary, Castlebar, 1880-1915', *Cathair na Mart*, vol. 18 (1998), pp 99-124

A.W. Rumney, *A Cyclist's Note Book* (London and Edinburgh: W. & A.K. Johnston, 1901)

A.W. Rumney, *A Hank of Cycling Yarn* (Keswick: A.W. Rumney, 1935)

A.W. Rumney, *Fifty Years a Cyclist* (Penrith: *Cumberland and Westmoreland Herald*, n.d.)

Ann Saddlemyer (ed), *Letters to Molly: John Millington Synge to Maire O'Neill 1906-1909* (Cambridge, Massachusetts: Belknap Press, 1971)

Annie MP Smithson, *Myself – and Others: An Autobiography* (Dublin: Talbot Press, 1944)

Katherine Tynan, *Memories* (London: Eveleigh Nash and Grayson, 1924)

'Velox', *Velocipedes, Bicycles and Tricycles: How to Make, and How to Use Them* (London: George Routledge, 1869)

A.J. Wilson, *Two Trips to the Emerald Isle* (London: Iliffe, 1888)

A.J. Wilson ('Faed'), *Riding Rhymes, or, Every Bicycle Club Its Own Music Hall, and Faed's Comic Almanack for 1880* (London: Etherington, 1880)

A.J. Wilson and 'Nym', *Duffersville: Its Cycling Chronicles and Other Sketches* (London: Iliffe, 1889)

W. Fitzwalter Wray, *A Vagabond's Note Book* (London: *Daily News*, 1908)

Secondary sources

Guides and works of reference:

H.A. Doubleday, Geoffrey H. White and Lord Howard de Walden (eds), *The Complete Peerage* (London: St Catherine Press, 1945)

Jim Herlihy, *Royal Irish Constabulary Officers: A Biographical Dictionary and Genealogical Guide, 1816-1922* (Dublin: Four Courts Press, 2005)

H.C.G. Matthew and Brian Harrison (eds), *Oxford Dictionary of National Biography* (Oxford: Oxford University Press, 2004)

Kate Newman (ed), *Dictionary of Ulster Biography* (Belfast: Institute of Irish Studies, Queen's University of Belfast, 1993)

Brian W. Walker, *Parliamentary Election Results in Ireland, 1801-1922* (Dublin: Royal Irish Academy, 1978)

Other published secondary sources:

Frederick Alderson, *Bicycling: A History* (Newton Abbot: David and Charles, 1972)

Roger Alma, 'Malvern Cycling Club, 1883-1912: Social Class, Motivation, and Leisure Use', pp 139-148 of Rob van der Plas (ed), *Cycle History: Proceedings of the 5th International Cycle History Conference* (San Francisco: Bicycle Books, 1995)

Sidney H. Aronson, 'The Sociology of the Bicycle', *Social Forces*, vol. 30, no. 3 (1952), pp 305-312

Kenneth C. Bailey, *A History of Trinity College Dublin 1892-1945* (Dublin: The University Press, 1945)

Linda May Ballard, *Forgetting Frolic: Marriage Traditions in Ireland* (Belfast: Institute of Irish Studies, Queen's University of Belfast, 1998).

Wiebe E. Bijker, *Of Bicycles, Bakelites, and Bulbs: Toward a Theory of Sociotechnical Change* (Cambridge, Massachusetts: MIT Press, 1995)

Bicycle Polo Association of Great Britain, *Bicycle Polo* (London: Bicycle Polo Association of Great Britain, n.d.)

Penny Bonsall, *The Irish RMs: The Resident Magistrates in the British Administration of Ireland* (Dublin: Four Courts Press, 1997)

Maurice Bourgeois, *John Millington Synge and the Irish Theatre* (London: Constable, 1913)

Angela Bourke, *The Burning of Bridget Cleary: A True Story* (London: Pimlico, 1999)

Patrick Callan, '*Rambles in Éirinn* by William Bulfin', *Studies* (1982), pp 391-398

Catherine Candy, *Priestly Fictions: Popular Irish Novelists of the Early 20th Century* (Dublin: Wolfhound, 1997)

Tim Pat Coogan, *De Valera: Long Fellow, Long Shadow* (London: Arrow Books, 1995)

Jim Cooke, *Ireland's Premier Coachbuilder: John Hutton & Sons, Summerhill, Dublin* (Dublin: Jim Cooke, 1992)

Jim Cooke, 'John Boyd Dunlop 1840-1921, Inventor', *Dublin Historical Record*, vol. xliv (Spring, 1996), pp 16-31

Jim Cooke, *John Boyd Dunlop* (Garristown: Dreoilín, 2000)

John B. Cunningham and Joe O'Loughlin, 'O'Loughlin's Cycle Shop, Belleek, Co. Fermanagh and the Coming of the Bicycle', *Ulster Folklife*, vol. 44 (1998), pp 94-99

Emily Lucy de Burgh Daly (ed), *Chronicles and Poems of Percy French* (Dublin: Talbot Press, 1922)

Miriam Daly, 'The Return to the Roads', pp 134-149 of Kevin B. Nowlan (ed), *Travel and Transport in Ireland* (Dublin: Gill and Macmillan, 1973)

M.J. Daunton, *Royal Mail: The Post Office since 1840* (London and Dover, New Hampshire: Athlone Press, 1985)

Arthur F. Dimmock, *Arthur James Wilson 1858-1945* (Feltham: British Deaf History Society, 1996)

Marcus de Búrca, *The Story of the G.A.A. to 1990* (Dublin: Wolfhound Press, 1990)

Ruth Dudley Edwards, *Patrick Pearse: The Triumph of Failure* (London: Victor Gollancz, 1977)

John Eglinton, *A Memoir of AE: George William Russell* (London: Macmillan, 1937)

Tony Farmar, *Ordinary Lives: Three Generations of Irish Middle Class Experience 1907, 1932, 1963* (Dublin: Gill and Macmillan, 1991)

Seán Farragher and Annraoi Wyer, *Blackrock College 1860-1995* (Blackrock: Paraclete Press, 1995)

Jim Gilligan, 'Murray's of Dunshaughlin, 1896-1910', pp 224-247 of Denis A. Cronin, Jim Gilligan and Karina Holton (eds), *Irish Fairs and Markets: Studies in Local History* (Dublin: Four Courts Press, 2001)

Ellen Gruber Garvey, 'Reframing the Bicycle: Advertising-Supported Magazines and Scorching Women', *American Quarterly*, vol. 47 (1995), pp 66-101

Maurice Gorham, *Ireland from Old Photographs* (London: B.T. Batsford, 1971)

W.F. Grew, *The Cycle Industry: Its Origin, History and Latest Development* (London: Sir Isaac Pitman, 1921)

Brian Griffin, 'The Early History of Cycling in Meath and Drogheda', *Ríocht na Midhe*, vol. xv (2004), pp 123-151

Brian Griffin, 'Cycling and Gender in Victorian Ireland', in *Éire-Ireland*, vol. xli, numbers 1 & 2 (Spring/
     Summer 2006), pp 213-241

Brian Griffin, 'Cycling Clubs in Victorian Ireland', in William Murphy and Paul Rouse (eds), *Sport and
     History in Ireland* (forthcoming)

Georg Grote, *Torn Between Politics and Culture: The Gaelic League 1893-1993* (Münster and New York:
     Waxmann, 1994)

Fred Hamond, 'Communications in County Down', pp 599-628 of Lindsay Proudfoot (ed), *Down
     History and Society: Interdisciplinary Essays on the History of an Irish County* (Dublin: Geography
     Publications, 1997)

Richard Harmond, 'Progress and Flight: An Interpretation of the American Cycle Craze of the 1890s',
     Journal of Social History, vol. 5 (Winter 1971-1972), pp 235-257

A.C. Hepburn, *A Past Apart: Studies in the History of Catholic Belfast 1850-1950* (Belfast: Ulster Historical
     Foundation, 1996)

David V. Herlihy, *Bicycle: The History* (New Haven and London: Yale University Press, 2004)

H.D. Higman, 'Founding of the Dunlop Tyre Company', pp 91-94 of Rob van der Plas (ed), *Cycle
     History: Proceedings of the 5th International Cycle History Conference* (San Francisco: Bicycle Books,
     1995)

Donal Horgan, *The Victorian Visitor in Ireland: Irish Tourism 1840-1910* (Cork: Imagimedia, 2002)

Patrick N. Wyse Jackson, 'On Rocks and Bicycles: A Biobibliography of Grenville Arthur James Cole
     (1865-1924) Fifth Director of the Geological Survey of Ireland', *Bulletin of the Geological Survey of
     Ireland*, vol. 4 (1989), pp 151-163

John Jamieson, *The History of the Royal Belfast Academical Institution 1810-1960* (Belfast: William Mullan,
     1959)

Michael Killeen, 'Harry Reynolds World Cycling Champion', *Dublin Historical Record*, vol. xli
     (December 1987-September 1988), pp 70-81

James T. Lightwood, *The Cyclists' Touring Club, being the Romance of Fifty Years' Cycling* (London: Cyclists'
     Touring Club, 1928)

Roger Lloyd-James, M.J. Lewis and Mark Eason, *Raleigh and the British Bicycle Industry: An Economic and
     Business History, 1870-1960* (Aldershot: Ashgate, 2000)

Patrick Loughrey, 'Commerce, Cycling or the Classroom?', *Ulster Local Studies*, vol. 8, no. 3 (Winter
     1983), pp 25-29

J.B. Lyons, *The Enigma of Tom Kettle: Irish Patriot, Essayist, Poet, British Soldier, 1880-1916* (Dublin: Glendale
     Press, 1983)

James McGurn, *On Your Bicycle: An Illustrated History of Cycling* (London: John Murray, 1987)

William Magan, *Umma-More: The Story of an Irish Family* (Salisbury: Element Books, 1983)

W.A. Maguire, *Belfast* (Keele: Ryburn Publishing, 1993)

W.F. Mandle, *The Gaelic Athletic Association and Irish Nationalist Politics 1884-1924* (Dublin: Gill and
     Macmillan, 1987)

Patricia Marks, *Bicycles, Bangs and Bloomers: The New Woman in the Popular Press* (Lexington: University of
     Kentucky Press, 1990)

Paul Mohr, *Wind, Rain and Rocks: The Discovery of West Connacht Geology, 1800-1950* (Indreabhán: Clódóirí
     Lurgan, n.d.)

Bob Montgomery, *R J Mecredy: The Father of Irish Motoring* (Garristown: Dreoilín, 2003)

John Moore, *Motor Makers in Ireland* (Belfast: Blackstaff Press, 1982)

Thomas J. Morrissey, *William J. Walsh: Archbishop of Dublin, 1841-1921* (Dublin: Four Courts Press, 2000)

Ignatius Murphy, *The Diocese of Killaloe 1850-1904* (Dublin: Four Courts Press, 1995)

James H. Murphy, *Nos Autem: Castleknock College and its Contribution* (Dublin: Gill and Macmillan, 1996)

John A. Murphy, *The College: A History of Queen's/University College Cork, 1845-1995* (Cork: Cork
     University Press, 1995)

Sean Murphy, *Pedal Power by Shannonside: The Story of Limerick Cycling 1876-1991* (Limerick: Limerick
     Treaty 300 Cycling History Committee, 1991)

Máiréad ní Chinnéide, *Máire de Buitléir: Bean Athbheochan* (Dublin: Comhar Teoranta, 1993)

William Oakley, *Winged Wheel: The History of the First Hundred Years of the Cyclists' Touring Club*
     (Godalming: Cyclists' Touring Club, 1977)

Anne V. O'Connor and Susan M. Parkes, *Gladly Learn and Gladly Teach: Alexandra College and School
     1866-1966* (Dublin: Blackwater Press, 1984).

Ulick O'Connor, *Oliver St John Gogarty: A Poet and His Times* (London: Jonathan Cape, 1964)

John O'Donovan, *Wheels and Deals: People and Places in Early Irish Motoring* (Dublin: Gill and Macmillan, 1983)

Pádraig Ó Fearáil, *The History of Conradh na Gaeilge* (Dublin: Clódhanna Teoranta, 1975)

Séamas Ó Maitiú, *Dublin's Suburban Towns 1834-1930* (Dublin: Four Courts Press, 2003)

Séamus Ó Riain, *Maurice Davin (1842-1927): First President of the GAA* (Dublin: Geography Publications, 1994)

Donncha Ó Súilleabháin, *Na Timirí i Ré Tósaigh an Chonartha 1893-1927* (Dublin: Conradh na Gaeilge, 1990)

Austin O'Sullivan, 'Pierces of Wexford', *Journal of the Wexford Historical Society*, no. 16 (1996-1997), pp 126-143

Arthur Judson Palmer, *Riding High: The Story of the Bicycle* (New York: Dutton, 1956)

Janet Phillips and Peter Phillips, 'History from Below: Women's Underwear and the Rise of Women's Sport', *Journal of Popular Culture*, vol. 27, no. 2 (1993), pp 129-148

Robert Lloyd Praeger, *Some Irish Naturalists: A Biographical Note-Book* (Dundalk: W. Tempest and Dundalgan Press, 1949)

Denis Pye, *Fellowship is Life: The National Clarion Cycling Club 1895-1995* (Bolton: Clarion Publishing, 1995)

Hilary Pyle, *Red-Headed Rebel: Susan L. Mitchell, Poet and Mystic of the Irish Cultural Renaissance* (Dublin: Woodfield Press, 1998)

Andrew Ritchie, *King of the Road: An Illustrated History of Cycling* (London: Wildwood House, 1975)

Andrew Ritchie, 'The Origins of Bicycle Racing in England: Technology, Entertainment, Sponsorship and Advertising in the Early History of the Sport', *Journal of Sports History*, vol. 26 (Autumn, 1999), pp 489-550

Derek Roberts, *Cycling History: Myths and Queries* (n.p.: John Pinkerton, 1991)

David Rubinstein, 'Cycling in the 1890s', *Victorian Studies*, vol. 21, no. 1 (Autumn, 1977), pp 47-71

David Rubinstein, 'Cycling Eighty Years Ago', *History Today*, vol. 28, no. 8 (1978), pp 544-547

Penny Russell, 'Recycling Femininity: Old Ladies and New Women', *Australian Cultural History*, vol. 13 (1994), pp 31-51

Robert A. Smith, *Merry Wheels and Spokes of Steel: A Social History of the Bicycle* (San Bernardino: Borgo Press, 1995)

Henry Summerfield, *That Myriad-Minded Man: a Biography of George William Russell 'A.E.' 1867-1935* (Gerrards Cross: Colin Smythe, 1975)

Eric Tompkins, *The History of the Pneumatic Tyre* (Lavenham: Eastland Press, 1981)

Margaret Ward, *Hannah Sheehy Skeffington: A Life* (Cork: Attic Press, 1997)

Trevor West, 'Football, Athletics, and Cycling: The Role of Trinity College, Dublin in the Evolution of Irish Sport', pp 137-146 of Sarah Alyn Stacey (ed), *Essays on Heroism in Sport in Ireland and France* (Lewiston, New York; Queenston, Ontario; and Lampeter: Edwin Mellen Press, 2003)

J.D. Williams, *Donegal County Council 75 Years* (Lifford: Donegal County Council, 1974)

Geoffrey Williamson, *Wheels within Wheels: The Story of the Starleys of Coventry* (London: Geoffrey Bles, 1966)

Sarah Wintle, 'Horses, Bikes and Automobiles: New Woman on the Move', pp 66-78 of Angelique Richardson and Chris Willis (eds), *The New Woman in Fiction and in Fact: Fin-de-Siècle Feminisms* (Basingstoke and New York: Palgrave, 2001)

Unpublished Secondary Sources

Tom Hunt, 'The Development of Sport in County Westmeath, 1850-1905' (unpublished Ph.D. dissertation, De Montfort University, 2005)

Paul Rouse, '1888: The First All-Ireland Hurling Final', paper given at Sports History Ireland Second Annual Conference, NUI Maynooth, 18 February 2006